Creating Futures

Scenario Planning
as a Strategic Management Tool

Published by Economica Ltd,
9 Wimpole Street
London W1M 8LB

© Economica Ltd, 2001

First published 2001

Printed in France

Michel Godet

Creating Futures
Scenario Planning
as a Strategic Management Tool

ISBN 2-7178-4189-X

MICHEL GODET

Creating Futures

Scenario Planning as a Strategic Management Tool

Preface by Joseph F. COATES

Translated by Kathryn Radford

⊕⊕ ECONOMICA

London • Paris • Genève

ACKNOWLEDGEMENTS

This book was translated with assistance from the French Ministry of Foreign Affairs, specifically the Scientific and Technical Cooperation Department, in order to help the French school of *la prospective* become better known in the English-speaking world.

The translation/adaptation of my work [1] owes much to the literary talent of Kathryn Radford (lecturer, Université de Montréal and McGill University), who gladly attended corporate workshops in Paris to see our futures-thinking techniques in practice. Sylvie Molina, whom I thank for her ever-helpful suggestions and cheerful rigor, prepared the manuscript for publication. Lastly, I am both grateful and honored to have one of the greatest American futurists, Joseph F. Coates, preface *Creating Futures*.

---

1. French handbook *Manuel de prospective stratégique*, Dunod, 1997.

CONTENTS

PREFACE

If clarity is a virtue, Michel Godet is a saint. Two features of Professor Godet's career show through clearly in his new *tour de force*. First, as a university professor, he admires and practices clarity, consistency, and intellectual integrity. As a consultant practitioner - one of the most eminent in France - he brings to his treatment of scenario planning as a strategic management tool, a truly admirable degree of practicality and flexibility. If adopted, his attitude and precepts would greatly benefit those using scenarios in planning and strategic management.

Anglophones have dominated the world of forecasting and its applications to planning for too long. Fortunately Godet has been a primary actor in turning that tide and bringing the French experience to an English-speaking audience. As one might except, there are cultural differences, but little that is fundamentally different when one looks past the differences in nomenclature and the difference in relative emphasis.

On the other hand, Godet makes a central point that must be emphasized: formal planning is rigor and rationality. He notes that "the situation appears all the worse given the sad state of affairs in the United States where rational or formalistic techniques have been passed over for essentially intuitive approaches". There is no doubt that he has hit a resonant, if perhaps a low base, chord there. There is far too much attitude, judgment, expert and lay sentiment entering into futures studies in general in the anglophone world, especially in the US and UK. Reflecting that situation is the underuse of formal techniques and quantification.

Godet highlights the fact that by being less rational (or what I prefer to think of as less systematic), the vocabulary becomes garbled or confused, and the processes muddy. Godet's approach and prescriptions would take us farther toward rationalizing and clarifying our approaches to the future. Being rational and rigorous does not necessarily imply greater time and cost, but rather a fuller commitment to a thorough examination of assumptions and possibilities.

His concentration on scenario-based planning will satisfy many executives craving clearer insights into the future and a more solidly based spectrum of alternative outcomes in terms of the choices that they must make. As a book, and to some extent a textbook, this work is beautifully organized. It begins with a smooth easy review of general factors and concerns then moves into a crescendo of detail to end with three outstanding chapters of case material. The cases are presented in enough procedural and substantive detail to convince the reader, at least this reader, that the processes Godet lays out and the technique that he describes will work in industry, e.g. aluminum and electric utilities; as well as the military, the private sector, and regional planning. His most extensive example is that of BASF facing agri-food and environmental challenges.

Godet's approach is easy to take because of the grace, style, and humor with which he presents his model. After an easy beginning, he considers key concepts in looking toward the future, including a general overview of "la prospective". He then moves into a popular topic - why experts so often get it wrong. After that he wages a brief war on clichés, emphasizing how paralytic they can be in organizational thinking. With that clearing of the stage, he discusses how to be rigorous in scenario planning, defining specific conditions and the tools that are essential to ensuring rigor. The core of his approach lies in these two chapters, followed by the case material. I am sure readers will enjoy, learn and definitely profit from Godet's latest work.

Joseph F. COATES
Coates & Jarratt, Inc.
Washington, D.C.

HOW TO THINK ABOUT THE FUTURE NOW

Action is meaningless without a goal. Only an approach like scenario building can point the way to action while giving it both meaning and direction. Similarly scenario building cannot readily be dissociated from strategy, hence the term "strategic scenario building" or "strategic scenario planning".

However, the complexity of strategic problems, as well as the need to resolve them collectively, means we require methods that are as rigorous and participatory as possible just to recognize the problem and then find acceptable solutions. At the same time, we must keep in mind the limits imposed by formalization and remember that people are guided by intuition and passion as well as logic. Our mental models are inventions of the mind and represent a world unwilling to be straitjacketed by equations. We say all the better because without this freedom, any will driven by desire would lead nowhere!

As a result, our conviction is to use all the powers of reason while remaining aware of both its inherent limits and virtues. We should remember that intuition and reason are not opposite but rather complementary faculties.

Planning, "la Prospective" and Strategy: What is the Difference?

The three concepts of *la prospective*, [1] strategy and planning are intimately linked in practice; as a result, *strategic planning*, *strategic management* and *the strategic prospective approach* will be mentioned throughout this book. Each of these approaches refers to a set of definitions, problems, and methods whose specificity is weak, given the vague terminology.

With all the buzzwords and false synonyms, some readers may wonder how we can make sense of anything related to the future. Some might ask if these approaches are not all quite similar. After all, do we not already have a series of practical methods that are actually more useful in that their limits are known? The answer is a resounding "yes". A toolbox for futures studies and strategic analysis does exist. Informed managers would be wrong to deprive themselves of this toolbox, because a common language could thus be created; the power of

---

1. With respect to terms, *la prospective* in French covers the concepts of *preactivity* and *proactivity*, as seen in Igor Ansoff's writings. The concept of *foresight*, another suggested translation, only partially renders the meaning of *la prospective* since in usage *foresight* is generally applied to technology with the inherent idea of a collective process surrounding anticipation (preactivity) of technological change, but the idea of proactivity is missing. Our current use of *la prospective* would best be translated by *strategic scenario building*.

collective thought, increased, and the inevitable biases, reduced. To achieve all this, however, there must be a return to the fundamental concepts and their history.

In order to be fruitful, the marriage between scenario building and strategy must be a part of daily life. It must be appropriated by all the actors involved, from the top of the hierarchy to the bottom. (Note that here the word *actor* is used as it is in management theory.) Although the union between scenario building and strategy may have been inevitable, it has certainly not cleared up any confusion in genres and concepts. Deep down, however, the ideas are much closer than is generally admitted. In fact the definition of planning put forward by Ackoff (1970), "to conceive a desired future as well as the practical means of achieving it" does not differ much from the one we suggest for strategic scenario building in which the dream infuses reality, where desire is the productive force of the future and where anticipation sheds light on the preactive and the proactive.

Managerial fads may come and go but they always have one common denominator – people need to be motivated through new challenges. Of course, the process of getting people involved is considered the goal to be reached no matter what the outcome. In this way strategic analysis can generate a synthesis of collective commitment, contrary to the ideas expressed by Henry Mintzberg (1994). Indeed, the real difficulty lies not in making the right choices but in making sure that all the participants ask themselves the right questions Remember the old schoolteacher expression: A problem well stated (and shared by those concerned) is already half solved. This is exactly what Michel Crozier meant when he said "the problem is the problem!"

With regard to managerial fashions, the rich heritage of strategic analysis remains with us. For example, the classical analysis using threats and opportunities coming from the general environment shows that we cannot limit our analysis to the competitive environment in the name of short-term profits, as the early writings of Michael Porter might lead us to believe. The fact that many uncertainties hang in the balance within the general context, especially over the long-term, underscores the need for broad scenario building to clarify the strategic options available and to ensure continued development.

In the past, the European management market was flooded by tools and approaches designed abroad, mainly in Japan and the USA. Examples abound, but the most outstanding was the Strategic Business Unit (SBU) approach. Indeed many American firms actually became victims of the SBU approach. Yet in the end, the relative or even absolute decline of entire sections of American industry, in comparison with Japan and Europe during the 1960s and 80s, made any debate over a classic American approach moot. As Marc Giget (1998) put it: "The revival in the 90s was generated from analyses labeled *Made in America* which were inspired directly by foreign models." Hence managers rediscovered the virtues of positioning themselves against the best (benchmarking), the value of a complete rehaul of processes and structures (re-engineering), as well as the importance of sticking to the basics (downsizing) and lastly, the power of innovation when it comes from the company's core competences. Therein lies the difference between winning and losing companies, as Hamel and Prahalad point out: "We had to conclude that some management teams were simply more foresightful than others. Some were capable of imagining products, services and entire industries that did not yet exist and then giving them birth. These managers seemed to spend less time worrying about how to position the firm in existing competitive space and more time creating fundamentally new competitive space. Other companies, the laggards were more interested in protecting the past than in creating the future." [1]

Let us reconsider some of the terms employed above. Strategy uses foresight and innovation while *la prospective* uses preactivity and proactivity, but we are essentially talking about the exact same thing.

Given this similarity, the term *strategic prospective* has been circulating since the late 1980's, especially in France. Better late than never, but we wonder how else a strategist could operate any other way than by "seeing far, wide, and deep, while taking risks and thinking about the human factor"? (See Gaston Berger (1964).) In fact we would add to the above "thinking unconventionally and collectively". We continue paraphrasing Gaston Berger who once remarked that "looking at the future disturbs the present". However, we add a conclusion to his remark: "but anticipation encourages action". By now we are convinced that scenario building is often strategic if not through its outcome at least through its intentions. Similarly, strategy calls upon futures studies to clarify choices made with the future in mind.

The Use and Abuse of the Term *Strategy*

The so-called "rise and fall of strategic planning" has not exhausted people's interest. (This may be a relief for an author like Henry Mintzberg (1979).) In fact there is no risk of a real fall because of the independent nature of each of its components. "An organization can plan (take the future into consideration) without actually committing to planning (a formal procedure) even if it does draw up some plans (explicit intentions)." In reality, the issue is not really planning but

---

1. Hamel G, C.K. Prahalad. *Competing for the Future*. Boston: Harvard Business School Press, 1994, Preface xvii.

rather the manner in which planning is carried out. The graft of strategic planning only takes root if it is integrated into the corporate culture and identity. To use another metaphor, the wheels of development depend not only on logic, but also on human emotion and behavior. Hence the idea of strategic management, which is almost a tautology according to Boyer and Equilbey's definition of management (1990): "the art of management is to make the organization serve strategy." Yet management in itself does not constitute a strategy. Strategy shapes management but also presupposes objectives and related tactics (contingent decisionmaking). One wonders how serious authors reject these distinctions. It is high time that these concepts be clarified so that the same word does not have different meanings and that different things are not named the same.

For traditional authors, such as Lucien Poirier (1987) and Igor Ansoff (1965) the notion of strategy refers to a firm's actions upon its environment and reflection on that action. Without hesitating, Lucien Poirier used the term *stratégie prospective* which we have called "strategic prospective" or strategic scenario building. Obviously, the two notions are distinct but often associated. However some authors, including Fabrice Roubelat (1996), maintain that *la prospective* has two sides to it. Roubelat bases his comments on Jacques Lesourne (1989) to conclude that "a strategic decision is either one that creates an irreversible situation for the entire organization or one that anticipates an environmental change apt to provoke such an irreversible situation". In other words, according to Lesourne, "a strategic decision would likely be a decision that forces the organization to ponder its very existence, independence, mission, and main field of activity." In short, this decision exists for a specific company and according to this definition, general forecasting sessions would not have any strategic value for the actor/company involved.

The main advantage of these definitions is that they avoid using the word *strategic* to qualify or inflate everything that merely seems important.

Of course prudence and common sense enter into the equation; consequently, our efforts are not limited to asking about risks of breakdowns or breakthroughs and strategy is not reduced only to decisions of an irreversible nature for the company. It is true that the borders are fuzzy here and impossible to redraw completely. The same may be said for decisions, for as Jacques Lesourne once put it: "major decisions are rarely made, they become increasingly improbable as the small decisions accumulate".

For any organization, *prospective* is not philanthropy but rather reflection with a view to clarifying action, especially action of a strategic nature.

The Five Basic Questions Leading to Action

Like fraternal twins, *prospective* and strategy remain distinct entities and it is necessary to distinguish between:

1) a time for anticipation, in other words, the study of possible and desirable changes, and

2) a time to prepare action: in other words, the working out and assessing of possible strategic choices so as to be prepared for expected changes (pre-activity) and provoke desirable changes (pro-activity).

The dichotomy between exploring and preparing a course of action implies the following five questions: (Q1), what could happen? (scenario building) (Q2), what can I do? (strategic options) (Q3), what will I do? (strategic decisions) (Q4), how will I do it? (actions and operational plans) and an essential pre-question (Q0), who am I? All too often ignored, the last question is the starting point of Marc Giget's strategic procedure (1998). However this preliminary identification also echoes Socrates' famous lesson, "know thyself".

Only the *prospective* approach with a preactive and proactive attitude focuses on the question "what could happen?" (Q1) It becomes strategic when an organization asks itself "what can we do?" (Q2) Once these two questions have been answered, the strategy goes from "what can we do?" (Q2) to two further queries: "what are we going to do?" (Q3) and "how will we do it?" (Q4) Hence the overlapping between scenario and strategy. There are, of course, future studies that contain no clear strategic nature whatsoever for an actor as well as strategic analyses of firms or sectors whose interest in the future is embryonic or even nonexistent. For the sake of clarity, the expression *strategic prospective* will therefore be reserved for futures studies having strategic ambitions and endpoints for those participating.

Five Attitudes towards the Future

Anticipation is a must in the modern world as a direct result of two factors:

1) the feeling that social, economic and technological change is speeding up, hence the need for a long-term vision. Gaston Berger, the spiritual father of the French futures school, expressed this situation best when he said "the faster the car, the stronger the headlights must be";

2) the factors of inertia inherent to various structures and behaviors oblige us to sow now if we want to reap a future harvest. As my grandfather used to say: "The longer a tree takes to grow, the earlier you have to plant it."

Lack of foresight in the past has led to the present situation in which yesterday's stupid questions become today's urgent matters that have to be settled quickly, even with bandaids, to the detriment of long-term development. Although reactivity is not desirable in the short-term as an end in itself, the ageless advice of Seneca rings true here: "There is no fair wind for the man who knows not where he is headed."

Anticipation enlightens action and lends it meaning as well as direction. If there is no direction for the future, the present is empty of meaning. Similarly, a dream is not the opposite of reality but rather the incubator of reality and, in that reality, any project must be driven by desire or will.

In this sense, people can choose from among five basic attitudes:

1) the passive ostrich, who accepts change;

2) the reactive firefighter, who waits for the alarm to put out fires;

3) the preactive insurer, who prepares for foreseeable changes because an ounce of prevention is worth a pound of cure;

4) the proactive conspirator, who acts to provoke desirable change;

5) the *anticipactive* actor who savvily combines all of the above but adopts an anticipactive attitude; in other words, a blend of the reactive, preactive and proactive attitudes.

Another analogy is the college football try-out. A passive recruit will soon be back on the bench; whereas, a reactive player will chase madly after the ball and rarely get hold of it. A preactive player will try to anticipate the right moves but often defensively and incorrectly. Remember the old saying: A strong offense is the best defense. The team's star has to outplay the opponent's tactics and not be fooled by players who are running interference; i.e., those who follow conventional thinking. Leading and scoring require offense. When you play proactively, the other team plays reactively.

Perhaps decisionmakers should remember the fifth attitude, which blends the star player's ambition with caution and urgency. Try this decisionmaking exercise, from now on, when you prepare an action plan, write down three columns in your matrix: one for reactivity, one for pre-activity and one for pro-activity. None of the three should be too empty or too full. Of course, in periods of crisis, reactivity will prevail while in periods of growth, changes must be anticipated and induced, particularly through innovation.

A Riddle: What is the *raison d'être* of the present and creative force of the future?

The world may well be changing but the direction of that change is not certain. Shifts and transfers trigger social, economic, and technological uncertainty that people and corporations have to integrate into their strategies for the future.

Futures-thinking exercises, *la prospective*, or strategic scenario building do not claim to eliminate uncertainty with predictions;

instead they seek to reduce uncertainty as much as possible and to enable people to make decisions in view of desired futures. It is above all a state of mind (imagination and anticipation) that leads to behavior (hope and will).

Historically, the attitude described above is a form of rebellion against determinism (Hugues de Jouvenel) and chance (Pierre Massé). This revolt rides on willpower. Of course there is no will without a goal and the goal is exactly that a particular desire will materialize.

By considering desire or will as a productive force for the future, we rehabilitate subjectivism and utopia, thus reuniting imagination and scientific logic. Like many terms, utopian is too often used as synonymous with impossible. Etymologically *ou-topos*, coming from Greek, means a non-place; i.e., a place that does not exist. However, this does not exclude an eventual future existence. Utopia as a virtual object of desire is the source where action takes its meaning or direction. We are thus able to understand why the structure of social relationships crumbles as soon as a certain level of restrictions conflict with desire and make life intolerable. In other words, the rather philosophical goal of any futures-thinking exercise is to erase the line between reality and possibility.

Once again we come up against the dream versus the reality when discussing the present *vis-à-vis* the future. Once again we turn to Gaston Berger's wisdom: "The future is the *raison d'être* of the present".

All this talk about the future, however, does not negate the past. We need to make the link between the past because what we regret about the past is the lost future. The image of an old couple comes to mind. "They do not want to relive their past love but to live their love now as they did before, when they had such a vast future ahead of them and which is now behind them. What they have lost and what they regret is not really the past but rather the future they no longer have before them." (Nicolas Grimaldi, 1971)

Generally what we suffer in the future is the result of past actions. Similarly, what we want in the future explains present actions. In other words, it is not only the past that explains the future, but also the image of the future which leaves an imprint on the present. As an example, one individual's consumption at any given moment does not depend only on his/her previous earnings or savings, but also on anticipated income, e.g. credit. This is precisely what Milton Friedman expressed in his permanent income theory. Decidedly, we have to look to the future to shed light on the present.

Five Key Ideas

Any form of prediction is a sham because the future is not already written in some big book in the sky. The future remains to be created. In this sense, it is plural, undetermined and open to a wide variety of possibilities. Whatever happens tomorrow depends less on heavy trends than on policies dictated in the face of these trends. If the future is indeed the fruit of human will, then the following five key ideas should be kept in mind at all times.

The World Changes but the Problems Stay the Same

Why? The problems stay the same because they are linked to human nature. The basic motivators, e.g. wealth, power, love and hate, function now just as well as in ancient Greece. Politicians know the number of traitors has not diminished since Judas' time. The only difference is that a traitor's life expectancy has increased!

We have to study and know human nature to understand what is happening around us. We need to find the memory of the past to shed light upon the future while keeping in mind the message of Visconti's movie, *The Leopard*, "everything must change so that everything may start over!"

In fact every time we find a problem that we encountered some five, ten, even fifteen years before, whether it be a concrete situation, such as selecting an airport site or a social issue like unemployment, the idea of change as renewal comes to mind.

As did the year 1000, the year 2000 has generated an excess of end-of-the-world predictions. Thinking about the future has always been the favorite time to let one's fantasies run wild as either dreams or nightmares. However, now that Y2K is yesterday's news, maybe we can stop the attempts to frighten or impress others with statements like, "two-thirds of tomorrow's products do not exist yet" or "the skills of tomorrow are unknown today!" In many respects, tomorrow's world will resemble today's. Children will go to schools where there are blackboards and chalk, even though their schoolbags will contain powerful portable computers.

Every generation has the impression that it is living in an era of unprecedented transition. Nothing could be more normal! The current era is exceptional to each of us because it is the only one we will know; hence, we tend to overestimate the speed and importance of changes, especially in terms of new technology.

Overestimating Technological Change

That which is technologically possible is not necessarily economically profitable or socially desirable. Let us take the example of telecommuting or the home office. It is improbable that telecommuting will develop to the point that it eclipses most office jobs. Many factors go against the grain in this maximalist hypothesis. First of all, the current layout of suburban houses does not make them suitable for full working days on a regular basis. Second, work also means socializing and fulfilling a need to communicate with others. Note in passing that this is a social need that appears increasingly difficult to satisfy.

People are looking for a social relationship and some kind of direction for their life. Their current despair stems from the solitude that they feel. The problem is particularly acute among the unemployed who are excluded from the social network that a job offers. The market niche of tomorrow is solitude and the need for human contact. Obviously the information highway is a deadend solution.

Internet: A Computerized Dumpster

The high tech mirage regularly rises and floats to center stage, e.g. "computers for one and all!" (fifth generation, of course) and now the internet. Like our colleague Bruno Lussato, we are tempted to see the internet as a computerized trash can or garbage bin. Following the analogy; indeed, there is anything and everything in a garbage bin, maybe even hidden treasure. However, that does not provide sufficient reason to spend one's time rummaging through the trash. There are skoupedologists trained to do just this type of sociological research.

Yes, we all need a wastepaper basket or garbage pail of some kind and electronic mail does represent progress, but many people boast of devoting hours daily to communicating with the rest of the world on the net while they are incapable of exchanging a few words with their nextdoor neighbor. How can we consider this stampede to surf the net as anything other than a sign of the times; i.e., feelings of tremendous solitude and the need for human contact? The main advantage of cybercafés is that they provide those who long to communicate with a place where they can talk amongst themselves and not only with a screen. Of course some people achieve the same effect by taking their dog out for a walk!

Technology is the Pandora's box of modern society in that information technology enables people to be closer, in contact with the entire world, but with no one next to them for a chat. Some people pay psychoanalysts a fortune just to have someone to listen to them. In terms of human contact, telecommuting does not really spell progress; hence, it will remain marginal.

Tomorrow's population will not work any less than today's. Tomorrow's workers will also try to find in their office job the kind of social ties and opportunities for mutual recognition that are needed for life to have some purpose. People do not want the life of solitude enjoyed by the nerd, hacker or cyberhermit who lives deprived of human contact.

Obviously, the world changes, but over time people's behaviour patterns have remained -- often sadly -- the same. When placed in the same situation, they react almost identically and thus predictably.

Let us not forget the human factor and that people are always at the core of any difference or change. There is no need to find a scapegoat in globalization or technology just to shirk our responsibilities. For many companies, regions or individuals experiencing difficulties, their troubles stem from internal insufficiencies and not some external force. The keys of success and causes of failure are initially internal.

The future of an individual or an organization depends largely on its internal strengths and weaknesses. We recognize the wisdom of the ancient Greeks, namely Socrates, who counseled: "Know thyself (we stress the second part; thyself first)". As we will see, this advice leads us to several key questions.

Deep down we know that there is no technological or economic solution to problems of another nature. Trying to apply technology or economics to a human resources problem is like giving candy to a child seeking affection. The major questions for the future are linked to social "fractures" or breakdowns and the spiritual void of a society in which economics can not give life meaning.

Yet people have selective short-term memory and fail to recognize the long-term and what it can teach us. The well-known expression states that history may not be repeated, but human behavior certainly is repeated! Over the centuries, people have adopted and kept eerily similar behavioral patterns that led them to similar situations in which they behaved in almost the same ways. Their behavior is thus predictable and the past thus provides us with insightful lessons for the future. Economic examples come to mind, such as cyclical scarcity and plenty in the food supply related to speculation on prices or long periods of inflation followed by deflation and lastly, the worrisome coincidences between demographic shifts and political/economic decline.

Structures and patterns are always characterized by heavy inertia, which should not be underestimated in terms of the potential forces of change. Unfortunately in futures studies we tend to consider that which could change by forgetting to systematically list all that which most likely will remain unchanged, especially if nothing is done. Some inertial forces actually act like a brake on adaptation and development and they then become rigid if change -- whether desirable or undesirable -- has not been prepared far enough in advance. However, other inertial forces play a healthy role and, as any driver knows, the brake complements the accelerator.

From Key Actors to Bifurcations

The future should not be envisaged as a single, pretraced line extending from the past. The future is plural and undetermined. This plurality and the degrees of freedom in human action essentially form a tandem.

The present is all the richer since the future remains open to a vast array of possible futures in which the desirable may dominate. In the words of Gaston Berger (1967), "old age is simply the shrinking of the field of possibilities". Phrased differently, whatever is no longer possible in the future is the fruit of our past actions; whereas, that which remains possible depends upon our present actions.

The broader the array of possible futures is, the greater the number of futures and the greater the uncertainty. Each possible future, or *futurible*, [1] is more or less probable but only certain ones are desirable to each actor. The actors' projects are partially antagonistic and the future actually created may be considered as the result of the balance of power among those actors. Of course the balance of power is not static and the actors' strategies serve to orient probable results toward desirable results. In sum, creating futures depends not only upon chance and necessity but also upon human will.

The so-called real world is much too complex for us to hope to generate a logarithm of any hidden determinism it may hold. Even if we could calculate such a formula, the uncertainty that is inherent in any measure, especially if social, would leave us with a range of possible futures at least in our minds. Yet since determinism is undeterminable, we have to go along *as if* no bets had been placed, as if the revolution of will could singlehandedly dethrone the tyranny of chance and necessity.

During the seventies, Ilya Prigogine and Isabelle Stengers (1979) based their work on theories and experiments in thermodynamics and physical chemistry to advance their own notions of *order by fluctuation* and *fertile chaos* (Prigogine, 1990). They demonstrated that when far from the initial conditions of equilibrium, bifurcations appear which lead to other states of equilibrium. Near these critical points weak fluctuations, either internal or external to the system, may prove decisive in moving towards one or another branch of evolution. When transposed to social systems, these weak fluctuations may be chance upsets or individual actions. At these critical points, the fluctuations become dangerous whereas elsewhere they would have remained insignificant.

How can we recognize bifurcations? "What events and which innovations will be inconsequential and which ones are liable to affect the

---

1. Neologism based on the words *futur* and *possible*, created by Bertrand de Jouvenel.

world order, determine an irreversible evolutionary choice? What are the zones of selection and the zones of stability?" (Prigogine, 1990) The same questions arise regularly in any futures-thinking exercise.

If we think about it, identifying the range of possible futures with scenarios is also recognizing the diagram of bifurcations. And if so, then the parameters of those bifurcations are also the key variables used in the analysis stage of futures-thinking.

Over the past few years, theories have converged towards a self-organizing concept that enables one to adapt them to whatever is "new" and to the creation of anything new. Everything happens as if the traditional arrow of time were reversed so that what we do today may be explained not by conditioning but by the goal that we have set and are striving to reach (Jean-Pierre Dupuy, 1982). Once again, the future is the *raison d'être* of the present. Let us add that desire is the force generating the future and the driving/guiding principle of self-organization.

Nevertheless, futures thinking is far from neutral. It depends on subjective choices related to how problems are approached, which hypotheses are tested, and what goals are pursued. In fact, starting a futures-thinking exercise and listing scenarios as part of actors' strategies is rather like a poker bid. Here we put our finger squarely on the ideological role that scenario building may play and on the danger of manipulation inherent in the process.

Political parties play with the future like Pavlov's bell that can be rung to mobilize or demobilize the masses. One example is to get people to accept the problems of the day more readily as a future project. Obviously a leader can hardly tell the nation to tighten its belt so that tomorrow will be even worse! If we take it to extremes, there is the theme of the sacrificed generations. In this case the ideological spin is incredible and political groups speak of the future as if speaking about the future made it true. (Yves Barel, 1971). The danger of manipulation will be lessened once futures-thinking exercises or strategic scenario building are accessible to everyone; i.e., all those concerned may take part not only managers or leaders.

The image of the future that we create for ourselves is invaluable and must be analyzed since questioning actors on their representations of the future reveals a great deal about their strategic behavior. Moreover, even if this vision of the future seems wrong to us, we still need to take it into account.

At this point, many will want to justify the usefulness and credibility of futures techniques or methodology. Let us employ the analogy of a gambler at the casino. The uncertainty of the future prompts him to place bets and, like a good gambler, a good strategic futurist/expert wins more often than he loses.

Simple Tools for Complex Problems

Are only complex tools capable of reading our complex reality? No. Modern history's great minds traditionally found relatively simple laws to explain the universe. Examples abound in the principles of thermodynamics or the theory of relativity. As the French mathematical economist and Nobel prize-winner Maurice Allais (1989) put it: "A theory in which neither the hypotheses nor the consequences may be squared with reality is of no scientific interest." Allais adds that a perfect model is impossible and that only approximative models of reality are possible. He points out that "of two models, the best will always be the one in which a given approximation will represent the data gathered through observation in the simplest manner." That should reassure readers who think all this is Greek to them and it should also shake up all those who confuse the term "complex" with "complicated" and hence simple with simplistic! The real challenge lies in convincing those who are used to making things complicated. It is always easier to complicate matters than it is to simplify them.

Here is one more definition: a system is not reality but rather a means to observe reality. Systems analysis is nothing more than a way of thinking observed as a way of thinking. It is also an act of epistemological faith since it supposes that the observer is capable of self-observation and observation simultaneously. In this sense a complex way of thinking, a complex vision of reality, does require a complex tool. Consequently we suggest confronting complexity with the simplest tools possible because a tool is there to reduce rather than increase complexity. We also suggest:
– testing complex tools on simple problems to be able to measure the added value of the complex tool versus the simple tool;
– approaching complex problems with simple tools in order to ensure that the complexity stems from the problem and not the tool.

It is worth repeating that an imperfect tool, be it an inaccuracy, a surplus or a lack of data, as well as the subjectivity of interpretations, is inevitable and encourages the use of varied, complementary approaches. Wherever possible, the sensitivity of the results generated by a model should be tested against the variation in input data and the use of another tool. Only solid, tested results should be considered credible.

If scenario building requires rigor to deal with complexity, it also requires tools that are simple enough to be appropriated. The following timeless recommendation rings true: "An operational imperfection is better than a non-existent perfection." In this respect, game theory has certainly advanced, at least theoretically, but it remains unapplied in corporations. On the other hand, the Mactor method (as seen in the case studies herein) used in analyzing actors'strategies may not be perfect but it is at least operational.

Ask the Right Questions and Quash Conventional Thinking

"The answer is yes, but what was the question?" Woody Allen

This famous line is all too often what happens when we forget to consider the validity of a question and rush like lemmings to find the illusory answers to false questions. Since there can be no right answer to a wrong question, how can we ensure that we are indeed asking the right questions?

Information is often stifled, as in a gag order, by conformism in the shape of consensus. Innocent-sounding enough, consensus may incite individuals to opt for the dominant opinion and reject the minority view. In the end, any one individual who sees clearly will not likely be heard. Of course that does not mean that wild predictions should be given more credence, but rather that many conjectures and preconceived ideas should be considered with suspicion. Yes, there is always some discomfort in rousing people from years of intellectual habits; however, the scenario planner or futurist must act like the cheeky child who dares to say that the Emperor is naked and definitely not wearing new clothes!

In the past we have often been right in exposing and tilting against conventional thinking. Through "mental re-engineering", or going back to square one of the problem, we managed

– to point out as early as 1978 that there would be a new oil crisis plus an energy surplus that would render nuclear energy less necessary; [1]

– dispute the thesis of the industrial decline of Europe in relation to the United States and Japan; [2]

– to cast doubt on the Japanese management "model of the week" fashion; [3]

– to question the regularly evoked thesis of Germany's decline (at a time when Germany had become the world's leading exporter of manufactured goods); [4]

– to denounce the myth of technology as the way out of economic crises. [5]

Strategy is also affected by conformism and conventional thinking. How many investment and site selection choices have been justified with the mantra "the company needs a critical size to compete internationally"? In reality, there are always smaller, more profitable com-

1. "Energy Horizon Keeps Receding?", *The Times*, 5 September 1978.
2. "The USA: Recovery or Concealed Decline?", *Futures*, vol. 17, n°3, 1985, pp. 196-201.
3. "Ten Unfashionable and Controversial Findings on Japan", *Futures*, vol. 19, n°4, 1987, pp. 371-84.
4. "Germany: Paradoxical Power", *Futures*, vol. 12, n°4, 1989, pp. 344-60.
5. "From the Technological Mirage to the Social Breakthrough", *Futures*, vol. 17, n°3, 1986, pp. 369-75.

panies even within the same sector. Why then does a company not opt to find ways to be more profitable without expanding? The correct question would be "how can we be more profitable at our current size?" The answer to this question may mean temporary lack of growth, like trees which are pruned only to grow back all the more beautifully. Profitability is really the best condition for healthy growth.

Despite a respectable track record in the futures field, we have few illusions about the impact of a statement or an article that goes against the grain of popular wisdom. However, we consider it almost a civic duty to say what others only think. Too many intellectuals keep quiet for the sake of their career, gobbing everything and prepared to sacrifice their own ideas for money, honor or reputation. Cowardice underlies the demure attitude of some, not to mention the "reasons of State", sometimes given as an explanation for remaining silent even about crimes.

Any good teacher knows that the best ideas or lessons are those that students find themselves. However, in the school of hard knocks, everyone knows that if the boss likes an idea and actually thinks it came from him or her, then it will go through. This is part of human nature. It is a fact of life that should be remembered whenever we have to convince anyone of anything.

From Anticipation to Action through Appropriation

Vision may be a buzzword, but we insist on using it here, especially since breadth of vision is needed if anything is going to happen, first, on a small scale, and then within the larger scheme of things. Mobilizing intelligence is all the more efficient if it takes place within the framework of a specific project known to all. Internal motivation and external strategy are thus like two sides of the same sheet of paper. They are also two goals that can not be reached separately.

Intellectual and affective appropriation is a compulsory stage if anticipation is to crystallize into effective action. We turn to the ancient Greeks to conceptualize this idea, the Greek triangle illustrated below. "Logos" (thought, rationality, discourse), "Epithumia" (desire in all its noble and not so noble aspects), "Ergo" (action or realization). The marriage of passion and reason, of heart and mind, is the key to successful action and individual fulfillment (the body). Let us turn to the cover to see the same message in color: the blue of cold reason mixed with the yellow of warm feelings produces the green of brilliant action. Of course in English we have the three as: Appropriation, Anticipation and Action.

The age-old phony war that pits intuition against logic and the link between thought and action appears clearly here. Once it is time to act, it is too late to think. Moreover, when one thinks, one should take time and not be rushed by an emergency. Action is commanded by a

The Greek Triangle

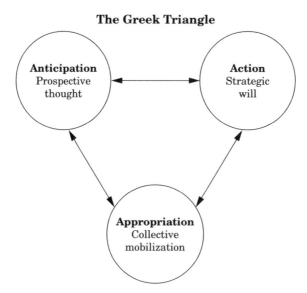

reflex whereas reason is generally dominated by intuition. This impression fools us into thinking that the reflex to act is just as fast and appropriate because the brain has been trained previously. This is not always the case for just like muscles, the brain needs exercise, too. In the end, there really is no opposition but rather complementarity between intuition and reason.

A Few Key Words

Prospective: Anticipate before acting. *La prospective*, an "intellectual non-discipline" (Pierre Massé) seeks to see "far, wide and deep" (Gaston Berger).

Prediction: Estimate of the future assigned a certain degree of confidence.

Projection: Extension or inflection into the future of past trends.

Scenario: coherent sets of hypotheses leading from a given original situation to a future situation.

Five Basic Attitudes toward the Future

1) Passive   Ostrich accepting change as it comes
2) Reactive   Firefighter waiting for the alarm to ring
3) Preactive   Insurance agent preparing for foreseeable changes
                          (An ounce of prevention is worth a pound of cure.)
4) Proactive   Conspirator (agent provocateur) who pushes for desirable changes
5) A combination of 2 to 4.

Planning

"Conceiving of a desired future as well as the real means required to achieve it." (R.L. Ackoff).

Strategy

Code of conduct for actors enabling them to reach their goals

Tactics(plur.) ways and means of reaching goals within a strategy according to the circumstances.

Strategic Planning

Concept launched in the mid-60s, notably by Igor Ansoff, to refer to the fact that corporate planning should take turbulence in the company's environment (often called strategic environment) into account much more and adapt its goals accordingly.

Strategic Management

Concept launched in the mid-1960s by Igor Ansoff in order to emphasize the conditions that enable structures and organizations to adapt to an increasingly turbulent world.

Strategic Prospective

Concept from the 1990s, French School, in which *la prospective* is applied to strategic action and the corporate vision. In this way; *strategic prospective* acts as a management tool from anticipation to action through appropriation. This is also the case of technological *foresight* in terms of public acceptance of change and policymaking.

2

WHY DO THE EXPERTS GET IT WRONG?

Tales of Error

History is full of paradoxes regarding the future. For example, it was during the sixties when forecasting was easier and less necessary that futurology, futures studies, and *la prospective* were developed. In those days, econometric models run through a computer could demonstrate, in practical terms, what people already knew: everything was more or less directly correlated to the national product, which was growing at 5% annually. No doubt about it, time was the best "explanatory" variable for what was considered a perpetual period of growth.

However since 1973, the future has stopped looking like the past. The horizon used in futures thinking; i.e., break points or discontinuities, had crept up on us. However no model based on data and relationships from the past could have foreseen these breaks or bifurcations because they were linked to the behavior of actors free to behave however they wished.

Although we might bruise a few egos in reviewing historical errors in forecasting, there are important lessons to be learned. In fact, it soon becomes obvious that errors in forecasting cause less damage than errors in analysis, diagnosis and prescription. The latter are created more by a lack of foresight and are thus worse than any false prediction. Canadian futurist Kimon Valaskakis uses a medical analogy to illustrate the potential for error in any futures exercise. The possibility of error lies at the following four points:

1) in diagnosing the disease;
2) in forecasting its development;
3) in prescribing the right drugs;
4) and lastly, in determining the correct dosage of prescription drugs.

The first error, a diagnostic error, is obviously the most serious, but numbers two through four are just as frequent. For most issues, for example, unemployment, the diagnosis was rendered public a long time ago, but the pill seems too bitter to swallow given the many socioeconomic taboos surrounding joblessness.

An effective futures-thinking exercise or forecast implies nonconformism, rigor, and consistency. Just trusting intuition, especially intuition unenlightened by logic, leads to desperate detours and even deadends. Remember that even while walking in the dark, we have to keep our eyes wide open and avoid preconceived ideas.

Whether errors in analysis come from models or not, they may be directly linked to experts whose erroneous viewpoints are spread on the simple basis of their reputation. The following historical example of conventional, conformist thinking and authority comes from Bernard Cazes (1986). In the fifteenth century, Christopher Columbus proposed his seafaring expedition to the King and Queen of Spain. The

enterprise was carefully examined by an informal commission presided by the Hieronymite brother Hernando de Talavera, Queen Isa-
bela's confessor. Four years later, the commission rendered its opinion
to the monarchs. To paraphrase Talavera, nothing could justify royal
assent for such an enterprise based on weak logic and seemingly
impossible to anyone with any knowledge whatsoever! The six arguments against Columbus' idea of a western passage to the Indies
appear to follow a logical structure:

1) a journey to Asia would require three years;

2) the (Atlantic) ocean is infinite and perhaps unnavigable;

3) if Columbus were to reach the ends of the earth, he would not be
able to return home;

4) there are no endpoints of land because most of the globe is covered with water and because Saint Augustine said so;

5) of five parts of the world, only three are inhabitable;

6) so many centuries after the Creation, it is unlikely that lands of
any interest could have remained undiscovered.

Although the expert committee was wrong, Christopher Columbus
was equally wrong. He remained convinced that between the end of
the Orient and the end of the Occident there lay only one sea. As a
result, he concluded that the Chinese coast was only five or six thousand kilometers from Europe. Columbus never did reach the Orient
and discovered America without knowing it. He went to his grave
claiming to have reached the Indies when he had only completed one-
third of his journey and the Antilles did not look anything like what
people knew of the Orient in those days.

Another historical example given by our colleague André Guillerme
involves estimates of the Earth's age up to the eighteenth century and
the catastrophic extrapolations that ensued.

Up to and including the year 1750, scientists estimated the Earth's
age to be 5,200 years. In 1750, a Frenchman named Buffon calculated
it to be one million years while his colleague, Cuvier, went as high as
ten million. Nowadays, the Earth's age is considered to be approximately twenty billion years. Right up to the mid-eighteenth century,
however, scientific calculations used five thousand years as a reference
point for their extrapolations. On the basis of the observable erosion
which had occurred over the past 5,000 years, they predicted that the
mountains would disappear within the following two hundred years
and that the planet would turn into swampland during the twentieth
century. Similarly, given a "Little Ice Age" at the end of the eighteenth
century, the same scientists thought that the Earth's temperature had
settled at 1,000° in 3000 BC and consequently should reach 10° in 1880
and then 0° in the year 2000. Reports of academic societies also proved
that the Champagne region of France was destined to become a desert
based on the supposition that heavy deforestation would continue. No
one anticipated the upcoming use of coal!

Well, that was then, some might say. Scientists of yesteryear did not have today's analytical tools. Granted, we are better equipped now, but often you would not know it from the results. Indeed, armies of economists focused their efforts on fuel and energy forecasting after the first oil shock. In hindsight, they were all wrong, dead wrong. Energy consumption in 1985 was actually half the amount regularly predicted in 1974.

That was then, but this is now. Can we say that current forecasts or predictions are any more reliable? The World Energy Conference (1993) forecast consumption rates of slightly more than 13 billion tons of oil equivalent (TOE).

Oil accounts for one quarter of that amount, in other words, only slightly more than what was predicted in 1985 for the year 2000. So far, the world demand has been systematically overestimated, especially for petroleum. Why? It seems that the slowdown in developed economies was never considered longlasting. In the future, of course, the opposite could arise if the probable upswing in several developing countries pans out. Remember that 1990 North American energy consumption of 8 TOE per capita was twice the Western European rate and five to six times that of developing countries.

Lastly, we know how a progressive increase in energy prices affects savings and increases the possibility of substitution. We can thus legitimately ask if the relative decrease in oil prices since the mid-eighties is not paving the way for new oil shocks that will be all the sharper because we have let down our guard.

Of course sometimes the experts get it wrong because they have biased information. However, often they simply attack false problems that mask the real issues. There are actually many possible causes of error. What follows is a summary and update of the classic list found in *From Anticipation to Action*, 1994.

The Four Main Causes of Error

Shortsightedness When Facing Change and Inertia

We have already mentioned two biases as sources of error: overestimating change and underestimating inertia. Overestimating change in 1965 led the Rand Corporation, Delphi expert survey in hand, to announce teaching machines and 100% accurate weather forecasts for 1975; automatic translation by 1979; household robots for 1988. (For more information on these much awaited future technologies, see Bernard Cazes (1986)).

This excessive extrapolation of technological possibilities continues in the third millennium, as seen in the emphasis placed on distance education and telecommuting or the mirage of a "communication society". Fortunately or unfortunately, many experts, managers and politicians forget that people crave social ties and that nothing replaces human contact. Think about how often you prefer to wait for the "real live" operator or a receptionist when you telephone a large business or organization!

Inversely, many technological changes considered inconceivable yesterday have become commonplace today. At the beginning of the twentieth century, American astronomer and mathematician, Simon Newcomb, thought that he had amply demonstrated the impossibility of ever seeing a device heavier than air fly. He considered the impossibility tantamount to a fact. (Denis de Rougemont, in Cazes (1986)).

One common denominator in technological change is uncertainty. Uncertainty prevails, and unexpected discoveries or innovations may arise, but we should never forget that what is technologically possible today will develop slowly because of inertia and socio-economic limits or restrictions. One example stands out: polymetallic nodules. Use of these nodules is technically possible but economically less profitable than existing mines, and, of course, there are considerable geopolitical issues. The life sciences and genetic engineering abound with examples of technically possible but socially or economically unacceptable changes.

Shortsightedness or myopia in the face of change leads to two types of symmetric errors: people either overestimate or underestimate the phenomenon. In our experience, the former occurs more than the latter. Urbanization, as the rural world has moved to an industrial one in only a few generations, can teach us a lesson in underestimating change. Again, the impact of television on families and villages has had a tremendous effect on structures and roles. Yet the family structures, e.g. authoritarian versus egalitarian, described by Emmanuel Todd (1983) seem to have existed for millennia. There are thus permanent features in life, despite the frequent appearance of structural changes.

Nevertheless, the prevailing *zeitgeist* of the twentieth century was that change had accelerated and that history constantly surprises us. One event that comes to mind is the fall of Communism in Eastern Europe (1989), crowned by the reunification of Germany in 1990. Only a few years, even months, beforehand, the domino collapse of several governments remained unthinkable. Yet the velvet revolution and equally surprising, although less smooth, revolts in surrounding countries rose from inertial forces like nationalism and cultural identity. These two forces had resisted decades of authoritarian efforts to stifle or eradicate them. Precisely because they were pent up, nationalism and cultural identity surged stronger than ever throughout Eastern Europe as if floodgates had been opened.

Of course an accurate appraisal of the forces of inertia and change depends on the horizon given in a study. It is important to distinguish among the short-, medium- and long-term, characterized by economic, trend-based, and structural variables respectively. In many fields, accelerated change shrinks the medium-term and brings the long-term closer. In other words, the horizon given in making many decisions may have changed. In some industrial sectors, like electronics, two to four years is already considered a long-term horizon whereas in aeronautics, inertia is such that ten to fifteen years must be used as long-term horizons.

Prophecies and Political Lies

Almost any published report on any development or change in a given area of our lives will provoke reactions which, in turn, affect that development. This is the prophecy effect at work. Some are encouraging prophecies that help complete the effect of a phenomenon, e.g. inflation. In inflation the anticipation and announcement of an increase usually triggers the multiplier effect. Whereas others are dissuasive or discouraging prophecies which produce a reaction that counters or prevents a development from occuring. We often talk of self-fulfilling or self-destroying (also called self-destructive) prophecies.

Ironically, a good prediction is not one that comes true but rather one that leads to action. The prophecy effect is not always wrong and may even be sought after to correct a situation or reorient a development in a more desirable direction. Hence "foreseeing a catastrophe is conditional in that it requires one to foresee what would happen if we do nothing to prevent it." (Pierre Massé, Gaston Berger, 1967).

Catastrophic demographic projections given during the seventies provide an excellent example of a normative prophecy. If effective, the so-called prophetic information should lead to measures or behaviors that correct an undesirable development. However, in this instance, the prophecy went unfulfilled. African countries did little to control their spiraling birthrates; whereas European countries did nothing to stop the decline of an aging population.

In economics, as Keynes (1936) pointed out, a simple forecast change can through its effects provoke an oscillation similar in shape to a cyclical movement. As a result, the mere mention of a coffee shortage or the unavailability of a children's toy often paves the way for an abundance of the product a few months or years later. Agriculture and the raw materials sector are particularly susceptible to this effect since many investments, e.g. the futures market, depend on the time margin.

In political economy, the prophecy effect is much sought-after by leaders or politicians who play a permanent bluffer's game of poker. Political parties use the prophecy effect in a form of "lying by objective". Governments are better informed nowadays, according to Jean-

François Revel (1988) in his book on lies and politics. As he describes it, the political lie has become a way to fool public opinion; whereas in the old days, the political lie was used to trick other governments.

Revel's blunt words should not discourage readers because we still have a role to play in creating futures. An anonymous political science professor once said that "one law deducted from the practice of pluralistic democracy is that a majority victory does not survive the application of its platform." The reason lies in the "broad margin separating an electoral platform from a governmental program. The platform expresses the desirable; the program, the possible." The supply is just meeting the demand. Who is to blame if – as Jean-François Revel (1988) put it – "the first force leading the world is the lie"?

Self-Censorship and Insufficient Information

Light will blind you, if you go too close. We all need to step back from the media floodlights and information overload in which secondary factors often take center stage. There is a real risk of "mind poisoning" from Garbage In, Garbage Out (GIGO). Not only is there useless, even deceptive information, there is also a lack of strategic information. This situation stems not so much from chance or progress as from countless petty struggles played out at the same time around the world. In fact information should often be considered like a series of bids, as in poker, the game in which a bluff may well count for more than the truth.

Given this state of affairs, Revel (1988) asks a serious question: How can we explain the rarity of "accurate" information in the free world when those gathering information seem to care more about falsifying it and those receiving information seem to care more about avoiding it? He does offer an explanation of sorts: "regulating the circulation of information (in a positive sense) is the determining element of power and the need to believe is stronger than the need to know. There is an ill will which leads us to take precautions and hide the truth from ourselves so that we are surer of our resolve when we deny it in front of others. There is a refusal to admit a mistake, unless we can attribute it to one of our qualities. Lastly, we have the capacity to put in our mind these systematized explanations of what is real, in other words, ideologies, which are like machines capable of both sorting favorable facts that suit our convictions and of rejecting all others."

Relevant information on either the future or past is a rare commodity. Spreading and exchanging information are not neutral, gratuitous processes. "Informing the other person, giving him elements that he does not have, is disclosure or showing one's trump cards rather than bidding." (Michel Crozier, Ehrard Friedberg, 1977).

Decoding information or misinformation according to the power dynamics within a society or a company means cross-checking, reviewing sources and filtering the data on the basis of the actors who create and distribute it. Otherwise anything goes. Clichés, hollow promises and motherhood statements abound simply because they meet the expectations of the reader or listener, "rub the right way" or fit the *zeitgeist*.

Never neutral, information must always be checked against the source and the channel. What is hidden is often more important that what is shown. The media and the government dazzle us with statistics and official commentary to the point where we become blind. Any skeptics should look up unemployment in the annals of the statistics department. They will find that unemployment is generally presented as a rate and a variation from one year to the next. Rarely, however, are any absolute values given so that the reader can calculate and compare one period to the next, one country to another. These figures do exist but happen to be less accessible and often are provided much later than the sacrosanct unemployment rate.

As a result, information or its omission often serves specific interests. Every reader really should ask two questions: what's to gain and who benefits here? Many desk drawers are lined with politically ill-timed studies. Many relevant reports are gutted or sanitized. Similarly, many realities remain unreported because no one dares to speak out. The most effective and powerful form of censure is the self-censure that researchers and managers adopt when they do not wish to displease their clients or superiors.

Faulty Interpretation

A prediction or forecast generally precedes from a single "reading" of a single situation or event when there are actually many possible interpretations. The resulting error in interpretation is a source of many forecasting disasters. As Bertrand de Jouvenel (1964) pointed out, "because Marx looked at history as a class struggle, the revolution of 1848 is in his eyes just a parody of the first French Revolution (...) but others see in this revolution an awakening of the nationalities which would soon spread across Europe." In essence, there is no reality free of perception and the perception of facts depends on the theory used in to reviewing them. Objective facts do not exist other than through our subjective perception. To paraphrase Oskar Morgenstern (1972): "Data do not become scientific information except through theory".

Errors in interpretation are more difficult to discern because a false theory can provide accurate predictions. Inversely, a valid theory may be proved much later or never. Einstein's theory of general relativity stands out as a brilliant example. An error in interpretation is acceptable in the sense that interpreting is like betting that one has accurately read a phenomenon and also that the reading will be verified. The wager is necessary here since there are no absolute truths and only relative ones. Any proposition is true, but so is its opposite. The most important thing is to retain a sense of proportion.

Misinformation – More and More!

Misinformation or disinformation, noted as a consequence of political lies and self-censure, makes us wonder about the media. Although not a systematic process, misinformation may be explained using the media's commercial goals, e.g. sales figures and audience ratings. One of France's finest journalists – one whose ethics remain impeccable – enlightened us in 1986 with the following statement: "The media are not there to inform but rather to make money on information." A sad commentary, indeed, but one that should not be ignored.

The sloppy reporting, sensationalism and self-promotion that run rampant in much of the media will never be headline news. Reporters may love to talk about themselves, as seen in hostage-taking episodes in Lebanon during the 1970s or the expulsion of certain journalists and confiscation of their cameras in various parts of FYROM. As in many other professions, there is a code of honor or even Omerta's law. Often journalists interview or quote their colleagues as part of the newscast. Some even go so far as to become both the source and the story! The viewer who zaps at news time or during weekly digest shows finds panels of reporters chatting amongst themselves. The painfully obvious diagnosis is that style and packaging (the container) has taken the place of content, especially when there is no content! In other words, the quality of information plummets and the media end up talking more and more about themselves.

Add to the media malaise, some say sclerosis, the mania for public opinion polls and the result is a debate over empty phrases coming from surveys on anything and nothing. Examples abound: a survey on the need to hold a referendum; i.e., a survey on a survey! Soon the telephone will ring at suppertime and someone will ask whether you would like to know what you think about what you want. The illusion of direct or participatory democracy hides direct demagogy.

Would any medium ever mention a book about the media mess? Would the author take the risk of being blacklisted professionally? Brave without being stupid, we think that the profession is egotistical enough to want to taste some criticism of the content not just the container.

The Abuse of Power

The press is often called the fourth column in a democracy, following closely the legislative, judiciary and executive. The label flatters members of the profession but the cliché reveals a danger in that only oppressive regimes claim to use the press as public opinion. The media's role is to serve as a spokesperson, a mirror of society, a relay between the people and their government. Given the journalist's professional duty to investigate, the media also serve to counterbalance the first three columns.

Politicians use the press for advertising while the press uses politicians to anchor its privileged status as spokesperson, or vehicle, in public opinion. The result: coverage of the political scene reaches the saturation point. What we usually see is staging or orchestrated events in which a few big wigs appear and make a sound bite which is then rehashed or interpreted by teams of reporters.

In the age of TV and computers, image counts more than sound. However, an image is only a partial, even a deformed, reflection of a whole. There are editors, mixers, graphic artists, and computer wizards involved, too. The reporter or anchor often passes off these clips as reality with no commentary. What is really eighty seconds of an interview is presented as a "special report" while someone who witnessed an accident gives a few impressions which become an "exclusive live-witness item". The less valuable the news content, the fancier the packaging with file footage or archive material to fill in the gaps.

Information as a Product

In television, the Nielsen or other audience ratings and the competition among major networks dictate what we see. A network's results may be measured in market shares which translate to advertising dollars. As a result, information is orchestrated to catch the public's attention. Hence information must surprise, shock, and then disappear but only to be renewed constantly. Competition pushes the networks to reduce the "shelf life", or air life, of a news item and to promote scoops or flashes instead, even though these may not be reliable or complete. Rumor thus replaces information. Fortunately there are some watchdogs who dare to point out such examples as the false news story about babies in incubators at an Iraqi hospital during the Gulf War, to name but one.

Information once was called the "oil of the 1990s" because of its cost and value. Given budget restrictions, the news covers a few subjects briefly. Many newsrooms and reporters rely on the same raw data, dispatched over the wire, without taking the time to crosscheck or complete the information. Overall the reporter, news anchor and journalist see their profession reduced to delivering anemic information pumped up with superlatives like *historic*, *exclusive* and *just breaking*. As a result, the average citizen is made irresponsible and bloated on a diet of non-information.

Yet rigor in processing information is of vital importance if people are to make relevant judgments. Unfortunately, misinformation feeds upon itself and becomes a habit tolerated out of ignorance or apathy. The public starts to think "wrong" using seemingly correct logic. One word is used for another and through false synonymy *resistant* is substituted for rebel and Eastern Europe now has only reformers. Communists are labeled conservatives, socialists, even liberals.

Effective misinformation alters judgment and wipes out basic common sense. It is insidious. Meanwhile the media are misinforming themselves and others through competition heightened by a lack of rigor and seriousness or even through laziness. The dictatorship of what is now and novel favors anecdotal events and stories to the detriment of trends and actions that really do make history. Moreover, many of these events are told rather than captured live. Of course this does not mean that filming a disaster equates explaining it. In the end, what good is a 20-second commentary given by a specialist questioned during a televised newscast? Based on our own experience, the audience remembers the face but not what was said or even the subject of the news clip. Even testimonials from eyewitnesses may be fraught with errors.

Credible but Unreliable Witnesses

Most facts rely on testimonials; unfortunately, accurate testimony is exceptional and jurists or criminologists know it. On this last point, Jean-Noël Kapferer (1987) concluded the following:
  – "witnesses give false information with the same assurance as they give accurate information, and always in good faith;
  – what we say we saw reflects stereotypes in our mind more than what we really saw;
  – if several witnesses concur, it it not necessarily an indication that their claims or declarations are true. It may mean that several people share the same stereotypes and mental clichés and yet they perceived the facts in an identical but erroneous manner."

How can we avoid analysis and forecasting errors with information that is insufficient and incomplete? How can we escape misinformation as clichés multiply and media sclerosis increases? For our part, the answer is doubt, verifications, and taboo hunting. On the part of the media, the answer is greater rigor and stricter ethics. Intellectuals also have some responsibility for misinformation but they know when to keep quiet especially when speaking out might harm their reputation or career which requires types of communication other than vulgarization. Silence or pseudo-scientific jargon makes many academics and intellectuals partners in the crime of misinformation. All too often those in the know remain silent. Consequently there is very little official censor because self-censorship operates so effectively.

In terms of growth, technology, competitiveness, employment and training or in demographics and ecology, common sense and experience soon clash with what is "politically correct". Anyone speaking out soon earns a reputation as an agent provocateur whereas it is reality that is provocative! By speaking our mind, we have often been told things like, "you're 100% right... but we can't say that! It would kill us in the polls". It seems sense is revolutionary. Saying aloud what many whisper deep down inside does not sit well in our conformist societies. The futurist must not, however, remain silent since the torchbearer of the future must point out the pitfalls so that we can avoid them.

What Makes a Good Expert?

Our answer is simple but does not make matters simpler or solve the problem. Bright lights are often in the minority, an enlightened few. We then have to ask which minority sees the most clearly.

In many fields, notably in technology, an expert's forecasting judgment is often the main information tool available. This characteristic explains the success of methods like the Delphi (see Linstone, 1975) which seeks the convergence of opinions through a consensus guided gently – some might say manipulated – by the organizers. These methods are appropriate when decisions are pushed forward based on the consensus reached; however, the same methods are often more misleading than helpful in forecasting or scenario building. Remember opinions converging in a consensus do not necessarily mean and, indeed, rarely imply statistical consistency. The fact that everyone agrees on one opinion does not lend it any additional credibility.

There is often confusion on consensus and expert opinions. The reader should consider the following analysis of experts' forecasts or predictions from the first half of the twentieth century.

It seems that the reliability of any expert reaches a point of diminishing returns. After that moment, specialists lose sight of the bigger picture or lack critical distance from their own previous opinions or recommendations; in other words, those which made their reputation.

In any field, it is easier to think like everyone else so as not to justify any divergent point of view. On the other hand, any divergent viewpoint does require justification. Here is a practical exercise: managers, consultants or leaders who state opinions should ask only those who think like they do for a justification and not ask those who doubt them. The results can be revrealing.

All in all, the isolated expert can really get it wrong, regardless of reputation. Statistically, it seems wiser to seek the services of a group of experts because we have often observed that the consensus of the group, or the average taken of the various individual views, will yield better results.

Evaluating the Experts

In Issue no.5 (Vol. 8, October 1976, p. 411-419) of "Futures", George Wise of the General Electric R&D Centre analyzed the accuracy of forecasts on technological progress and the effects of various American innovations from 1890 to 1940. The author based his study on a corpus of 1,556 forecasts related to the following:
– technological progress (confirmed or not) in 18 specific technological areas;
– social, economic or political impact expected from these changes.

From the bulk of Mr. Wise's study, we can draw five conclusions:
1) Authors of long-term predictions (10 yrs +) were wrong more often than they were right.
2) Experts view the situation slightly more accurately than do the non-experts.
3) Predictions by experts outside their own field are no less accurate than those from specialists in the field studied.
4) Forecasts related to a continued *status quo* in technology, at any particular time, are not more accurate than predictions on innovation.
5) Effects of technological progress are less foreseeable that the changes themselves.

3

Hunting down cliches

No Right Answers to Wrong Questions

Three Mirages from the 1970s and 1980s
From Energy to High-Tech: One Mirage Replaces Another
The Computer *versus* the Chalkboard
The Diploma Disease
Made in Japan

Current Real Questions and False Problems
Globalization and Governance
How Far Can Globalization Go?
Waves of Europtimism and Europessimism
Europe: A longstanding Marketplace
Sustainable Development, With or Without Mankind?
Risk of a Demographic Implosion
The Missing Link
A Major Issue: Food Safety

Although some may consider it an easy intellectual exercise or a wild goose chase, hunting down clichés is a fascinating sport. Admittedly, nowadays it seems like one simply has to oppose dominant or preconceived ideas to earn celebrity status overnight. However beyond the spotlight, the real world is another matter. In fact, the wide and even wild variety of clichés out there proves just how much intellectual curiosity is needed to ensure a broad view of the future. That big picture has long been part of *la prospective*, or the French school's approach to scenario building, and we know from experience how much effort it takes to "swim upstream".

Naturally the newness of the various subjects studied makes the task all the more challenging. Our own experience is diverse ranging from energy to agriculture; from education and technology with statistics on unemployment, through to economic growth, and ecology in places like Japan, Germany, and the European Union. New fields are only one challenge. There is also the challenge of entry barriers erected by the recognized experts in any particular discipline. Obviously it is in their best interest to block a new arrival, in other words, a competitor, who represents a form of double jeopardy in that he/she challenges the ideas which form the very foundation of the established experts' field of activity.

Hunting down clichés thus remains a risky endeavor in intellectual terms. It will never be easy to speak frankly without making enemies, and the coalition of "well-intentioned" thinkers will inevitably try to marginalize any deviant or disturbing point of view. Usually only those who are not involved or not affected appreciate unconventional thinking for the "not in my backyard" (NIMBY) syndrome persists. As implied in the previous chapter, the French media published scores of articles that went against the grain of conventional wisdom over the past twenty years without mentioning, however, the media's own malaise.

No Right Answers to Wrong Questions

No doctor can prescribe the right remedy based on a faulty diagnosis. Unfortunately managers, politicians and even experts run the risk of diagnosing a situation incorrectly when they follow popular or fashionable ideas.

Consultants and leaders have to go against the tide of popular wisdom and conventional thinking to see clearly and ask the right questions, even if it hurts. Yet the majority of experts are conformist and conservative. Sticking with the majority is a comfortable choice because that way the others can do all the explaining. Often the correct forecast; i.e., that is the one which sees the situation correctly, comes form a minority of imaginative, daring experts. Of course it may be difficult to recognize the "right" minority point of view among the others. For the futurist and scenario planner, the lesson remains simple: "If it is difficult, even risky, to defend a new idea among other possible ideas, fear not! Go ahead and challenge the dominant vision; test the rationale behind prevalent ideas."

The consultants, managers, in fact all participants in a futures-thinking exercise, must question what they may take for granted and the "wisdom of the day" that consensus rarely checks. French Nobel prize winner, Maurice Allais points out the tyranny of dominant ideas and adds that only through the constant questioning of the established truths and flourishing of new ideas flowing from creative intuition can science advance. Yet all real scientific progress clashes with the tyranny of preconceived ideas within the major institutions which uphold them. Allais (1989) points out that the more widespread the thinking, the more stubbornly rooted it seems to be in human psychology, and consequently, the more difficult it is for a new concept to be accepted, regardless of its potential.

Light throws shadows. We should add here especially spotlights. Logically then, if the media promote certain problems, they mask others or make them disappear.

Let us use the theory of statistical testing as an analogy. There are three possible risks of error. The risk of error lies in...

1) preparing for something which will not happen and giving empty answers to false problems. This risk frequently arises in environmental and agri-food issues;

2) not preparing for something that can happen and is anticipated: a real question thus remains unanswered;

3) not asking the right questions because they might disturb people or they are politically incorrect, e.g. the demographic and economic implosion of Western Europe.

For example, it has not been proven that global warming is the result of human activities. However, if the principle of precaution requires hard decisions made on the basis of soft information, these decisions should not be too hard and should not be based on information that is too soft. The principle of precaution, or precautionary principle, must not rein in innovation. The future must be kept open and experimenting should continue, even with genetically engineered products, also called genetically manipulated organisms (GM products or GMOs). The same principle should be applied to demographics and economic growth. Although not yet demonstrated, it would be better to consider a possible link between the two and begin researching the various causes and effects. Otherwise, young people in the West (especially Western Europe) will remain a minority, sacrificed on the altar of conventional thinking. The main risk threatening Western societies today has little to do with the environment but everything to do with the demographic and economic implosion related to the "baby bust or crash" which has followed the famous baby boom. On the Old Continent, nothing has been done to prevent this major risk. In terms of retirement programs, every possible solution has been studied, except a plan to rejuvenate populations through an increased birthrate and more immigration. Why? Both birthrates and immigration remain taboo issues in countries like France and Spain.

The first mental habit to cultivate is doubt. Doubt leads to questioning, investigating and confirming. Descartes, whose Cartesian spirit has fallen out of fashion these days, considered doubt his first premise. "[I] never accept anything as the truth unless I knew it obviously to be thus. In other words, I painstakingly avoid precipitation and prevention and do not understand anything more than that which, in my judgment, was so clearly and distinctly presented that to my mind that I had no opportunity to doubt it."

Three Mirages from the 1970s and 1980s

Not long ago, during the 1970s, energy was the cause of all human woes. Only yesterday, in the 1980s, technology was humanity's savior. As a result, in the 1990s training became a priority but it was renamed a "nonmaterial investment". Europe fell victim first to the technology mirage and then to the education mirage.

From Energy to High-Tech: One Mirage Replaces Another

Lest we forget, readers, recent history shows that in 1974 the economic crisis was explained primarily in terms of energy. In a nutshell: Get out from under the limitation of energy to recover and start strong economic growth. This rationale explains how the French nuclear energy program began.

With hindsight, it is worth observing that in both the North and South, the most economically dynamic countries e.g. Japan, Germany and South Korea, remained heavily dependent on others for energy. Countries with oil, e.g. Great Britain or OPEC members, stagnated industrially. Moreover, not one of the OPEC countries belongs to the group of newly industrialized countries, once popularly referred to as NICs. Everything happened as if the limitation were a stimulus and as if the oil money had led to a lackadaisical, laisser-aller attitude. It is also worth noting that from 1974 to 1977, technology in general – excluding energy technology – was virutally a non-issue in the debate on how to get out of the economic crisis.

From 1978 onward, before the second oil shock, the technology mirage chased away the energy mirage. During this time, official reports resounded with the phrases "new technology and society" or the "new technological society".

The technology mirage justified an enormous waste of public funds. Note the past tense is used in this case, but the mirage still floats around. The main idea was not to be left behind during this third industrial revolution. This kind of thinking led to schools equipped with computers which soon became dated and unsalable thus contributing to the failure of the "computers for everyone" plan. After "computerizing the classroom", as this phase was called, long-distance teaching in which the computer replaced the chalkboard was discussed. Educational television was yet another idea, one that led to more channels and less quality on the air. It seems that the same inverse ratio of quantity and quality applies to technology.

On another front, did governments really have to dig into the public coffers to finance research on high resolution TV and cable television? Perhaps there are needs that are not real needs as well as basic needs that are not well served. What about the need for security, human contact, living space, and peace of mind? Whose needs are really being met in our society? The answer is not clear when we think of how the elderly are treated sometimes or how the countryside is ravaged.

Initially, major corporations also fell victim to the technology mirage. For example, in the early 1980s. Renault attributed its sagging productivity rate to technological causes. It soon became apparent, however, that with a comparable level of automation, Renault's performance remained half that of the Japanese carmakers. The difference lay not so much in technology but in individuals and organizations; i.e., the human factor.

The above observation shows just how relative the importance of technical, and financial solutions can be in the development strategies of a company. Any strategy based solely on modernizing technology appears more often that not to be a bottomless pit sucking money. More importantly, this type of strategy diverts management's attention from the real problems of competitiveness that are not only technological but also socio-organizational. The techno trend can be traced throughout management literature starting around 1982. Before then, technology was scarcely ever mentioned, to the point that the term does not appear in the index of corporate strategy manuals. In the end, however, it is not the volume of material or immaterial investments that matters but rather their effectiveness.

The technology mirage continued, buoyed by a new mirage called training, rebaptized "intellectual investment". However, a shiny new label does not change the contents of an old box. Training remains an expense which must be both suitable and effective. Many trainers should be trained or retrained themselves! And nothing can top collective self-training because only when you teach someone something do you really learn it yourself. The same movement can be traced in modern pedagogy.

The Computer *versus* the Chalkboard

Most major industrialized countries dived headfirst into beginner computer courses given at school during the 1980s. Each country wanted to "keep up with the Joneses" so that the phenomenon spread quickly, especially in countries that produced hardware, like France and Great Britain. Modernizing education, adapting the school system to the new technical and economical context tempts commissioners and politicians to provide material solutions (more computer labs, more consoles and workstations) to problems that are of another kind.

Educators fear a generation of computer illiterate children, but the real risk lies in creating a generation of computer users who are simply illiterate. The computer remains a container that can process information. The wealth and value of that information comes from the computer user or designer. The rationale in training children in computers at the end of the twentieth century resembles that of teaching pupils auto mechanics at the beginning of the century. As Bruno Lussato (1988, 1996) said "the issue of using the computer in the classroom is no more important than that of using chalk."

Yes, new information technology may facilitate the transmission and acquisition of basic knowledge. However, it seems increasingly obvious that the image on the screen does not enhance learning and that nothing can replace the direct human contact of traditional teaching practices.

In reality, new information technology should not revolutionize the education system any more than traditional media did. After all, the media have a different mission; i.e., sell information and attract an audience or a readership. Ironically television channels multiply like fruit flies, but no one has developed a successful educational channel, at least not in Europe. The stellar success of Internet will do little to change this situation. Although access to data has become almost unlimited, it takes time and knowledge to sift through the information, just to separate the sheep from the goats. Think for a moment about how many people have an encyclopedia at home. And just because they have it, how many consult it regularly? The encyclopedia meets an infrequent need while many other needs must be met and within the twenty-four hours available daily!

These new media may, nevertheless, prove useful in developing parallel training systems that would allow those who do not live within the geographical territory of a school board or those who do not want an imposed system to try their luck by paying for this additional service. The "new media" may inject a competitive spirit into a compartimentalized marketplace and, as a result, correct the serious regional disparities existing in education. Other outcomes might be a form of quality control (upstream) through centralized production and efficiency (downstream) in lower dropout rates or higher graduation rates.

Yet the original question of how to integrate new information technologies into the educational system has become secondary to one of the new stakes; i.e., the development of parallel educational systems organized by local groups, companies or associations, thus introducing new forms of competition on an educational market heretofore protected by distance or limited access.

The Diploma Disease

The true story (Michel Godet, sworn witness) began just as a fairy tale should. One fine day in the early 80s, a top French civil servant was touring Honda's auto plants in Japan. He found out that 90% of the Japanese auto assembly line workers had attended school up to the age of 18. He heard the words "final year" and understood high school diploma. Remember that all of this conversation was held in broken English by a Frenchman and a Japanese executive. The civil servant returned to France to tell his minister that obviously the Japanese were outperforming the French in the automobile sector because they have high school graduates on the lines whereas France has illiterate manual laborers. And thus the slogan "80% of a generation with a high school diploma" resounded throughout the Hexagon.

Alas like Cinderella's pumpkin, it soon came out that everyone goes to school in Japan until the age of 18, but no one is failed so that "face" and the social cohesion of groups are maintained. The real selection process begins after what could be called the last year of American high school. Fierce competition begins then as difficult entrance exams for admission to the major universities must be sat. Training for these entrance exams starts with evening and summer courses at a very early age. Those working on the assembly lines are those who could not get into university.

However the real question that French civil servant should have asked is: How do our German neighbors build Mercedes with Turkish guestworkers? The answer lies in training, not in geography or schooling. When the major French industries closed their training facilities, they gave themselves an additional handicap *vis-à-vis* their Bavarian competitor, who benefits from a system in which State and industry share responsibility for training.

As the new millennium began, France already had almost 75% of one generation at the high-school leaving level. Perhaps the next Education Ministry objective should be that 80% of the next generation of those high school graduates know the three Rs! Irony aside, the stakes are high here. What France needed to do was follow the German example and develop training and apprenticeship programs, not a general education imparted by teachers who have little life experience other than teaching. According to the OECD, France has 8 million illiterates; i.e., people unable to read and understand an administrative document. (Of course many administrative forms mystify scholars with post-graduate degrees!) Nevertheless, it is continuing education or training that should be promoted as the true source of social and economic renewal because reinforcing basic education only accentuates the initial social inequalities.

Strangely enough, the education mirage has not completely replaced the technology mirage. Instead one feeds the other. The rationale is that the children must be prepared for the third industrial revolution. Horse feathers! Tomorrow's jobs will require a high level of professionalism not more skills. What does "professional" mean? Essentially it means liking what you do and wanting to do it well. In other words, the opposite of the uninterested, bitter graduates that the diploma disease generates.

Confusion over words and meaning in training creates the illusion that knowledge equals skill and that skill is equivalent to experience. Why then do companies not recruit executives over the age of fifty or simply adjust retirement programs accordingly?

The paper chase in general education is all the more difficult to justify given that tomorrow's jobs are not only in new or high technology as many people believe. Technological change in industry and service translates to an increased need of high-level specialists but the number required is limited. There will be more positions filled by less skilled workers who will monitor machines and provide services; in other words, the tertiary sector. There will be a tremendous need for secretaries, healthcare workers, sorters, wrappers or packers, waiters and waitresses. In these jobs "book learning", as sanctioned by a diploma, will not be as important as cooperative behavior, attention to detail and creativity in applying various skills or techniques. Training in the workplace or in company training centers is the main vector leading to the professionalism needed for the "jobs of tomorrow" or even today! Hire to train rather than train to be hired should be the byword.

Made in Japan

Now here is a label that may be interpreted in many ways. Some fifteen years ago managers in Europe and North America were chanting the same mantra: imitate the Japanese management model to catch up with Nippon productivity rates. Ironically the French automaker, Renault, bought Nissan in the mid-nineties.

Of course while the fascination with Japan Inc. was at its peak, I made comments that clashed with the popular ideas of the day. Nevertheless, my analysis from the end of the 1980s stands today. [1]

---

1. See "Ten Unfashionable and Controversial Findings on Japan" in *Futures*, August 1987.

Basically, any attempt to explain the fierce competitiveness of Japanese industry at that time must take into account the overwhelming desire to work in order to escape the scarcities that Japan knew in the 1950s. The country had no resources other than its people and their labor.

The Japanese concepts of productivity and quality had been imported from the USA during the 1950s. At that time, American productivity rates were the highest in the world. As the proverb says, no man is a prophet is his own country, so American management specialists like W.E. Deming and J.M. Juran, considered the fathers of quality, saw their ideas applied in Japan. (See Dimitri Weiss, 1988.) Initially Japanese companies created small groups mandated to improve processes and products to the latest levels. The idea of *total quality*, which was originally the concept of quality *all together* as a collective goal or shared responsibility, made the concept of *quality control* redundant. American authors would use the word *excellence* later on. Quality became a resounding success in Japan for various reasons, including prevention. Remember that Japanese products were exported around the world with no need for an expensive after-sales service network.

Other cornerstones of the Japanese management system were put forth as reasons for success. First of all, lifetime or lifelong employment. This aspect of the Japanese corporate world only affected 20% of the salaried workers, but it does reveal the strong sense of almost feudal loyalty that Japanese employees had towards their employer.

Similarly, the individual is perceived as a member of a group or clan in Japan. Hence we find another pillar or cornerstone of the Japanese management system: consensus. Group or peer pressure explains the apparent social harmony that reigns in Japanese businesses. Japanese proverbs like "hammer down the nail that sticks out" may apply to consensus-building, too. Of course in the Japanese system, workers who got out of line would hear from both their superiors and their colleagues.

Who would not toe the line under these circumstances? Do like the others becomes the golden rule. In other words, the famous Japanese corporate consensus is a result of collective self-censorship more than any form of debate or negotiation. It is better to give up one's ideas rather than rock the boat. In any event, an individual Japanese worker could never live down the loss of face created by rebellion or dissension.

Another Japanese cliché in manufacturing: longer working hours. Official statistics reveal theory more than the harsh reality, given that production restrictions and the strains of belonging to a group are such that many employees "spontaneously" stay late at night and come in on their weekends off to reach the goals set by the company. Peer pressure is so strong that employees do like their colleagues and give up a large part of their leisure time.

Motivating and mobilizing human resources was also at the core of the Japanese management system. At Honda, for example, the employee who could come up with the most proposals on how to improve productivity received a handsome bonus. Despite all the clichés that readers may have heard, the Japanese miracle stems from basic production organization. The idea was to do well what had to be done through order, method and, of course, tremendous staff motivation. None of the above lay beyond the reach of any company of any nationality. In fact Japanese-owned and managed electronics plants in France's northern coastal region, Brittany, actually achieved better performance rates than their counterparts in Japan.

As in show business, we have saved the best for last – a finale of sorts. One of the most famous Japan Inc. management anecdotes ruffled politicians' feathers and made headlines. Like an urban legend, it probably would have circulated via Internet had Japan not sunk into an economic crisis in the early 1990s.

The background almost surpasses the story itself. Everything started with a shocking remark attributed to the Japanese president Matsushita. It translated roughly to "We are going to win and the industrialized West will lose. You can not do much about it because you carry your defeat within you. Your organizations are Taylorian and what's worse your minds are too (…) we are post-Taylorian."

Quoted variously but broadly in the mid-eighties, Matsushita's remark worked like intellectual electroshock therapy. Suddenly the Japanese lead could be explained by a management model which one needed to understand in order to emulate. Yet we have known since 1987 that the famous quote is a historical half-truth. A French author, Henri Sérieyx, revealed the other half in the preface to Isabella Orgogozo's 1987 book and reconfirmed it in his 1989 publication entitled *Le zéro mépris* (a clever punning title like "Zero Intolerance").

The Japanese management system became a true fashion based on a false analysis. Rather like a rumor reflects one facette of reality or the old adage "where there's smoke there's fire". Moreover everyone knows that Japanese politeness resembles false modesty and may actually mask a certain arrogance. Given the Japanese reputation, Matsushita's remark was plausible. Imagine, a Japanese leader was finally telling us what he really thought! Of course this was not the case and the real story now begs to be told or retold.

Once upon a time, we were invited by the Management Centre of Europe (Paris, 1990) to speak before three hundred top managers from around the world. The panel included renowned experts like Henry Kissinger. Among the other speakers was R.T. Pascale, a Harvard professor and the premier specialist in Japanese management. Halfway through his presentation in English, he quoted Matsushita's famous remark. Astonished, even embarrassed, I wondered what to do as a colleague and conference participant. I opted to ask questions and check sources like a good reporter. In speaking with one of Professor Pascale's assistants and co-workers, it came out that he had only started using that quote two or three years prior. In fact, his last conversation with President Matsushita took place in 1982. Curious, even stubborn, I discretely buttonholed the professor himself. Slightly red-faced, to his credit, he said that he had read this ten-line quote one day in its English version. He added that when he met Matsushita in 1982, the elderly leader spoke scarcely audible English. The whole episode sounded like the children's game of broken telephone. Nevertheless Professor Pascale said that he believed what he understood that day from the Japanese president to correspond exactly to what he read later.

Somehow the quote, like a rumor, has already done its job and discrediting the statement means little now. Moreover, Sérieyx's book has not been translated into English and even the francophone professor had never heard of it.

The one redeeming feature of Matsushita's supposed prophecy is that it triggered a real revolution in Western corporate minds. Results included quality circles, corporate projects, and self-training, to name a few. Someday history will cover the Japan Inc. period and show the healthy albeit unexpected role that the Japanese model played in the West.

Current Real Questions and False Problems

The three mirages – energy, technology and education – they may well rise up and hover vaporously above us again. Remember the myth of critical size, rather like critical mass, of a company. This popular idea goes against concrete reality in which there are always smaller and more effective companies in any given sector. The real challenge for any company is to be effective at its current size. What better way to grow? Otherwise one company has to join forces with another or form networks. Critical size has been integrated into the grander globalization myth which translates into mergers and acquisitions plus urban planning policies that promote massive metropolises as technopoles for activities and jobs. Ironically we do not even know whether employment is the cause or consequence of these policies.

European decline is yet another myth that rears its ugly head in between phases of euro-optimism. However the 1990s were marked by new mirages recognizable by the buzzwords "globalization" and "governance".

Globalization and Governance

The absolute value of a power does not prevent its relative decline. This strange equation applies to the United States which today represents only 25% of the world's Gross Domestic Product. Although not powerful enough to impose its will as regulator, the USA is powerful enough to play the troublemaker. The USA does prevail worldwide and can prevent any other regulator from imposing its will.

Since the early 1990s, the United States has experienced a renewal of power. Yet the USA could be to the twenty-first century what Great Britain was to the twentieth century: a decadent power. In fact this point of view is often expressed by Japanese experts. On the other hand, Japan does not have the vocation to become the center of a new world economy.

Yet another myth that persists with no basis is the one about Japan at the heart of the Pacific. This is a Japan that relegates the Old Atlantic World, hence Europe, to its periphery.

In the end, numbers speak louder than words. Statistically, Japan accounts for 18% of the world's GDP; in other words, one-third less than that of the USA or Europe. Of course growth in newly industrialized South-East Asian firms is spectacular but corresponds to these countries' time lag in development. For example, the GDP per capita in terms of purchasing power, in South Korea is generally half of Japan's but three to four times that of China or Indonesia.

The Pax Nipponica will not take the baton from the defunct Pax Americana because Japan lacks the necessary military power. Japanese-American co-management of the world system would be a more realistic hypothesis. However, the United States would have to reindustrialize successfully. The Japanese are doing their part through their investments but they are losing faith in the American capacity to lead. Hence Japanese criticism of American economic and monetary policies, which can not ensure stability in times of change, has grown harsher.

Indeed, Japan might find more responsible partners in Europe, especially in Germany. The Japanese slogan could be "Out of America, into Europe". The jury is still out on this hypothesis but Japan is showing renewed interest in Europe. This interest further encourages the Old Continent to modernize its production systems.

The slumbering giant to the east remains a greater mystery. China has experienced impressive development over the past few years with rising annual GDP rates and double-digit exchange figures, but this is a period of catching up with the rest of the world. A massive effort is required given the enormous delay in China's development. Between 1950 and 1988, China represented less than 1% of international trade. However the figures tripled in less than a decade (1988-1998). In fact,

China was eleventh, just ahead of South Korea, in the ranking of world exporters by 1995. In terms of international trade, Japanese figures are triple and French figures double the Chinese. With trade rates growing at 30% annually, situations certainly change fast. China will have to keep up its exponential growth rate to keep up to Japan in the year 2010.

Of course history has its lessons and there is always the long run. China has previously, even regularly, opened up to the outside world only to close its doors suddenly and brutally. The explanation for these cyclical openings remains the same: the development differential between the maritime provinces and the interior provinces is enormous and threatens to break up the middle kingdom which turns inward once again. China's main economic partners in the region know this all too well and tread carefully with their neighbor. The Japanese are particularly reticent because of their conflictual history with China. The Japanese sacking of Nankin in the mid-1930s remains part of the collective memory. Relations with former colonizers are never easy, but may be particularly tense when the economic and cultural hierarchy in the region are inverted. Remember, the Chinese transmitted their culture to the Japanese through the Koreans!

No country or intergovernmental agency appears ready to carry the baton of Pax Americana. The lack of a regulator is all the more damaging given the increasing interdependence of economies through "globalization", a phenomenon that should be reweighed, even renamed, because what is occurring is an "integration" within major economic regions of the world. Here is a riddle: If a country like France exports 25% of its production, what happened to the other 75%? Answer: It was consumed in France. In fact, 70% of France's exports go to Western European countries (Western in broad terms), where social conditions are comparable to those in France. The bottom line is that over 93% of everything stamped *Fabriqué en France* is also consumed in Europe. A similar pattern can be seen in other Western European countries, in Japan and the United States. The term should be "regionalization of exchanges" rather than the ubiquitous term "globalization". The impact of globalization on the economy of Japan, France, Canada or any developed country should be reevaluated. It is likely not greater than the impact of multinationals in the recent past.

How Far Can Globalization Go?

The liberalization of trade flows has generated unprecedented growth. Ever since the General Agreement of Taxes and Tariffs (GATT) went into effect in 1947, the average customs tariff has decreased by nearly 90% among industrialized countries. The average number of trade transactions has increased fifteenfold and world production has increased eightfold. Only by attacking non-tariff barriers and protectionist practices in countries like the USA can these levels be surpassed.

However the Americans want to control or terminate governmental assistance in sectors where they lead, like agriculture, entertainment and services. For all the other areas, the Americans do not hesitate in protecting themselves through unilateral anti-dumping measures, as in the case of European steel, or through pressure to impose self-limiting export agreements.

In any event, it would be risky to regulate trade and production according to employment rates because certain countries have a reciprocal advantage although it may not be distributed equally. Through trade, countries grow rich mutually. Through protectionism or by closing borders, they become impoverished and do not progress. In the long run, protecting national companies is neither healthy nor helpful. As in athletics, competition requires training which develops muscle. Think about your tennis or golf game and notice how you improve when matched with a player slightly better than you.

The real stakes lie elsewhere because organized retreats into greater specialization are profitable. Hence it is easy to import large quantities of objects of low value, requiring little skilled labor balanced off by a small number of products with added value requiring intelligence and skill. The Germans knew this equation well and maintained a foreign trade surplus before reunification. Indeed, this was the recipe for the two famous German advantages of a high salary and plenty of leisure time. In fact, Germany will probably return to this formula once the reunification process has been absorbed economically.

All countries benefit from trade, it seems, even if jobs are lost in certain sectors, overall wealth is gained. The accusations leveled at the newly industrialized countries (NICs) should be stopped now. Ethically, how can a bloc of countries ask weaker countries to accept the laws of competition when it suits the bloc and then refuse others the same laws when it does not? If countries play at opening up to trade then they must accept to import products manufactured at low salaries (the main competitive advantage of NICs). Yes, there are limits; child labor comes to mind first. However, overall, the best way for a country to develop and improve its social context is by opening up its economy to increased trade.

Global economies are not necessarily leveling the playing field or scaling living conditions downward; nevertheless, less developed countries (LDCs) can only catch up to the developed countries if the latter carry out economic and social restructuring which will become all the more painful if not anticipated.

There are a limited number of instances which merit protection in a free trade context or agreement, for example, those in which a country's identity is challenged. This category includes defense, security, culture, the environment and, of course, agriculture. Of course in highly advanced countries including Japan, Switzerland, Austria and Norway, agriculture continues to be protected through subsidies exceeding 80%. Nevertheless these countries manage to function fully in the international specialized marketplace. The issue of subsidies and marketing boards raises many unanswered questions. For example, should Japanese consumers be penalized and obliged to pay five to ten times the current international price for rice? Would it not be better to accept to pay for farmers' non-commercial production; i.e., a human presence and nature conservation in the countryside?

What other solution is there? Why not simply recognize the fact that there are protected sectors within international competition, essentially localized services requiring someone on site, and also a limited number of sectors that should be protected from international competition. Architecture, for example, should be considered in this light. Otherwise the world will look like every city was molded from the same steel and concrete, a cookie-cutter look that would eliminate variety. Variety, the spice of life, must be preserved if the Earth is to retain its wealth, exoticism and fascination. Imagine, if every place looked the same, tourists would never need to leave home!

Waves of Europtimism and Europessimism

At the end of the 1980s, Europe, the largest solvent market on Earth appeared as if the El Dorado for the 1990s. Europessimism, prevalent until the mid-80s, went out of fashion and the arrival of a single market, January 1, 1993, was heralded as a sign of increased growth and job creation. At least this was the message emanating from the Commission in Brussels.

The prophetic effect, or self-fulfilling prophecy, of this vast domestic market and the perspective of monetary union infused the Old World with new confidence. However this renewal was buffeted by the recession of the early 1990s.

Like a bad penny, the European decline myth reappears periodically. In the 1960s a false alarm was sounded by J.J. Servan Schreiber's book Le Défi américain (The American Challenge). Oddly enough, at this time Europe was experiencing growth greater than that of the United States. From 1973 to 1993, economic growth in both regions was comparable, although since that time growth has been greater in the US. Nevertheless, the Americans are living beyond their means with record-breaking deficits in the country's balance of payments. When American figures are compared to Japan's previous foreign trade surpluses, the picture becomes clearer: Japanese savings are financing American consumption. Europe, on the other hand, generally presents stable balance of payment figures.

Many readers will remember that in 1984, during an upswing prematurely called the American economic revival, there were record exchange rates for the US dollar. At this time the knee-jerk reaction was to point to Europe's technological delay, weaker growth rates and rigid socio-political structures. Some observers actually claimed that the term crisis had disappeared from the American business vocabulary only to be replaced by *Europessimism*!

The analysts who diagnosed Europessimism and "sclerosis" forgot that a crisis may be an opportunity to surmount inertia and break the habits that block or slow down change and adaptation. Adapt or die sounds more like evolutionary biology than economics. However this expression describes what most European nations managed to do during the last two decades of the twentieth century; to wit, conquer inflation by reducing the indexing of wages to prices, by ensuring better distribution of added value and thus favoring companies, demonstrating flexibility in job and wage issues, and setting limits to the welfare state's role as protector.

Zeitgeist? L'air du temps? Whatever the word, the mood swings from Europessimism to Europtimism appeared schizophrenic at times. As a manager, investor or consultant, the best response is to step back and consider the long run. Europessimism is generally based on short-term considerations whereas structural evolutions, with the notable, essential example of demographic decline, have long promoted a logical, cautious *Europtimism. Europtimism*, as we coined it, is based on the following:

1) Europe has maintained its status as a hub in international trade. In fact one-third of all international trade passes through Europe, which makes this continent the main supplier as well as market outlet for most of the world's other regions (exception: Asia). Europe has even reinforced its integration since the number of intrastate transactions (internal trade) has increased.

2) Non-oil-producing European countries have significantly reduced their energy dependence (the ratio of consumed fuel to imported fuel). For example, France's and Germany's dependency is only 55% now. Here they have performed better than Japan which remains dependent at a rate exceeding 80%.

3) Europe achieved relative stablility in its monetary system within a turbulent international environment. The European Monetary Union (EMU) is already prepared and being implemented gradually. In fact the European Monetary System and Union both became credible once the Treaties of Maastricht and Amsterdam were ratified.

4) Europe holds the greatest scientific potential in the world and has shown how profitable cooperation in R&D can be, e.g. the Airbus planes and Ariane satellites.

5) Industrial redeployment on the Old Continent's shores resulted in investment and increased productivity with rates higher than those

in the USA. (Note that this was the upside of minimal job creation.) With substantial public support, Europe has managed to hold strategic positions in key industrial sectors, e.g. aeronautics and satellite communication. In fact Europe has even hunkered down to maintain its ranking in traditional sectors like agriculture, chemistry and transportation.

6) European socio-cultural diversity, often cited as a weakness and a hurdle to cohesion, represents a potential advantage in adapting to the uncertainty of the future. In fact diversity may offer opportunities. Consider business travel for investors and managers. Standard destinations used to be California or Japan, but companies are now rerouting to Southern Germany, Northern Italy, Catalonia and the French region of Britanny.

Europe: A Longstanding Marketplace

The saga of modern European integration could be summed up as a permanent confrontation between the European Community's will to integrate politically and economically versus each state's individual concern about maintaining national sovereignty.

Since the 1987 Single Market Act, the rule of unanimity has become the exception and the European Council rules by majority as qualified by the Commission's proposal and in cooperation with the European Parliament. However the struture is not monolithic and monopolizing; unanimity is still required on indirect fiscal decisions as well as those related to the free circulation of individuals, and the rights and interests of wage-earners.

As the Berlin Wall crumbled on November 9, 1989, and Germany began its reunification process, the builders of the new Europe pushed to beat the clock. Of couse the timeframe was set out in the Maastrich Treaty, drafted to implement a single currency at the end of the twentieth century, for those European states meeting several established economic criteria. History continued being made as the European Union was created in 1994 and then enlarged to include Sweden, Finland and Austria that same year. Time has not stood still and former Eastern bloc countries are waiting in line to join.

Some wonder if it is better to consolidate Europe before enlarging it. The question comes too late. The greater the number of member-states, the wider the democratic circle, but Europe will also become less governable through a majority vote since the interests of the various countries will multiply and diverge.

Geopolitics determine monetary issues and there are no examples of a single currency zone being established without settling sovereignty and defense issues beforehand. Perhaps starting with a common currency and developing the private use of the euro would have been the best way to start.

The dominant impression is that the road to a unified Europe is more narrow than ever, that the easiest obstacles have been surmounted and that the players should move ahead now by giving up components of their national sovereignty at monetary, fiscal and social levels. However the various member-states are not prepared to do so. "Europe's unity lies in its diversity", Fernand Braudel observed ironically. His words reveal that the European identity feeds on a variety of cultures, references and models. Think only of the Olympic Games. No one would consider replacing national flags like the French tricolor or the Union Jack with the European circle of stars! Centrifugal forces may prevent harmony and convergence, but they can not be ignored. The example of Catalonia stands out. In this autonomous province of Spain, it is increasingly necessary to speak Catalan for business purposes. In Italy, the North does not question joining the rest of Europe but rather whether to separate from what it considers the Mafia-ridden South.

The resurgence of nationalism witnessed throughout Europe may overflow, as seen in the brutal, bloody battles waged inside the former Yugoslav republic. Former artificial federations of peoples have simply shattered. New states rise up from old regions. Questions also arise, however, when the West applauds the independence of Baltic republics or Slovenia while rejecting the Basque people's right to self-determination. The warning should be heeded so centrifugal forces previously contained within nation-states are not unleashed, awaking particularities in peoples seeking a lost identity.

In the end, the answer is "yes to Europe", but which Europe? Is it a clubhouse, a confederation or a federation? Is it the Europe of 15 or a structure containing 80 or 30 countries, as evoked by former EU president Jacques Delors? Should countries really give up entire components of their national sovereignty for a technocratic and ungovernable Europe?

The dream of a united Europe should not turn into a nightmare that leads to the breakdown of the continent into micro-nation-states. It would be much more realistic to refocus European construction on a limited number of countries.

Sustainable Development: With or Without Mankind?

The media tend to preach gloom and doom so we often miss or forget the brighter news. Risk prevention certainly falls under the sway of this media fashion, as seen in the examples of acid rain and catalytic converters. In fact Olivier Postel-Vinay (1994) describes the situation as follows: "at the end of the 1970s and early 1980s, the dominant theory was that deforestation in Europe and North America was caused by factory emissions of sulfuric dioxide. Dozens of measures implemented at the international level were supposed to limit the damage caused by pollution. Five years later, the theory had changed. Now the guilty party was no longer acid rain but rather the deadly effects of ozone. The sun and car were to blame. As a result, the European Union decided to impose catalytic converters on vehicles within its member-states. No sooner had the ink dried on the law, than experts had to admit the unthinkable: the forests were suddenly on the mend, in even much better condition than in previous decades. Of course by that time, two collective errors had been made and two important industrial policies had been implemented. The winners in both cases were the laboratories specialized in analyzing the lower atmosphere or forests. This was only the beginning of the sweeping tide of "scientistic ecology" (See Postel-Vinay (1994) for historical details.)

Given the all-mighty power of modern society, some people actually believe that from now on they are responsible for global warming. Perhaps someone should remind these well-intentioned folks that the dinosaurs did not need humans to push them into extinction. The jury is still out on global warning and there is no proof that it is related to human activity.

All too often people forget to consider the logic behind the questions asked. Instead we rush like lemmings towards the illusory answer to a false question. As mentioned earlier, if we opt to err on the side of caution, we should not take too many hard and fast decisions based on overly "soft" information.

Remembering Past Climatic Variations

Variations in the climate have less impact on developed countries than did economic and demographic fluctuations during the early Middle Ages. Technological progress has neutralized many effects of minor climatic changes. Actually, in major modern cities, residents are currently exposed less frequently to seasonal changes. The urban population lives inside with artificial light and air. People travel in underground passages and malls. Nevertheless everyone's morale depends to a great extent on the weather, a standard feature of any news broadcast. Imagine what it was like in Europe where people spent most of their summers by the fireplace because of constant rain, as was the case in 1816. Consider what would happen if two-thirds of the walnut trees froze, as in the winter of 1709? Or, better yet, if there were eight soggy years in a row, as from 1313 to 1320 during which most of Western Europe waded up to its knees? Emmanuel Le Roy Ladurie (1983).

The same author-historian reminds readers that during "these eight wet years, 1313-1320, in which the entire Western world was up to its knees in water, the rain ruined the harvest, made seeds scarce and led to horrible famines from 1315 to 1316. "The floods during these two years provoked irreversible damage and loss of grains. Never was the number of dead as high in the one-hundred years from 1245 to 1347 as it was during those two years alone. There were also scorching summers during which the crops seared underfoot, as in 1666. In September 1666, the wooden structures of London houses were so dry that the tiniest spark would turn them into a tinder box. The Great Fire of London in 1666 was no coincidence."

Modern madness (in the media and elsewhere) certainly throws a wrench into nature's work. The real force at work here is end-of-the-millennium angst or early century blues. Links between global warming or the greenhouse effect and human activity have not been shown. Little is currently known. However as Jean-Paul Dufour said in an article in the French newspaper, *Le Monde* (January 11, 1986), "Although new record highs were hit in 1985, past examples make it difficult to interpret the average increase in temperatures observed over the past century. Most researchers are awaiting new clues before rendering their verdict (…) as long as there are unknown factors in the way the world climate functions. The past reveals that major variations may arise cyclically without any long-lasting deregulation."

It is true that Alpine glaciers have lost one-third of their surface areas since 1860. It is also true that this warming of less than one degree within one century follows the cooling of the Little Ice Age that lasted from 1550 to 1850, including a strong glacial thrust between 1600 and 1710. The Western World is far from the optimal average temperature of the period between 800 and 1200. It needs at least one or two degrees and even five to recover the *Warmzeit* conditions of 100,000 years ago. In fact, in the year 1000, Greenland was indeed green, ice-free and colonized by Vikings. The globe is much colder today and its warming has been noticeable only since the mid-1800s. Nevertheless, this too may simply be a minor fluctuation within the cycles that have already experienced major shifts in amplitude over the past millennia. (Cf. Emmanuel Le Roy Ladurie, (1983)). Those shifts and fluctuations are not linear since there was a slight cooling between 1955 and 1975 which made some people fear another ice age.

Although there is some probability, doubts remain as to whether the natural oscillations of the some climatic system have indeed been affected by human activity. Of course nothing prevents researchers from wondering and studying the matter so that we all behave in a more responsible fashion and prepare for the unavoidable and unpredictable.

Yet how can we behave responsibly when the unknown factors in the environment are such that we may doubt the data and solutions put forth. As Haroun Tazieff asked: Will the famous hole in the ozone layer, whose size and growth have been documented, continue in the usual uncertain way, according to volcanic rhythms? In fact the author added that the threat of stratospheric ozone disappearing simply is not there. "Those who have been trying to make people believe otherwise are betraying a scientific truth".

Who benefits from this doubt? Researchers, who obtain more funding, or projects and governments, who take advantage of the situation to play the "good international citizen" with little effort or spending. Meanwhile the same governments are unable to solve national problems and qwell public anger.

The Risk of a Demographic Implosion

Sustainable development has been trendy for a while now. Its origins may be found in ecology, especially in the English-speaking world where the term was coined. Sustainable development combines a mixture of often antagonistic notions, from sustainability based on the environment to social acceptability. The two concepts are at loggerheads: the old greens, for whom growth is bad, and the modern greens, who know that there is no creation without destruction. Mother Nature herself is cruel and does not let humans play the sorcerer's apprentice.

Everyone must be made aware of the risk of a scientistic and green dictatorship and should keep in mind the Heidelberg Appeal launched by hundreds of scientists from around the world, at the closing session of the Rio Conference. According to this Appeal, *"... we want to make our full contribution to the preservation of our common heritage, the Earth. We are however worried, at the dawn of the twenty-first century, at the emergence of an irrational ideology which is opposed to scientific and industrial progress and impedes economic and social development. We contend that a Natural State, sometimes idealized by movements with a tendency to look toward the past, does not exist, and has probably never existed since man's first appearance in the biosphere, insofar as humanity has always progressed by increasingly harnessing Nature to its needs and not the reverse."*

The appeal lacks a key component, though. It needs Man to work for both Mankind and the future of humanity. We hereby subscribe to an "eco-realist" vision of sustainable development with a human face and a social dimension.

As a result, the development of megalopolises or mega-technopoles cannot be considered sustainable if social tension inevitably rises and even increases in tandem with the stress of various imbalances and inequalities.

In urban clusters, the number one endangered species is actually the *homo sapiens*, who can not thrive without dignity, autonomy, social ties and some meaning or sense of direction in life. Humans need space to live and play. They need clean air, suitable architecture and social relations. All of the above should also be part of any real sustainable development. Risk prevention should be considered here, too, for in many fields an increase in quantity triggers a decrease in quality.

What should be condemned are those short-term practices which are implemented to rationalize expenditures yet lead to depreciation in future values (positive and negative) and also overvalue the present. In other words, the inflated growth (flux) to the detriment of heritage (stocks). It may seem normal to consider the current value of a very far-off, albeit great, advantage as negligible. But do we have the right to treat the risk of major drawbacks in a similar fashion using the excuse that they are far-off?

Such practices will leave future generations a heritage of cities, forests and waterways that are disfigured or polluted. Species have already become extinct and hazardous waste continues to accumulate, Members of the next generation will be obliged to pay for the sins of their parents, who behaved as if tomorrow would never come. Yet Lester Brown told them that the earth was not an inheritance from our ancestors but rather a loan from our descendants. Was anyone listening?

In any event, development can not be sustainable if there is no one left to maintain the diversity of our landmarks, memories, languages and cultures. Unfortunately the effects of the "baby bust", or crash, particularly in Southern Europe, indicate that this diversity is threatened. The slow suicide of the Old Continent through low birthrates may not be as significant as the stockpiling of radioactive waste. It is also difficult to consider the population issue in a world dominated by what is considered politically correct.

Yet what would ecologists say if the fertility rate of whales plunged to a level less than half that of the renewal rate? They would surely alert the population to this ecological disaster of global proportions. Ironically this is exactly the pattern in Northern Italy and Catalonia where fertility rates are lower than one child per woman. Perhaps one day what is politically correct will defend children and adults as fervently as whales.

Those who delight in seeing vast green spaces transformed into virtual nature preserves with no humans in sight are condemning themselves to a sad existence in anarchic urban clusters. In short, development will never be sustainable if people continue to feel threatened in their diversity by the forces of uniformity and by the leveling off of the very differences that they themselves have put into place.

Sustainable development necessarily keeps the future open-ended for the generations to come. It can not be planned or organized without considering humanity. Planners, developers, leaders, all of these people should be just as attentive to humanity as they are to nature.

Young people should no longer be sacrificed on the altar of "affirmative action" invented specifically to protect threatened minorities.

Youth should benefit from this form of discrimination, for as the humanist Jean Bodin said back in 1576, "the only wealth is human-kind". Let us rediscover the path of population renewal. Let us lift demographic taboos and renounce, as did Jean-Claude Chesnais (1995) when he described "this implicit, absurd, suicidal consensus adopted by all the social partners" and "this idea of the rising social-ization of the cost of old age and rising privatization of the cost of youth."

If young people are to remain a minority, imagine their solitary old age!

The Missing Link

Economists readily recognize the link between growth and job cre-ation. Hence those who ponder which mechanisms encourage growth usually cite demand and innovation or the lack thereof. Very few, how-ever, make the connection between economic growth, job creation and demographics. Somehow economists refuse to see the link and there-fore do not even test or confirm it.

Yet the baby-boom went hand-in-hand with economic growth and the powerful American economy *vis-à-vis* the European may be explained by innovation as well as greater demographic growth. For the past twenty years, the fertility rate in the United States has been two children per woman versus a rate of 1.5 in Europe. Meanwhile the American population, through immigration as well as number of births, has continued to increase steadily while the European popula-tion has stagnated.

These troubling correlations reveal that the industrialized coun-tries which have created jobs and reduced employment the most are also those whose population has increased the most dramatically. It was a pipe-dream to think that everything would fall into place after the year 2000 because of a decrease in the active population in Europe. On the contrary, the demographic implosion, within a context of granny-boom and baby-crash will only heighten social and economic tensions.

The Active Population as Reflected in Employment Figures

The strong positive correlation between variations in population fig-ures and job creation is truly spectacular. There is an almost exponen-tial link between the demographic dynamics and job creation, espe-cially in the USA and in Japan where employment is rising twice as fast as the population. The following chart confirms this situation with figures from the OECD on population and jobs for the period 1975-1997. The following chart reveals that the United States and Japan, the two countries that have created the most jobs (45% and 26%

respectively), are also the countries in which the population rose the most, in relative terms (up 24% and 13% respectively). Inversely the five main European countries demonstrate weak demographic growth in both absolute and relative terms given the lack of job creation and significant increases in unemployment figures. Their populations increased moderately (7%) and jobs increased by less than half that figure (3%).

Naturally this type of correlation between demographics and economic growth only suggests causality. The hypothesis must be tested. Nevertheless, these averages disguise serious disparities among the various countries and regions compared. In fact, for any given population, growth does depend on innovation, job creation, entrepreneurial spirit and labor market conditions.

Variation in Population and Employment 1975-1997

	Variation in the population		Variation in jobs	
	Millions	**%**	**Millions**	**%**
USA	50.8	24%	39.1	45%
Japan	14.7	13%	13.4	26%
Five European countries	17.2	7%	3.1	3%

Five main European countries: France, Germany, UK, Italy and Spain.
Source: OECD.

Given the stakes involved, the principle of precaution so often cited in ecological matters should also be applied to demographics. Why are the statistics bureaus wearing blinkers? Statisticians should consider the link between demography and economic growth just as they considered the relationship between human activity and global warming. Why not start studies that test causality hypotheses and, in the meantime, take conservative measures to promote higher birthrates.

Let us remember that Europe's main market is Europe. Statistically, the Old Continent consumes 93% of what it produces. The rapid graying of Europe can hardly stimulate growth given that in order to invest and consume one must need to set up a household or company and be confident about the future. Unfortunately these traits decrease with age. In sum, the perspective for Europe is soft, variable growth.

Dynamic Demographics as a Condition for Growth

The demographic implosion in Europe will certainly be dramatic. In 1975, France had 1.7 million more youths under the age of 20 than it does today. In Northern Italy and the Catalan region of Spain, the fertility rate has remained stagnant at less than one child per woman for two decades! In other words, 2.1 children per woman would be required just to ensure reproduction of the current generation. European countries resemble orchards that have reached maturity after producing fine harvests for forty years. Unfortunately no one ever thought to replant!

In 2025, the "Europe of Fifteen" will have approximately the same number of inhabitants as in 1999 (380 million) and will be surpassed by the populations of southern and eastern shores of the Mediterranean, which will have doubled by then! Within the category of developed countries, the demographics of Russia, Japan, and Eastern Europe will deteriorate more than those of Western Europe.

Among the developed countries, only the United States will continue to be the exception. From 1999 to 2025, the American population (over 63 million) will continue to rise in absolute terms, comparable with Brazil's (over 50 million) or Indonesia's (75 million) and in contrast with the Japanese and Russian populations which will decrease by 6 and 8 million respectively.

In Europe, efforts to stimulate market demand by encouraging adults who are already settled to replace products will not compensate for decreases in consumption, and especially not a decrease in the dynamic spirit inherent in youth. European leaders have simply not understood that there will not be a durable economic revival without a demographic revival.

Indeed, demographic growth and job creation reveal a shared zest for life which translates into economic initiatives and childrearing. It seems that the entrepreneurial spirit is closely related to the family spirit! Economic revival is a major preoccupation among government leaders who, unfortunately, have done the opposite of what was needed by giving bonuses to car buyers and not to cradle buyers. Fortunately immigration has compensated for population decreases. Nevertheless, we can not ignore the value of educated citizens. If we are to integrate the maximum number of children arriving from elsewhere, we need plenty of native-born children in the schools!

Lastly, let us remember history's lessons and ponder the fact that the spectacular demographic decline of the Roman Empire (a drop of 50%) preceded its economic and political fall.

A Major Issue: Food Safety

In the past, European farmers organized as a collectivity with the help of the Common Agricultural Policy (CAP), to win various battles, be it productivity or modernization. Yet, by increasing the number of hectares and the number of bushels per hectare over the past thirty years, the same farmers have lost half their neighbors and have lost touch with the "old ways". These traditional ways were perhaps less efficient but usually more respectful and more attuned to the seasons and the environment. There was an awareness that some resources like the soil, water or scenery could not be treated indefinitely as a steady, ever-renewable flow while the inventory is decreasing in terms of both quantity and quality.

The influence of the media in the early 1990s combined with a general awareness of pollution led us to question the artificial nature of agricultural practices. Think back to the Mad Cow crisis, the rise of new technology like genetically engineered food products, not to forget the Belgian chicken and pork episode in 1999. These events made food safety a topical issue not just a sensationalist headline.

Caught up in the race to be productive, farmers have turned to illogical practices like the extensive use of growth hormones, adulterated food or even unnatural foodstuffs. One example of this frenzy is raising chickens in under five weeks when nature requires five months! Perhaps that infamous cow would not have gone mad if she had stayed out in the field!

We have opened up Pandora's box and can not close it. From now on, all problems must be brought out into the light properly, openly and with transparency. Otherwise, each new scandal revealed by the media will fuel the public's distrust. The tainted blood scandals should make officials prepare to act and fast! After the Belgian chicken crisis, are we waiting for the sequel, will it be "Senile Salmon"? Note this possibility should not be discounted among fish raised artificially who are fed everything that is prohibited to animals.

Consider the use of herbicides like atrazine, which is highly restricted in Germany but found in massive amounts along the roadside or near railroad tracks in France. As if the trickle down effect into other fields did not exist! There are also fields of good potential farm land that must be erased from the agricultural map because of long-term contamination by urban waste, including heavy metals.

Despite past errors, we should not become Luddites who reject technological progress and preach a back-to-basics philosophy. If overall life expectancy has risen, it may be due to the fact that our food is healthier and more balanced than before. The all-natural state is not without danger, too. For example, in the past people died after consuming a grain parasite, the ergot. Moreover, without pesticides, people could not eat as much as their appetite dictated. Although natural, all-natural or health food sounds better, even safer, the consumption of "bio" products also implies risks. For example the very symbol of healthy eating, an apple, can develop deadly toxins if not treated against certain diseases.

However, the intensive use of fertilizers and pesticides has its limits. It would be better to protect the water table and to optimize the use of such products with a more "logical" form of agriculture. Technology provides new answers with GM products, or various forms of genetic engineering, which seek to modify plants genetically thus avoiding the use of pesticides. Nevertheless, these answers or solutions are full of question marks and some anxiety. By manipulating nature, Man may lose control as did the gothic character, Frankenstein. Not surprisingly, the English-speaking press coined the term *Frankenfood* to describe France's reaction to British beef and related agri-food safety issues.

Society's attitude towards risk is often paradoxical, even schizo-phrenic. Genetically engineered or manipulated products, sometimes called GM products or GMOs, scare people. Moreover, those who reject these products as a precaution are correct in refusing a risk which pro-vides no tangible advantage in return. Consider, however, that no one has criticised the Limagrain group who genetically modified tobacco to produce an artificial blood component for humans (a form of hemoglo-bin). The GM products have not yet killed anyone; nevertheless they give rise to protest and opposition while a new drug like Viagra is socially accepted, despite the deaths associated with it. Why? Viagra presents a real usefulness for those who take it. The genetically manipulated product will be probably be accepted only when "pharma-foods" developed using genetic modifications considered beneficial to human health hit the shelves.

In any event, the choice should be left to the consumer while non-GM sectors are also being developed. As always, the principle of erring on the side of caution must also keep the future open. In this sense, the experimental production of GMOs must continue, even if only to keep up with technology. It is ridiculous to pretend to prohibit genetically modified wheat, maize or corn crops in a country like France, for exam-ple, while continuing to import tons of American soya, which has been genetically modified, for animal fodder. If the danger is really there, then logically the entire chain or channel must be protected!

As in the genetically modified product or in the genetic engineering issue, the stakes have reached a geopolitical and ethical level around the world. The questions will not be answered at the national level; in fact, more than ever, the European dimension is necessary. Once again, Europe will have to speak with one voice to play on the same field as the United States with its powerful companies that set the rates for the world agricultural market and dominate agricultural research, e.g. Monsanto.

The new challenge has already been given in the European Union's Agenda 2000. Not only will production assistance packages be decreased in accordance with legislation, but they will also be linked to limits and objectives in agricultural practices. In fact, it is in this spirit that territorial contracts and logical agriculture (integrated farming) will be applied. The over-arching goal: preserve the potential for devel-opment for future generations. In other words, pave the way for sus-tainable development.

Yet logical agriculture, called integrated farming in certain contexts, is an obligation only in terms of method, it does not guarantee results. Quality and safety require development in agriculture, as has been established successfully in the industry through quality insurance and certification systems, which, in essence, assume that products may be traced from table to stable. Only through transparency and consistency across the agribusiness sector, will farmers gain in terms of consumer confidence and popular opinion. At the same time, they will also have more confidence in their own future.

Given the many unknowns in the environment, doubt and prevention should be encouraged so that the long-term remains present in popular opinion. Risk prevention must also create a hierarchy of concerns and keep mankind, as well as the future of mankind, a priority. In any event, development can only be sustainable if people are around to maintain the diversity of landscapes, memories, languages and cultures.

4

HOW TO BE RIGOROUS WITH SCENARIO PLANNING

Five Conditions and the Tools to Ensure Rigor

More and more scenario planning functions as a collective thinking exercise or the mobilization of many minds when the winds of change blow through a company's strategic environment. It is also being successfully applied to regional organizations and local groups. The popularity, appropriation and increased use of scenario building means that specialists no longer monopolize the techniques. Sadly, however, there has been a decrease in methodological know-how and rigor.

The situation appears all the worse given the sad state of affairs in the United States where rational or formalistic techniques have been passed over for essentially intuitive approaches. Although commercially successful, these fuzzy approaches do not justify the meandering and detours involved. In this sense, if there is indeed a rationale to the procedure adopted by a group (Simon, 1982), a futures-thinking exercise must remain heuristic as opposed to either an algorithmic or a guesstimate approach. Of course that does not preclude the use of rigorous techniques when appropriate. This is the perspective of scenario building as "the art of the long view" to borrow Peter Schwartz' title (1991).

Despite the fine quality of Schwartz' book, not very many people have a mind as brilliant as his or the ability to execute this fine art without any method or technique. The philosophy and steps presented in his approach come close to ours but his lack of technique makes "the art of the long view", difficult to appropriate or reproduce.

This general loss of rationality coincides with a loss of memory to the point where words and names are forgotten. Too many would-be futurists and budding consultants dive headfirst into scenario planning with no background knowledge. Little wonder they look surprised, even bewildered, when someone mentions morphological analysis or probabilization.

At the end of the 1980s, French economist Jacques Lesourne, (then at the EDF, France's national power utility) sent out an important message. He called for more research in the field of scenario planning. Then, just as now, people tended to confuse simple and simplistic tools. The times have not changed. Nevertheless the scenario method, as designed twenty years ago, remains useful because it imposes a minimum of intellectual rigor through the qualitative and quantitative analysis of heavy trends and actors' strategies. Moreover it highlights seeds of change, conflict and tension, and allows for the construction of complete, coherent scenarios.

Scenarios: Use and Abuse

If you had a penny for each time you used scenario, you could still get rich soon since the word remains fashionable. Unfortunately its scientific nuance in futures-thinking exercises has been diluted.

Given the context, two questions must be asked:

1) Does simply baptizing *scenario* any combination of hypotheses make an analysis, even the most convincing analysis, credible in terms of managerial science?

2) Is it absolutely necessary to draft full, detailed scenarios in the planning process?

The answer is *no!* "No!" on both counts because scenarios and planning are not synonymous. A scenario is not a future reality but a way of foreseeing the future, thus throwing light on the present in terms of all possible and desirable futures. Reality as the acid test, combined with some concern for efficiency, should be used to guide futures thinking in order to gain a better mastery of history.

In other words, we have to ask the right questions and form real hypotheses that are key to the future in order to gauge the consistency and feasibility of the possible combinations. Otherwise there is the risk of leaving 80% of the probable futures unexplored. With the methods used in calculating probability, e.g. the Smic-Prob Expert, we can evaluate the probabilities in an exercise that takes little time for a working committee.

Ironically, the true value of a tool can often be seen when it almost went unused. This was our experience of the iron-steel industry in the early 80s. The probable scenarios remained unexplored because of conventional wisdom or clichés which blur the vision of futures-thinking groups or scenario-builders. In fact without probability testing, managers and consultants alike can pen nice tales more suited to Hollywood than to any company. In Brussels, administrative capital of the European Union, the Forward Studies Unit's report *Europe 2010, Five Possible Futures for Europe* appears to have fallen into this trap. [1]

It seems obvious, but a scenario is not a future reality. A scenario is simply a means to represent a future reality in order to shed light on current action in view of possible and desirable futures. The test that only reality provides combined with concern for efficiency guides futures thinking so that scenarios are only credible and useful if they meet the following five conditions that we believe instill rigor: relevance, coherence, plausibility, importance and transparency.

The last condition, transparency, is vital to appropriation. Without dwelling on transparency, which unfortunately became a buzzword in the 1990s, we point out the contradiction of consultants who do not submit their rationale to any system or tool that could detect errors or inconsistencies. This is not to say that probabilization of scenarios solves all problems. It is important to consider the much less probable scenarios which may be important in terms of breaks or bifurcations and the major impacts implied. Actually, transparency is vital to the

---

1. Godet, Michel. *Foresight*. vol. 2, n°1, Feb. 2000.

credibility and utility of the scenarios produced. Transparency reminds us of old-fashioned teachers who preached that clear writing was clear thinking. Another traditional schoolroom lesson: A question well asked is half answered. This last chestnut certainly applies to scenarios.

Yet all too often reading scenarios becomes a chore as the busy reader must make an effort to tease out the relevance and consistency of the scenario. The frequently low literary level of the scenarios does not help matters. Usually the reader skims through the scenarios without looking for the contradictions and since a few scenarios already seem relatively credible, he/she stops there.

Without the fifth condition, transparency, there can be no appropriation by the actors, players, or even the public, the very people who we often want to be sensitized through the scenarios. Of course transparency and attractive scenarios do not guarantee quality. There is also the risk of what is known as scenario entertainment, rather like "infotainment". Catchy titles, emotional terms and high anxiety do sell, as in Alvin Toffler's *Future Shock*; however, the genre remains fiction similar to Orwell's *Nineteen-Eighty-Four* and does not help a company or region in creating futures.

Let us go back to our second question: Is it absolutely necessary to draft full, detailed scenarios? We answered with a resounding *no* before. Why? Once again we underscore the difference between scenario planning and scenarios in general. Many futures-thinking exercises get bogged down when a working committee decides to dabble in the scenario method. People lose their focus and forget that a scenario is not an end in itself. A scenario only acquires meaning or direction in the form of results and consequences, in other words, action.

The scenario method implies a long timeframe that may extend to 12 even 18 months. Of course that estimate does not take into account the time needed to strike a committee, build a team and make it operational. Even participants in the Organization for Economic Cooperation and Development's three-year program, Interfuturs (1976-79), regretted having too little time to get to the end of the various scenarios. (For details on this program, see Lesourne, Malkin, 1979.) Of course in an ideal world, we would add a year to follow up the collective process by distributing and evaluating the results.

As a rule, working committees, groups or teams must produce a final report after one year of meeting. The other extreme may also happen and as a result, executives start a futures or scenario planning process that lasts only a few weeks. Although rarely ideal, any opportunity to reflect as a group allows participants to shed at least some light on their decisions for as the proverb goes, "it is better to light one candle than curse the darkness". In the end, common sense dictates the following pre-questions:

– what can we do in the time allotted and with the means available?

– how can we ensure that the results are credible and useful for the participants or report recipients?

The French Iron and Steel Industry

An Example of Scenario Building to Reduce Collective Biaises
Between 1990 and 1991, several months of participation in a futures-thinking exercise on the iron and steel industry in France (horizon 2005), enabled participants to identify six relevant and consistent scenarios constructed around three general hypotheses: H1 (low GDP growth, below 1.8%); H2 (severe constraints on the environment); H3 (strong competition from other materials).

Black (S 1)	poor growth in GDP and strong competition from materials
Morose (S 2)	poor growth in GDP with no strong competition from others materials.
Trend-based (S 3)	continuation of the current situation.
Ecological (S 4)	strong constraints from the environment.
Pink Steel (S 5)	strong growth of GDP and competition favorable to steel.
Pink Plastic (S 6)	strong growth of GDP and competition favorable to other materials.

Use of the Prob-Expert software enabled participants to pick out just six scenarios which covered only 40% of the field of probables:

S5 Pink steel and S4 Ecology	(010) = 0.147
S1 Black	(101) = 0.108
S6 Pink plastic	(001) = 0.071
S3 Trend-based	(000) = 0.056
S2 Morose	(100) = 0.016

Three new, far more probable scenarios thus appeared which the experts had not even selected, let alone identified, because these scenarios went against implicit or shared conventional thinking. This type of consensus, all the stronger since it remained unstated, is the source of major collective biases. Of the three remaining hypothesis configurations (60% of overall probability), each has an implementation probability superior to the most probable of the scenarios previously retained.

S7 Ecological black	(111) = 0.237
S8 Steel green	(110) = 0.200
S9 Plastic green	(011) = 0.164

The pair (11) in the two scenarios (S7 and S8) had been eliminated because, in a context of low growth, serious constraints from the environment seemed to be an improbable luxury. The pair (11) had also been eliminated because serious constraints from the environment (H2) seemed somewhat favorable for steel. But why did no one imagine plastics that could be bio-degradable with greater efficiency as suggested by scenario (11)?

From this point of view, it would be preferable to limit the number of scenarios to a few key hypotheses, perhaps four to six. Beyond six

(and sometimes even beforehand) the combinations become mindbog-
gling and participants give up. On the other hand, reducing the number of scenarios to four by combining two hypotheses (a technique suggested by some) oversimplifies matters. Scenario building on the basis
of five or six fundamental hypotheses will provide the group with a
backdrop for strategic thinking, and questions like what to do if x? or
what to do so that xyz happens? This shortcut does, nevertheless,
require some reflection ahead of time, especially consideration of the
key variables, trends and actors' strategies.

As mentioned, one inevitable logistical problem in scenario building
and method choice is time. Worse, if there is a change of team and captain, the project suffers. In fact, few futures studies or scenario planning
efforts survive the departure of the leader or originator of the project. In
major corporations, where mobility has become part of working life, a
one-year limit or scheduled intermediary results make a lot of sense.

Confusion of Scenarios and Strategies

Pure synonymy is rare in any field hence the confusion in management over terms like *scenario* and *strategy*. One point to remember is
that scenarios depend on the type of vision adopted, e.g. exploratory,
normative and plausible. Whereas strategies depend on attitudes
toward possible futures.

It seems that the normative concept creates the most confusion. As
a result, we prefer to speak of *anticipatory* scenarios. In the case of scenarios, normative is taken in the sense of retroprojective, or working
back from the future. Expressed bluntly, there is no "goal scenario";
there are only strategies. The following chart illustrates how attitudes
affect scenarios.

Attitudes towards the future	Corresponding scenarios	Corresponding strategies
Passive	None	Go with the flow
Reactive	None	Adaptive
Preactive	Trend-based	Preventive
Proactive	Desirable alternatives	Innovative

It is always tempting to take our desires for reality. However just
because certain views of the future or scenarios appear desirable, we
do not have to draft the strategic plan of an organization according to
this proactive vision alone. We need to be preactive too, in order to prepare for expected changes in the future corporate environment.

Remember that all possible scenarios are not equally probable or
desirable. In fact uncertainty may be gauged in the various scenarios

which can then be plotted on the field of probables. Essentially the higher the number of scenarios is, the greater the uncertainty. However this ratio stands only in principle since the content of the various scenarios may be very different. The most probable scenarios may be either very similar or very contrasted.

Experience shows that in general one-third of all the possible scenarios cover 80% of the field of probable futures. This translates to ten scenarios out of 32 possible scenarios for five basic hypotheses. If uncertainty is low; i.e., there is a limited number of scenarios that cluster on the graph, that concentration forms the main part of the field of probable futures. In this case, a risky strategy could be selected, rather like a gambler's bet, on one of the most probable scenarios. If uncertainty is high, over half the possible scenarios are needed to cover 80% of the field of probable futures and the most probable are highly differentiated. In this last case, a flexible strategy would be best. In other words, a flexible strategy that includes the maximum number of reversible choices. The risk here is to refuse to take a risk, to adopt a strategy that rejects risky but potentially quite profitable options and then turn inward sticking with choices that bear yields as low as the risks involved.

Again, it seems that success may spoil the term scenario. More than a terminological nuance, there is a difference between scenarios applicable to the general environment of a corporation and actors' strategies. We cannot stress this distinction enough and we remind managers, executives and decisionmakers of all stripes to distinguish between phase one, exploring future stakes, and the normative phase two, defining possible or desirable strategic choices in order to face the future. The distinction between these two phases becomes all the more important because the choice of strategy depends on the level of uncertainty – high or low – weighing upon the scenarios and on the degree of contrast among the most likely scenarios.

We also warn against confusing scenarios, which basically project desires and anxiety onto the future, with strategic options, which imply ambition and reality in foreseeable developments within the corporate environment. Why this warning? Because the actors found on the front lines are simply not the same as those in the back office. The anticipatory phase which looks at change should be collective with the participation of as many of the players as possible. Hence the need for futures studies or scenario planning as tools that help organize and structure the collective process and eventually the evaluation of strategic options in a transparent, efficient manner.

Of course, given legal issues like confidentiality, the strategic choice phase relies upon a limited number of people, usually the company's officers or board of directors. This last phase does not really need any specific method. However decisions must be made after consultation and some consensus among the executives, according to the corporate or group culture and the personality of the management team. One last reminder, the tools are useful in preparing choices but should not become a straitjacket.

The Nail and the Hammer

Although our problems may appear unsurmountable, we are not stuck in the stone age without tools. We do not have to reinvent the wheel since yesterday's tools are still useful today as long as they fulfill the following five conditions that we have set:
- stimulate the imagination;
- reduce inconsistency;
- create a common language;
- structure the collective thinking process;
- enable appropriation.

Of course intellectual tools do not come with a manufacturer's guarantee! We must always remember their limitations and respect freedom of choice. The simple hammer and nail analogy sums up the situation. We either ignore the hammer when we have to bang in a nail (the nail's dream) or we think that every problem resembles a nail and use only a hammer (the hammer's pitfall) while the nail happily stays put.

The key words here are appropriate use and appropriation. Paradoxically, as consultants, we spend half the time encouraging the use of strategic tools like scenario planning; the other half, discouraging beginners from misusing the same tools.

Of course we are not claiming that these tools equal the formulae used to calculate material resistance or magnetic fields in physics or biochemistry. Instead, the toolbox that we have humbly developed enables decisionmakers to consider realities full of unknowns as objectively as possible. Moreover, correct use of these tools is often hindered by the lack of time or money inherent to collective thinking exercises.

Why then do we insist on these tools at all? The answer in one word, rigor. Their main common feature is that they inspire intellectual rigor which, in turn, encourages participants to ask the right questions and reduce inconsistencies in their own logic. In other words, they meet the five criteria which we feel inspire and guide people in their reaction to the future. Naturally there is also the talent of the planner or consultant who can add a dose of common sense. In fact using these tools makes sense only in group futures-thinking exercises where they structure thought and provide participants with a common idiom. The tools are not like a deck of cards used for a game of solitaire. Indeed, working in isolation, a futurist or a management consultant can really only count on his or her own intellectual rigor. Since collective exercises require rigor to deal with complexity, the tools should be simple enough to be appropriable by the group.

Tools to Reduce Inconsistencies and Collective Biases

Scenario building enables managers, decisionmakers or entrepreneurs to keep the mind active and the intellect sharp. Time-tested methods ensure the effectiveness of strategic planning. In fact the common heritage of strategic analysis and futures studies serves us best when we want to show how various approaches converge or complement one another and may be organized in one super toolbox, rather like an old-fashioned fishing tackle box. Once the problem has been recognized, this intellectual toolbox helps us organize our thoughts while remaining creative.

The toolbox was set up according to a problem-based system which enables users to start the futures-thinking process which may lead to scenario-building. The five types of tools enable users to ask the right questions and identify key variables, analyze actors' strategies, scan possible futures, reduce uncertainty, obtain a full diagnostic of the company in terms of its environment, identify and evaluate strategic choices and options. The following list of tools reveals how practical the toolbox can be. Naturally this list is not exhaustive and there are other equally effective tools. However, we decided to highlight the ones that we had developed and used successfully. In this way we can vouch for the increased rigor and greater communication that these tools generate when used with the right blend of caution, common sense and enthusiasm.

A Specific Toolbox for Futures Thinking

Initiating and stimulating the process
– strategic prospective workshops

Making a complete diagnosis of the firm in relation to its environment
– competence trees
– strategic analysis tools
– strategic diagnosis

Asking the right questions and identifying key variables
– structural analysis and the Micmac method

Analysing issues and actors' games
– the Mactor method

Scanning the field of possible futures and reducing uncertainties
– morphological analysis
– the Delphi method
– the Régnier Abacus
– the SMIC Prob-Expert method

Evaluating strategic choices and options
– relevance trees

Multipol and multicriteria evaluation

Scenario Planning: An Integrated Approach

Given past and potential oil shocks, the eighties and nineties witnessed a boom in the use of scenarios for strategic planning at large corporations within the energy sector, e.g. Shell, Electricité de France and Elf.

The French School and *la Prospective*

The French school's approach, which relies on the analysis of trends and the risks of discontinuities (breakdowns or breakthroughs), shakes up the present and calls for strategic action. Strategy, or strategic analysis, covers possible choices and the risks of irreversibility in decisionmaking, and refers to scenarios. In fact, as Michael Porter's books show, scenarios have been a major reference point since the 1980s. We focused on developing the tremendous synergy between scenario building and strategic analysis in the early 1980s, starting with the combined use of competence trees, as developed by Marc Giget (1998), and the scenario method.

The integrated approach to scenario planning blends futures scenarios, competence trees and strategic analysis. This approach to scenario planning seeks to recenter the corporation in its environment while taking full account of its specific traits, especially its core competencies. The objective of this approach is to suggest strategic orientations and actions on the basis of a company's competencies according to scenarios applicable to both the company's general environment.

In order to compete for the future, as Hamel and Prahalad (1994) suggest, companies must rely on their core competences and mold them into key factors for commercial success in their field. It is not always enough to struggle for greater performance and increased market share. Through benchmarking, a corporation must also innovate, drawing again upon its core competencies to create new leadership activities. The modern strategic approach sounds like the ancient Greek motto, "know thyself". Simple as it may seem, corporations that do not know their own strengths or weaknesses can ill-prepare for future development. Without sounding like a self-help book, the only way to know what you wish to become is to know what you are, where you have been and the history behind it all. The same applies to a corporation.

By combining these two diagnostic techniques, a company can start to position itself within its competitive environment. However we have to go beyond the simple analysis of the company's portfolio of strategic activities. Here the competence tree helps us picture the company in its entirety with a growth dynamic in the form of environmental scenarios.

From Five Resources to the Competence Tree

The diagnosis of a company's resources and competencies must take place before anyone can consider its general and competitive environments. If we are to ask intelligent questions about changes within the strategic environment, we have to know the company's products, markets, techniques, staff and background, if only to home in on the environment under study.

Traditionally the internal diagnosis includes the financial, operational and functional components to which we add two more categories, technology and quality. These last two highlight the strengths and weaknesses of the five basic resources needed if a company is to succeed.

Five Basic Resources

An organization, be it a small firm or a major corporation, may be defined as a legal and economic production entity generating goods and services. As such, this entity comprises five basic resources which can be categorized as human, financial, technical, productive and commercial. They all play a role in the goals and limits of the entity. As an organization, this entity must simultaneously do the following:

– make the capital invested profitable while financing further or future development (idea of operationality and profitability);

– stimulate research to encourage innovation in processes and products that are likely to both meet market needs and guarantee lasting competitive advantages;

– turn basic products into finished or semi-finished products efficiently (idea of productivity and added value);

– sell as much as possible at a profit (idea of market share, sales figure and sales margin).

As a human collectivity, this commercial entity can create, adapt and grow but may also decline and die out. Strategic management of our hypothetical business must ensure a coordinated shift towards a sought-after or desired future through its five resources. Objectives, strategic tools and tactics may be associated with each of the five resources. Nevertheless, these objectives (technological, economic and social) are contradictory. In this sense strategic management is an ongoing negotiation between divergent objectives within a more or less turbulent environment.

Of course given a particular financial structure and level of profitability, the value of a company as perceived by its owners or administrators depends on the perspectives within the areas in which the company is active and also on the trust that the administration has in its managers or executives who should be capable of providing some vision and of forging a coherent strategy.

Value Chain, SBA, Core Competence and Competence Tree

Any production (output), be it goods or services, requires an input that may be transformed, processed, or enhanced. This creates a functional chain that originates in R&D, snakes it way through design, production, distribution and ends in after-sales service.

This functional chain is normally associated with the "value-added chain", a concept revived by Michael Porter (1985). However the notion of added value/value added is in part an illusion given that until the product is sold, the company knows only the additional manufacturing costs related to the product. To paraphrase Michael Porter, "value is what customers are prepared to pay". Actually, it would be more accurate to speak of "added-cost chains" and then the division of added value (difference in value between the sales price and the added costs) throughout various functions of a company.

Core competences here refer to the technological, financial and administrative know-how that a company has. A function may be described as a relatively homogenous field of activity or competence. For example, the same department or professional function usually does *not* produce items with high and low unit-prices, with long as well as short shelf-life, both mass manufactured or handcrafted, for both a mass-market and industrial clientele.

The competence trees created by Marc Giget in 1983 seek to represent the company in its entirety without reducing it to its products and markets alone. In these trees, the roots, (generic skills or competencies and know-how) and the trunk (manufacturing capacity) are just as important as the branches (product-market lines). The representation of a company as a competence tree grew out of the strategic analysis of Japanese firms. It seems that implictly or explicity most organizational structures in Japan were presented in tree formation. For example, three concentric circles would symbolize research, production and merchandising. The result was a one-dimensional tree.

Illustrated is an economic view of the competence tree. Here we can see the difference between technological trees in which the trunk (manufacturing) does not exist. Also the branches appear to spring directly from the roots. As Marc Giget (1989) points out, these are two concepts with distinct aims. Technological trees were usually drawn up by the research or communications departments which appreciated the simple, positive form presenting a coherent, exhaustive image of the company's activities to outsiders/the public.

The full competence tree requires considerable effort, especially an exhaustive listing of data on the corporation itself as well as its competitive environment. This comparative gathering stage is vital to the strategic diagnosis of the tree, e.g. the strengths and weaknesses of the roots, trunk and branches. The diagnosis must also be retrospective, in other words, it must look back before looking forward.

The tree image works well in that it shows how a company should not die with its product. Just because one branch is diseased, the forrester does not saw off the trunk. If a branch is sick, the sap of its competences should be redistributed to new branches, new activities, that share its genetic code. There are some famous examples like the manufacturer of cigarette rolling papers who converted to special packaging or the slide rule distributor who switched to selling calculators.

However the tree image has its limits, too. The dynamics of a tree are not unidirectional from the roots to branches only. As in nature, the branches feed the roots through photosynthesis as well as humus, a mulch formed by dry dead leaves and soil. There are incredible biological combinations but there are also inescapable incompatibilities. If we stay with the tree analogy, a pine cannot become an oak and a cherrytree cannot grow pears.

Strategic planning and management, based on competence trees, required a competitive environment to complete the picture. The need to see the big picture hence the need for other tools reflects the strength of the French school (la prospective) which has been enriched by tailoring techniques (scenario method) to meet a real demand.

Origins and Definitions of the Scenario Method

As the title of this book indicates, there are many possible futures and no single path leading to one or the other. The description of a possible future or *futuribles* plus the path to that future make up a scenario.

The word scenario was introduced into futures studies and common management parlance by H. Kahn over a quarter of a century ago in his book *The Year 2000*. Given the literary genre, the term was associated with the imagination applied to either a rosy or apocalyptic prediction. Of course there was a rich futuristic or Science Fiction tradition already established, from Jules Verne *(The Time Machine)* and Anatole France *(Ile des pingouins)* to George Orwell *(Nineteen-Eighty-Four)*.

In France the scenario method was first applied by the DATAR, a governmental organization, during regional futures studies. Ever since then the method has been adapted to many sectors ranging from agriculture to industry and services, and also applied to various geographical or political levels, e.g. regions, states, countries, or even the entire world.

In the United States, researchers like Coates, Gordon, Helmer or Dalkey developed several rather formalistic methods for scenario building. Most were based on expert advice or opinion, e.g. the Delphi questionnaire and Cross-Impact Matrices. Naturally their findings were published regularly in *Futures* (UK) and *Technological Forecasting and Social Change* (USA).

The rigorous method of scenario building dominant in France uses tools developed primarily for systems analysis. Many of these tools were developed in the early 1970s at the Rand Corporation in the United States and later in France at the Sema, a private consulting group, as part of Futuribles International, at the French army's centre for futures and evaluation, and at the DATAR.

The approach that I have personally developed in various posts with various teams over the past three decades stands apart because of its use of mixed systems analysis tools and procedures. There are tools or methods like the Micmac which identifies key variables; the Mactor which analyses actors' strategies; morphological analysis which helps build scenarios and the Smic-Prob-Expert which helps determine how feasible scenarios are. Yet these very helpful methods – mathematics in general – remain underused.

One vital message that we spread in workshops and classrooms is the potential of these tools. As we pointed out earlier, they stimulate the imagination; reduce inconsistencies in thinking; create a common language; structure the collective thinking exercise and enable participants to appropriate the techniques. Of course tools should not serve as a substitute for reflection and should not restrict freedom of choice.

Strangely enough there is no single scenario method but rather a host of ways to create scenarios (von Reinbitz, 1989; Schwartz, 1993, to mention a few). Scenario-building techniques range from rather simplistic to more or less sophisticated. There does appear to be consensus, however, on restricting the label "scenario method" to a process requiring a certain number of very specific steps. The usual steps are systems analysis, retrospective analysis, actors' strategies, and scenario drafting. They flow into one another logically as seen in the following figure.

Usefulness and limitations

Traditionally scenarios have been classified as possible, plausible and desirable. Their classification usually corresponds to their nature or probability as trend-based, reference, contrasted or anticipatory.

The trend-based scenario, probable or not, corresponds to an extrapolation of trends at all the points where a choice must be made.

Often the most probable scenario continues to be called trend-based even if it does not correspond to a pure and simple extrapolation. Yesteryear when the world changed at what seems a snails's pace now, the most probable scenario was in fact the continuation of trends. However, today when looking torward the future, the most probable scenario in many instances seems to correspond to deep breaks or even breakdowns in current trends.

Extrapolating from trends may lead to a much more contrasted situation with regard to the future. In this case the trend-based scenario is also an exptrapolation from trends and not the most probable scenario. No wonder words become confused in usage. To be more precise,

The Scenario Method

Prospective workshops	**The problem formulated The system examined**
Structural analysis Micmac method	**Search for key variables (internal-external)** Retrospective, trends, Key actors
Analysis of actor's strategies Mactor method	**Strategic stakes and objectives** Actors' positions Balance of power Convergences and divergences
Morphological analysis Morphol method	**Scanning the field of possibles** Preferences or exclusions Selection criteria
Expert inquiries Smic-Prob-Expert method	**Key questions for the future** Probabilised sets of hypotheses
	Scenarios Paths Images Forecasts

we call the most probable scenario a *reference* scenario whether it is trend-based or not.

On the other hand, a *contrasted* scenario is the exploration of an intentionally extreme theme, in other words, a future situation determined ahead of time. A trend-based scenario corresponds to an exploratory operation probing development heading in a particular direction for a specific situation. Inversely, a historical, contrasted scenario cor-

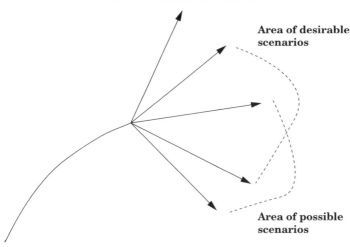

responds to an anticipatory operation that is both normative and imaginative. In this case we usually set a future scenario that is highly contrasted in terms of the present and then we work backwards to reach that future. In doing so, we draft the developmental/evolutionary scenario which may lead to that future.

The desirable scenarios may be found somewhere in the possible cone but they are not all necessarily plausible and all the plausible scenarios are not necessaily desirable.

Our Rediscovery of Morphological Analysis

Just when everyone was ready to reinvent the wheel, morphological analysis resurfaced. During a futures-thinking exercise with the French military on future weaponry at the end of the 1980s, we rediscovered morphological analysis and it became the most used tool in that case.

Oddly enough, morphological analysis had long been used in technological forecasting but very little in economic or sectorial futures studies. As a tool, however, morphological analysis works well in scenario building and in generating strategic profiles. (See chapter 6, ICW case study.)

Since the early 1990s, morphological analysis has been used systematically in future studies on air transportation, computerization in Europe, development in the Catalan region of Northwestern Spain, and scenario planning at AXA Insurance. (Please see the full AXA case study in chapter 7.).

The usefulness of morphological analysis became all the more apparent when the French Corn Growers Association came to us in 1998. Their time was limited to four or five business days. Not the ideal timeframe, but it was feasible. We suggested using morphological analysis for the two classic stages: scenario building and strategic planning. The first analysis provided development scenarios related to what would be at stake in the future of corn growing, especially the technological, economic and regulatory environments of this particular sector. Each scenario asked corngrowers strategic questions which could have different possible answers. Once again morphological analysis enabled the participants to organize their thinking as a group on the most relevant and consistent strategic responses.

Relevance, Coherence and Plausibility of Scenario-Building through Morphological Analysis

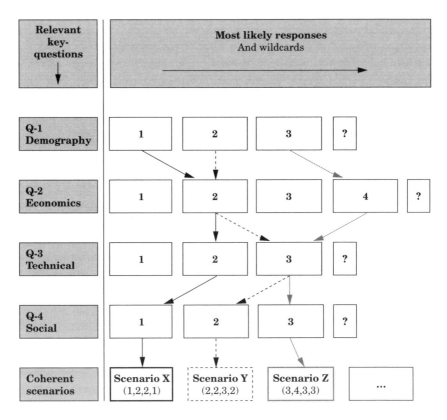

? stands for all other possibilities
At least 320 possible scenarios : $4 \times 5 \times 4 \times 4$

Relevance and Coherence of Strategies
through Morphological Analysis

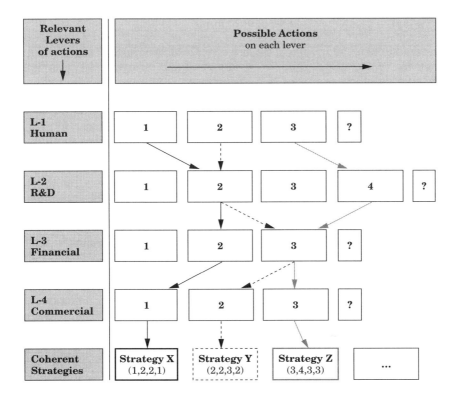

? stands for all other possibilities
At least 320 possible scenarios : 4 × 5 × 4 × 4

Morphological Analysis: Usefulness and Limitations

The areas of application of morphological analysis are many: exploratory scenario building, areas of innovation, and R&D.

Although the method has been used primarily in technological forecasting, it lends itself well to the construction of scenarios, in which the demographic, economic, technical and social dimensions, or components, can be characterized by a certain number of possible states, or hypotheses (configurations). A scenario thus becomes nothing more than a path, a combination bringing together a configuration for each component.

Morphological analysis stimulates the imagination and enables users to scan the field of possibilities systematically. There is just the very real risk of being swamped by the various combinations. It takes a bit of navigating to get through the morphological space using the selection criteria provided by the Morphol software.

The first limitation of morphological analysis stems from the choice of components. By leaving out one component or simply a configuration that is essential to the future, you run the risk of leaving out an entire facet of the range of possible futures. Note, however, this range is not restricted and evolves over time.

The second limitation, of course, stems from the sheer bulk of combinations which can rapidly submerge the user. One of the solutions is to introduce selection criteria, constraints such as exclusion or preference factors, and to exploit the useful morphological subspace.

Scenario Method and Strategic Planning

The integrated approach outlined here combines the scenario method and competence trees. The core scenario method appears in boxes 1,3,4, and 5 in the figure on page 82.

The first of the four steps seeks to analyze the problem put to us and to set the parameters of the system that we are studying. Here the scenario method or any futures-thinking exercise must be placed within the organizational context. Workshops generally serve to start up the process.

The second step is based on a full X-ray of the company, from its know-how to its product lines, illustrated in the competence trees.

The third step is to identify the key variables of the corporation and its environment using structural analysis.

The fourth step seeks to capture the dynamics of a company, a retrospective look at the company within its environment, its development, its strengths and weaknesses *vis-à-vis* the main actors in its strategic environment. By looking at the corporate battle field and the strategic stakes, we can ask key questions for the future.

Step five attempts to reduce the uncertainty weighing on key questions for the future. Various methods may be used at this point, for example, surveying experts for their opinions so that we can pinpoint the heavy trends, faultlines or breaks and tease out the most probable environmental scenarios.

Step six highlights the coherent projects, in other words, the strategic options which are compatible both with the corporate identity and the most probable scenarios, given the corporate environment. Step six flows into step seven, or the evaluation of strategic options. A rational approach to strategy should use a multicriteria method, but this is rarely the case. Step seven ends with reflection in anticipation of decisionmaking and finally action.

Step eight is crucial in that the participants move from thinking to deciding. The strategic choices and hierarchy of objectives come from the board of directors, executive committee or administrative equivalent.

Step nine is devoted to the action plan. This step involves drafting "goal" or "objective" contracts, setting up coordination and monitoring systems, and a strategic watch (*veille* in French, or vigil) that looks outside the company.

Steps eight and nine involve a smaller group within the company but they are important in that the decisions must be followed up with action. Although fewer people are involved in these steps, the information, decisions and objectives have been enriched through the consultation process. They crown the efforts of a group united in its efforts and motivated through a collective process designed to shed light on future action.

Note that the integrated approach is not completely linear and that it does offer several possible feedback loops. Sometimes implementing the action plan and the results of the strategic watch can lead participants to reconsider the dynamics of the company within its environment.

The Advantages and Disadvantages of the Approach

The integrated approach can be a double-edged sword. It combines logically and sequentially most of the tools used in futures studies, scenario building and strategic analysis. Each of these tools works, but the logical order within the approach may not always be followed completely. Similarly, the scenario method is rarely followed through from A to Z, usually because there is not enough time. Fortunately, as in any good toolbox, the tools may be used separately or in combination.

In any event, the choice of method is not dictated by the nature of the problems but the means (time and money) available.

As the previous figure shows, the integrated approach provides the rational skeleton but does not prevent the irrational circulation of ideas. Appropriation of the tools by the group paves the way to successful action without opposing the limits and confidentiality of strategic decisionmaking.

Scenario Planning Complete Process

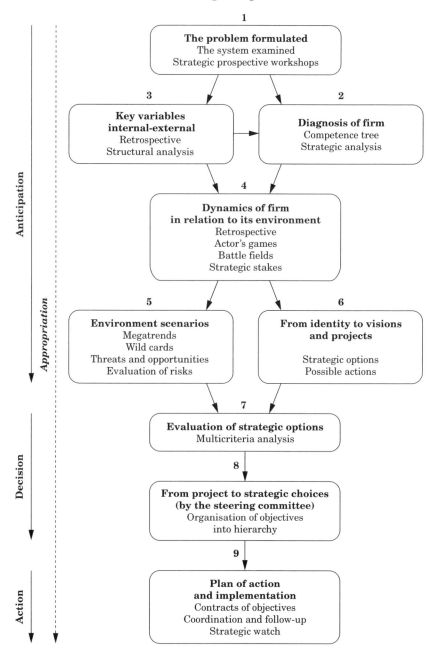

© Marc Giget (Euroconsult) Michel Godet (Cnam) 1990.

The integrated approach initially provided companies with a way of representing their structure as a competence tree. It has also been adopted by groups working on the future of territories or regions like Catalonia. There are, of course, many other general or sectorial issues for which the classic scenario method suffices.

The shift from futures-thinking to strategic action supposes appropriation by those involved. In other words, the personnel – not only the executives – should be as active as possible in the various steps of this process without altering the confidential nature of certain strategic choices. Success in moving from anticipation to action means moving through the three corners of the Greek triangle. (Please see chapter 1 and the front cover for color version.)

There really is no need to start all over again, as we already have tools that enable us to improve the pertinence, consistency, plausibility, importance and transparency when thinking about the complexity of our various futures.

Scenarios as Strategic Management Tools

There is a major distinction to be made between companies that carry out highly restricted futures studies for their executives' use in making strategic choices and companies that use scenarios as a collective tool, a way to mobilize people and intelligence because of turbulence or change. Major corporations like Lafarge, Péchiney, Mercedes and Nestlé belong in the first group; Renault or federal ministries, e.g. supplies and services, in the second.

The obvious difference lies in communication. In the first category, a group like Lafarge, provides an example of a traditional futures-thinking exercise which had an impact on strategy. Already by the mid-seventies, this group had foreseen a decline in the use of cement (– 1% annually by the year 2000). Lafarge decided to invest in an up-and-coming field, biotechnology, and bought the Coppee group, another capital-intensive business. This common financial feature was not enough to build a common future and Lafarge has since chosen to refocus on materials. Companies like Lafarge are always looking to the future and, indeed, Lafarge has already anticipated the consequences of European construction and a more open Eastern Europe.

For companies belonging to the second category mentioned above, a futures-thinking exercise serves as a means of mobilizing and managing people. In the examples mentioned, especially Renault, staff involvement allowed this corporation to face changes with greater awareness. It seems probable that restructuring at Renault in the 80s (one-third of the personnel downsized between 1985 and 1989) was facilitated by the awareness achieved through a program called MIDES (acronym for Industrial, Economic and Social Change). Thousands of executives and managers participated in this collective futures exercise. In this type of situation, transparency is mandatory. In fact Renault produced a workbook specific to the program. The workbook served as a sounding board and bullhorn for ideas generated by the futures studies group at Renault.

Between the two extremes lies one common point and several inter-mediate situations. The common point is the cyclical nature of futures studies, accentuated every four, five or seven years. The long-term backdrop must, however, be sturdy enough to last several years. If we adapt the traditional car analogy mentioned in the first chapter, an extra highbeam makes the road ahead easier to navigate.

The intermediate situation is that in which a company is using futures-thinking exercises to mobilize its managers or as a tool to determine strategy This was the case for Shell and Elf, two corpora-tions that have been using scenarios for over twenty years and even consider this practice a key component of strategic management.

On a patriotic note, we have to mention that the scenario tradition at Shell was started by Pierre Wack, a Frenchman. Indeed, Wack (1985) drew upon concepts introduced by the founders of the French school (de Jouvenel, Berger, Lesourne). Their ideas were little known across the channel and unknown across the pond. It is worth noting that Shell was the not the only one to anticipate major change in the oil sector. Another French pioneer, Jacques Lacoste at Electricité de France, the national power utility, presented a report entitled *An Abundance of Oil but for How Long?* to a futures group within the the "General Commissarat of Planning", an organ of the French govern-ment.

Planning à la Shell

This timeline illustrates exactly how Shell shifted from highly quantified linear predictions to an acceptatnce of uncertainy and descriptions of possible futures based on analysis by scenario.

1945-1955	Physical planning
1955-1965	Planning by projects selectively
1965-1972	Unified Planning Machinery (UPM System)
1967	Start of the Shell study using 2000 as a horizonline
1969-1970	Exercise called "HorizonYear Planning" (15-year horizon)
1971	Scenario experiments at the London Head Office
1972-1973	Introduction of the scenario planning method
1975	Introduction of cyclical scenarios for the medium-term
1976-1977	Further exploration of societal analysis in planning
1978-1979	Further exploraton of geopolitical and political risk in plan-ning
1979-1980	New approach to the long-term plus development of plan-ning skills within the Shell Group.

The method Pierre Wack described now operates like a well-oiled machine. The planners at the Shell Group acquired excellent experience in analyzing crucial factors impacting their field of activity, identifying the relations between the various actors and describing the processes of change in the balance of power among these actors. All analyses were presented to decisionmakers within coherent plans for further consideration.

Scenarios were developed on an international level by one department at the Shell Group. This particular department operated like an observatory monitoring the environment around the globe. It also produced world scenarios for the development of the economic, energy, and other environments. In these scenarios various events or phenomena were analyzed, e.g. demograpahics, political shifts of power, trends in values and lifestyles, technological and economic changes, monetary issues, energy demand on the basis of the preceeding factors, energy supplies, the special position of petrol, possible developments in relations between oil-producing and oil-consuming nations, price structures for crude oil and hypotheses on how these prices might change.

Using the international environmental scenarios presented by the Group, Shell's subsidiaries would draw up their own scenarios that included specific national/local aspects that could affect their business activities.

Designed as tools to help people think strategically, national scenarios must not be too numerous but they must come from an indepth, rigorous analysis, be usable, cover a full array of possibilities while remaining probable.

One of Pierre Wack's spiritual sons is Peter Schwartz who actually took over from Wack at Shell in 1984. Two years later Schwartz returned to the United States and set up the Global Business Network (GBN) a network of futures consultants and scenario planners who serve an international club of businesses. Peter Schwartz popularized scenarios in the English-speaking world and, somewhere in the eighties, even convinced his friend Michael Porter to integrate scenarios into his own methods.

Scenario Planning (adapted from Peter Schwartz, 1991)

1. Identify the focal issue, question or decision.
2. Pinpoint the key forces in the micro-environment.
3. Determine the driving forces (drivers) in the macro-environment.
4. Rank by order of importance and uncertainty.
5. Choose the "logics" or rationale behind the scenarios (axes).
6. Flesh out the scenarios.
7. Consider the implications of those scenarios.
8. Select the "signposts" or leading indicators.

In 1981, all oil companies stocked up reserves of crude oil in anticipation of the recently errupted conflict between Iraq and Iran. Thanks to the method mentioned above, Shell managed to get rid of its surplus before the market became saturated and the prices started to plummet.

Correct Use of Scenarios: The Elf Example

Without wearing out the French flag, we have to describe the textbook case of Elf, a large fuel company. Elf carried out three futures-thinking exercises over fifteen years; that is once every five or six years. In 1969, the first effort had a 1985 horizon; in 1978 the horizonwas 1990 and the last meetings through 1985 to 1987 had a 1995 horizon. We were fortunate to be involved in a new exercise begun in 1996 with a horizon of 2010. At this point, professional ethics prevent us from going beyond the methodology used at Elf. For more details, interested readers may refer to François Didier's report on the Elf case, published in French by Paul Alba (1989). What follows is a brief outline of the Elf experience.

In 1969, a small team of internal and external consultants was created. The team, led by research director Bernard Delapalme, produced a report. Looking back now, we see that although the oil shocks had not been foreseen, the vulnerability of Elf's position on Algerian oil had been seen. Hence the team's recommendations to diversify geographically, e.g. the North Sea, and sectorially, e.g., chemicals and pharmaceuticals. These recommendations were followed with the known outcomes. In terms of technology, however, the development of combustible fuel batteries, e.g. electric cars, and artificial proteins were vastly underestimated. In fact two or three years later, Elf interrupted its research in this field. Of course the rise of computers and growing awareness of environmental issues had been foreseen and an information and research centre was already in place. Overall, the report card for this first exercise was good. The team recommended doubling Elf's size in terms of the competition by 1985 and this goal was reached. [1]

Second Exercise in 1978-1979 with a 1990 Horizon

Elf's strategy manager, François Didier, took over this futures study and had eight people working fulltime over several months. The objective was to define strategies according to three identified global growth scenarios (conveniently labelled as grey, rosy and black). As in the previous exercise, changes in the energy sector went undetected. Although the West was in the throes of an oil shock, the price per bar-

---

1. In 1999 Elf was purchased by Total, a smaller, more profitable challenger.

rel was dropping in constant dollars. However, this time caution was applied on the topic of technology. Nevertheless, the focus was placed on innovation, not only technological but also economic and organizational.

Also stressed was reorganization of chemical activities while developing the biotechnological axis with Sanofi, a pharmaceutical. One recommendation in particular stands out from this study – Form the GRETS (acronym for groups for reflection and study on strategic themes). Some such twenty groups did operate throughout the eighties.

The Third Exercise in 1985-1987: Elf with 1995 as a Horizon

Still under the direction of François Didier, the study lasted 18 months and involved several dozen people. It took place in two stages: exploratory, to build environmental scenarios; normative, to define strategies given these scenarios.

Throughout the exploratory phase, a dozen teams per branch and by transversal theme (environment, research, geopolitics) were created. Throughout the normative phase, three typical strategies were studied: natural resources, commodities and "high tech-high growth".

Like the previous exercises, this one was carried out without any special methodology but with tremendous professionalism in terms of group animation and respect for deadlines. The collective effort was broadbased at key moments and included various meetings with the president, with division managers, and other levels or functions.

We were fortunate enough to follow the exercise as an invited consultant answering to the steering committee. The consultant as observer plays a thrilling yet sometimes challenging role. It involves listening without speaking for hours and then making a report, possibly critical, on what was said by the various participants, some high up on the corporate ladder.

In this case, two external consultants were used in another constructive way: they were offered – not imposed – as facilitators to teams in need of leadership. As P. Alba (1989) worded it in his conclusion on the Elf experience: "Once a company is very large, it cannot just hop up and down at will." Elf Aquitaine thus opted to base future development on its three industrial axes (oil, chemicals, health or hygiene products) and only those three axes. It is worth noting that this last exercise included a message written by the company president and distributed to all personnel on July 17, 1987.

Both Elf and Shell use scenarios regularly because of the high level of outside involvement they have developed. Errors in strategic diagnosis and forecasting have been made, though. And as any process may be improved, we think that these groups could benefit from using existing futures tools more often to enhance the pertinence, consistency and feasibility of their analyses. With regard to the issue of transparency in this case, not much more could be done for the collective memory at Elf without risking the confidential nature of that which should remain confidential.

Correct use of scenario building and strategy has been part of the corporate culture at the Parisian Transit Network (RATP) since 1972 and Electricité de France (EdF) since 1985. We will see just how EdF used scenarios in chapter 6.

Examples of Specific Tool Combinations

In the late 1980s, the French military carried out a futures-thinking exercise on an individual weapon for foot soldiers for the year 2010. As consultants to the General Direction of Armaments (DGA), we went back to square one in a structural analysis project that had been dragging on for three years. By creating a hierarchy of 57 variables with the Micmac method, we managed to narrow the list to 15 key variables. Upon reflection, we realized that nine of these key variables were features of the weapon itself, e.g. type of projectile, energy source, and range. Six of the variables were criteria to judge arms (cost, competitiveness, antipersonnel effectiveness). Morphological analysis of the nine components of this weapon, each component generating several configurations, led to 15,552 theoretically possible technological solutions. By using the Multipol method for multicriteria selection and the Morphol method to take into account the restrictions of exclusion and preferences, we were able to reduce the morphological space to fifty and then twenty solutions worth exploring futher in terms of both cost and technological know-how. Ten years later one of these solutions made headlines in France. It was the PAPOP or "polyarm-polyprojectile". This weapon enables a hidden foot soldier to fire on a sitting, moving or armored target with a specific projectile. (See chapter 6 for the full ICW 2010 case.)

Recommendations for the Future of Territories

We have had various opportunities to hone and test the tools mentioned thus far in several futures-thinking exercises on territories as diverse as the Basque region, Ile de la Réunion, France's Lorraine region, and the Ardennes, to name but a few. In this brief section, we show how lessons can be learned from both the successes and the failures.

The credibility, utility and quality of a territorial exercise require the strictest respect of various conditions. One condition that must be respected is the role of the outside consultant. Participants should never outsource the entire thinking process on a region's future.

In any study, regardless of its quality, the final report counts less than the process leading up to it. Hence the need to use local expertise and take advantage of the exercise to create a desire for change, at least intellectually. In this situation the study is almost secondary to the participatory thinking process that it brings about. Actually, by encouraging this type of futures-thinking exercise at a local level, we do spark a desire to bring together ideas and find consistency around one or two projects designed for that territory.

Participatory Yet Confidential

Although some futures studies must remain confidential, especially analysis of actors' strategies, the overall process must be considered one of appropriation. Each participant is an actor and this applies throughout the company or territory. The process has to prepare people mentally for desirable change in the company's environment and culture.

This decentralization in the process implies a minimum of centralization around the company's strategic poles. There must be some consistency and usually the steering committee ensures that there is. Generally the steering committee reports to the board of directors or executive committee depending on the company's structure. The latter organizes and coordinates the technical teams or groups within the collective futures exercise and ensures that the various orientations are taken into account.

In principle, an anticipatory process may be open to all personnel. In fact, experience shows that success is greater when there is freedom of expression and individual motivation within the limits of the strategic objectives put forward by management. These objectives may be detailed in a "charter" unveiled at the launching of the futures exercise. This charter usually outlines the rules of the process. If the rules are posted from the start and respected throughout the process, participation will not usually interfer with the confidentiality involved in strategy and will perhaps even make a strategy more acceptable.

The following comments, collected after a strategy seminar held by a major corporation in the service sector, sum up the desired effect.

"Participants were not only consumers but also producers of thoughts on the future… working in small groups enabled participants to be actively involved and to generate an avalanche of ideas that were not only diverse but expressed freely. Over a hundred factors of change were identified."

The rapporteur went further to add that *"the groups strove to distinguish two dimensions that are often confused: the importance of change and the mastery of change. We talk a lot about some changes but they are not important only because we "know how". Inversely there are important stakes we do not even talk about because they are taboo. The workshops showed that the company masters changes the best when they are technological. On the other hand, the company does not really master social or economic changes."*

To this last point, we add that changes in mentality or behavior, in particular, management rules in the human resources department, are the keys to competiveness and flexibility.

Lastly, futures studies and scenario planning, whether for a company or a region, provide a unique opportunity for participants to get beyond short-term restrictions and contradictions in order to become aware of the need to modify habits and behaviors in anticipation of future change.

However if this collective process is to be successful, internal expertise must be tapped and the futures-thinking exercise should be used to crystalize the competences often scattered throughout an organization. After our workshops the problems are usually better formulated, thought out and understood. The exercise has hopefully been a group effort that involved not only those who will continue the work but also those who requested it in the first place!

Instead of rushing headfirst into building general environmental and competitive scenarios, participants should remember Seneca's words, "know thyself". We humbly add "as completely as possible". In other words, a full diagnosis of the company in terms of its environment and the use of appropriate strategic analysis tools extend ancient philosophy to creating futures.

A Few Concepts

Megatrends
Movement affecting a phenomenon over a long period. Examples: urbanization, globalization.

Seed Events/Weak Signals
Factors of change which are now barely perceptible but will make up tomorrow's heavy or megatrends. In fact a latent variable is what P. Massé called a "seed event, or a miniscule sign given current dimensions but immense in its virtual consequences".

Actors
Those who play an important role in the system through variables which characterize their projects and which they more or less control. Example: the consumer society, multinational companies, to name a few, are actors in the energy sector.

Event
Notion defined by E. Borel as "an abstract being whose sole characteristic is that it happens or does not happen." We can consider an event as a variable that can take only two values, usually 1, if the event takes place, 0, if the event does not occur. Such an event would be called an isolated event.

5

INITIATING THE ENTIRE PROCESS

The Strategic Prospective Workshop

Workshop Outlines
Anticipating Change and Inertia
Hunting Down Clichés
Negotiating between the Short- and Long-Term
Drawing Competence Trees

Illustration: Regulation of the Telecommunications Industry (Horizon 2010)
The Context of Futures Thinking
Major Changes and Clichés Detected during the Workshops
From Key Issues to Actors' Strategies
Leading to Four Initial Scenarios

Practical Guide for Strategic Prospective
The Components and Functions of the Technical Group
Starting with Workshops
Practical Advice

The *Strategic Prospective* Workshop

How did the futures workshop develop? To answer that question, we think back to a period of several years when we trained forty-odd newly promoted executives at Renault. The seminar topic was "future watch" *(vigilance prospective)*, or a form of foresight similar to techno-logical foresight. In 1985, we were asked to design a more participa-tory method so that the attendees would be more than consumers of foresight and actually become participants actively thinking about foreseeable change and the strategic consequences of such change. The following three types of workshop took shape:

　　1) Anticipating and mastering change;
　　2) Hunting down clichés (conventional thinking);
　　3) Negotiating the short- and long-term.

From 1989 to 1990, a fourth type came naturally from the concept of competence trees, e.g. the past, present and future of an organiza-tion or a territorial collectivity. In this sense what began as a training tool, the competence tree, became a full futures-thinking exercise for a group, be it a corporate department or regional council. Creating the tree enables members of the group to outline problems and priorities according to the stakes, identify possible strategic actions and, most of all, simulate the entire process; in other words, outline within a few hours what would later take place in detail over several months. That group, be it a working committee or an informal assembly, is thus bet-ter prepared to become aware at least of potential obstacles. The group can then lay out an efficient plan adapted to the specific nature of both the problems at hand and the approach adopted by the group.

Futures workshops, or futures-thinking exercises, are suitable for groups of ten to one-hundred people with a shared experience or inter-est. They must be people who want to think together about possible and desirable changes with a view to charting a common course and mastering those changes.

The ideal number for a group is thirty. The main group can always be broken down into sub-groups or cells of five to ten. These sub-groups can then participate in different workshops. The laws of group dynamics tend to support at least two sub-groups on anticipating change. This division allows the group leaders or facilitators to later reconvene the two groups as one and compare notes. A sub-group for the clichés or conventional thinking workshop is a must. This work-shop usually provides participants with a chance to release tension and speak more openly than usual.

In an ideal world, there would be 30 workshop participants meet-ing over two days. Obviously thinking about the future requires some mental preparation, a bit of a warm-up and a break from routine thinking. Given the logistics, the actual workshops should start only in the afternoon of the first day to end in the evening of the second day.

The morning of the first day should be an introduction with debate about futures thinking. This initiation includes analysis of the causes of forecasting errors, warnings about clichés and landmarks in planning, e.g. probable trends and major uncertainties. It also shows participants how behavior and structures must be adapted, even transformed, in times of change. This introductory lecture should be thought-provoking, not dry or academic. Ideally participants will want to roll up their shirtsleeves and get started.

Overall, this two-day seminar aims to present the most important, most easily appropriated concepts and tools to participants. Through immersion, the futures workshop seeks to harness the collective thought process and apply it to strategic action. The workshops themselves allow participants to identify and prioritize as a group the stakes that their company or region has in its future environment. Note that the environment may be general or competitive, local or international. After two days, participants are ready to define their priorities and goals, draw up schedules, list methods and organize the follow-up to the workshops.

We have presented these workshops a hundred times over the past fifteen years. Each time the process must be adapted to the context, but little else changes in terms of alternating the participants' passive consumption and active production. The two-day format is preferable for tapping into the group dynamics without overwhelming participants and losing their attention. One day is simply not enough to introduce, explore and apply the concepts and tools mentioned above. And the last thing we want to do is frustrate participants who have just discovered their role in creating futures.

Futures-thinking exercises can spark incredible interest and enthusiasm in participants, as best seen in the BASF example. (Please see the full case study in chapter 8). In short, BASF Agriculture in France met with its distributors over three to four years. The process began with an initial encounter in Venice in 1995.

The workshops serve initially as a launching pad for two processes: collective thinking and mastering change. In some instances, however, it seems that the workshops actually are useful sooner than expected. In the case of BASF, it seemed smart to translate future stakes (results from workshops in terms of related goals), the identification of sub-goals, courses of action, projects and studies contributing to these goals (determined with pertinence trees) and to align the potential reality with studies and projects already under way. As a result, we soon could pinpoint the projects or research missions already undertaken but with an unspecified aim and the main stakes that required new courses of action.

Workshop Outlines

One of the most valuable pre-seminar tools is a basic questionnaire asking participants to list:
- changes that they have confronted in the past;
- ways in which they reacted to change;
- changes that they expect in the future;
- ways in which they expect to react.

Usually anonymous, the input provides the facilitator or group leader with a crash course in the company's problems or background plus the position of each participant. A summary may be prepared and presented at a plenary session before the workshops begin.

What follows below are thumbnail sketches of the four workshops mentioned earlier.

Anticipating Change and Inertia

This workshop takes place in two phases, exploratory and normative. The first phase answers the question "what can happen?" while the second leads to the question "what can I do?".

Anticipating Change (Exploratory Phase)

List the technological, economic, social and organizational changes that each participant perceives or wants. Each participant then makes his/her own list (15-20 minutes). These ideas are collected and regrouped as each participant around the table is called upon to comment. The entire workshop should take one to two hours.

A simple point system enables everyone to see the five or ten main changes and future stakes among the fifty to seventy originally listed. Although simple, this system places the ideas in a matrix which could be called generically "Importance × Control". The selected changes are graphically displayed and the current level of mastery is evaluated, too. The axis (ordinates) gives the importance of the so-called critical changes while the abscissa (coordinates) gives the current mastery of those changes.

Mastering Change (Normative Phase)

- Identify strategic objectives in terms of stakes.
- Take actions and choose the means to reach objectives.
- Assess the strategic gap or, roughly, the difference between an objective and what will happen if you do not act.

During the normative phase, participants ask the following questions:
- Who are the other actors (players) involved by these changed?
- What "levers", "drivers" or "brakes" are involved in the actions?

– How can we improve our control when dealing with important changes?

– How can we reduce the impact of changes that we do not control?

– In short, how can we reduce our weaknesses and maximize our strengths?

Position with regard to changes and inertias
Matrix: importance versus control

○ Critical changes & inertias
How to reduce their importance?
How to increase their control?

The four zones break down as follows:

Zone A : Critical changes affecting future stakes. These are important changes that we do not master at present.

Zone B : Important changes well mastered

Zone C : Moderately important changes that are not mastered but it does not matter. (Guiltless Weaknesses)

Zone D : Relatively important changes that are mastered. We probably talk about them more because we master them. (Useless Strengths)

From critical changes to action

Critical Changes	Stakes for Company	Corporate Objectives Given These Stakes	Ideas to Apply
1: ...			
2: ...			
3: ...			

Hunting Down Clichés

A cliché, whether true or false, is generally accepted without questioning. As a result, you may have often heard remarks like...
- "Young people don't know as much as previous generations did";
- "Americans (Brits, Spaniards, etc) are not good at learning languages";
- "Consultants are expensive".

In this workshop, participants list individually and then collectively examples of conventional thinking that they hear in their field. Sometimes mentioning a few clichés breaks the ice. Participants soon catch on, though!

The Top Ten from Various Workshops

1. The customer knows best
2. Might makes right
3. Women take more time off work than men
4. Consultants are expensive
5. A good consultant intervenes very little
6. Medicine is not a product like other products
7. Bigger is better
8. Change has to start at the top
9. Decentralization makes more people responsible but also dilutes responsibility.
10. Insurance companies are a band of thieves

The facilitator then asks the following questions:
- can some of these examples of conventional thinking be considered partially true, at least?

If so, why and which ones?
- how do you explain the popularity of these clichés, this type of thinking?
- what results do you see from this type of thinking?
- is there a lesson to be drawn from this analysis?
- what can be done to correct a cliché if it is negative and what can be done to utilize a cliché if it is positive?

Here is a personal favorite: "Consultants are expensive".

Does this idea have any foundation in fact? Why?

- Gray matter has no price tag
- Service exceeds the billed time (e.g. proposal writing, research, analysis, reports)
- The cost-benefit ratio must always be considered
- It is a net cost for the company
- The consultant has a high level of expertise

– The consultant is efficient and knows how to deal with the problem quickly.

Why does this idea prevail?

– Daily rate versus a salary.
– Recommendations seem obvious when *expost*.
– Weight of history.
– Misunderstood profession.
– Advice is not considered and investment.
– It is not easy to judge what the ROI (return on investment) will be.
– Some recommendations are not followed and thus become expensive!
– Quantity is favored, e.g. the thickness of the report not the quality.
– The consultant's look.
– Since it is expensive, cost is a good excuse for not using a consultant's services.

Consequences of the above

– Undervalued profession.
– Image problem.
– Potential for quick earnings attracts new consultants.
– Small-to-medium-size firms seldom use consultants.

Lessons to be learned...

– Clichés and conventional thinking are based on incomplete and biased information.
– Resistance to something new is strong partly because people have a system of references that they know and trust.
– Any excuse may be a good one to avoid asking difficult questions.

Negotiating between the Short- and Long-Term

Here we ask participants to draw upon their experience.
– What are the advantages and disadvantages of a course of action set out over the long-term, e.g. beyond one year?
– What are the advantages and disadvantages of a course of action set out over the short-term?
– What problems in choosing the short or long-term have you experienced in your field?

Although used less frequently than the others, this workshop suits audiences who admit that futures-thinking exercises hold little appeal for them. We have met negative reactions to futures-thinking among comptrollers as well as human resources directors. Yet no matter what their thoughts on the future may be, they have all faced choosing between the short and long-term in buying equipment, e.g. credit conditions, cost amortization, or in hiring people, e.g. which skills will we need in the future? This workshop provides decisionmaking criteria that enable participants to weigh the advantages between the short- and long-term.

Drawing Competence Trees (Past, Present and Future)

In the1980s, Marc Giget, head of Euroconsult, came up with the concept of a competence tree to assist managers in strategic thinking. Competence trees serve to analyze and evaluate the overall technological, industrial and commercial skills of a company. Properly used, this tool enables one to mobilize the key people involved at a corporation as well as quantify accurately and exhaustively that company's competences.

The purpose of the exercise within a workshop is not to come up with a detailed analysis and exact evaluation but rather to use the principle of the competence tree so that the participants or working committee develops a collective vision of reality for the company, city or region under study.

The workshop outline goes as follows:

1) Draw the past tree (20 years) and the present tree according to
– roots (vocation, competence, skills, know-how);
– trunk (implementation, organization);
– branches (product or service lines, markets).

2) Pinpoint the strengths and weaknesses on the tree according to the company's environment, the actors and implementation of strategies.

3) List major changes in the environment, e.g. technological breakthroughs, socio-economic shifts and political movements, that could affect the tree. Note whether these changes are desired, feared or perceived.

4) Match up the parts of the tree (roots, trunk, branches) that correspond to these changes and outline the advantages and limitations of other actors.

5) Build a competence tree for the future, e.g. which products or skills should be kept, discontinued or further developed.

The Competence Tree and Its Dynamic

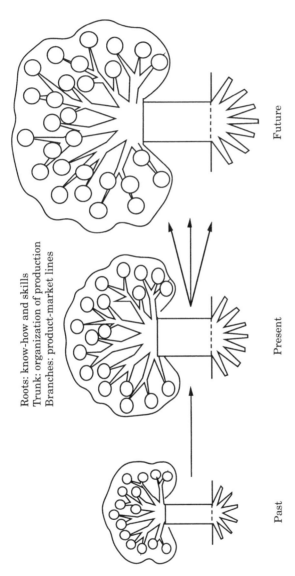

Roots: know-how and skills
Trunk: organization of production
Branches: product-market lines

Past

Present

Future

The past is unique; analysing it allows us to understand the constants and continuity of the company's business, to improve our knowledge of the company project in its historical reality

The future is uncertain; its analysis allows us to identify the threats and opportunities presented to the company, and to define the issues and challenges it faces, in order to determine its desired future and to incorporate this into the company project.

Source : Marc Giget, *La conduite de la réflexion et de l'action stratégique dans l'entreprise* (Euroconsult, 1988).

Illustration: Regulation of the Telecommunications Industry (Horizon 2010)

The results presented in this section come from a futures-thinking seminar called "Determining Factors in Regulating the Telecommunications Industry (Horizon 2010)". This event took place February 3-4 in 1999 at the French Secretary of State for Industry. The comments and opinions expressed in our report and this section present the different points of view of those in attendance. Nevertheless the opinions are those of the author and co-author, Stéphane Leroy-Therville and do not necessarily reflect those of the specific department or companies involved. Note the full report of this futures-thinking exercise was published in French in the LIPS working paper series, Cahier n°12 "The Future of Regulation in Telecommunications".

The Context of Futures Thinking

The legislative document which establishes the French federal secretariat of industry, information technology and postal service gives the Sub-Directorate of Telecommunications Regulations responsibility for analysis of the future of those sectors falling under its mandate. Sub-directorate management took the initiative of launching a series of futures-thinking exercises on regulation of telecommunications companies for two reasons.

First of all, the Telecom Review, a revision of the European regulatory framework was starting that year, so France needed to define its position. What was needed was a snapshot of the current situation and an idea of how circumstances may develop along with possible orientations. At the national level, it soon became apparent that principles of economic doctrine were needed to take into account increasingly numerous technologies, converging networks and services, as well as the specific a nature of the local network, often called *last miles*.

Another vital component in this process was sharing experiences and exploring ideas. This was achieved by bringing together representatives from all the various units of the system under study. In fact representatives from the telecommunications regulatory bodies and administrations from the French telecommunications regulatory body (ART), from the European Union, and also various users such as the French telegraph and telecommunications union (AFUTT) took part. Consultants along with certain experts known in the field also participated. Operators, industrials and distributors were either consulted, later on, or brought on board later as participants in working groups.

During the seminar itself, two workshops (Anticipating and Mastering Change and Hunting Down Clichés) were held. The results from the workshops are presented here first, followed by overall comments or observations.

Major Changes and Clichés Detected during the Workshops

1) Converging services and infrastructures in telecommunications, computers and audiovisual equipment. The main feature that was immediately noted was the mobile versus traditional stationary distinction.

2) Regulatory model, in other words, the level and basis of regulation.

3) Balance between sectoral regulation and competition.

4) Development of e-business/e-commerce.

5) Globalization, in other words, the spread of networks and markets around the world.

6) Sectorial and trans-sectorial alliances among companies involved in the information society.

7) Technological developments (digitization, packet-switching, Internet protocol).

8) The local system and ungrouping, last miles, legal rights, etc.

9) Consideration of market demand and pressure.

10) Standardization, in terms of harmonization, be it *de facto* or already underway.

11) Importance of satellites, groups of satellites and geostationary satellites.

12) Development of added value from transmission to content.

13) Role of the State: Actor or Arbitrator?

All of the above appears in the following diagram.

Hunting Down Clichés about the Telecommunications Sector

This workshop follows the format of the so-called change workshop. The first step involves listing clichés or pearls of conventional thinking both individually and collectively. In this exercise, a cliché, or preconceived idea, is part of what we call conventional thinking. It is an idea that has been accepted by the participants or by the public without any debate or critical thinking.

Proving or Disproving Clichés

The process of confirming clichés and debating them proved very stimulating in this field. The following charts show how the process goes right to the core of each cliché.

Among the 17 main clichés, the first one was:

"Promoting Internet access for all is vital to France's competitiveness."

Statements that disprove...

This is only one dimension among many.
The economic rules affecting the Internet have not yet stabilized.
The Internet is not safe and does not make the public feel safe.

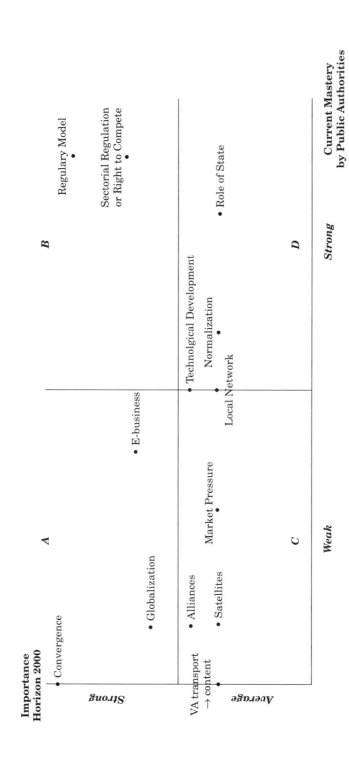

Zone A: critical changes, future stakes. These are the major changes that are not mastered currently. One strategy here might be to increase mastery or reduce the importance of the stakes in this zone.
Zone B: Major changes well mastered.
Zone C: Relatively important changes, not well mastered (no serious consequences).
Zone D: Relatively important changes, well mastered (do not focus on this zone).

There is the danger of building a virtual society.

It is just a fad.

France is not behind.

The important thing is to master usage and not spread the tools.

Internet for all plus illiteracy?

Statements that prove...

There is an increase in business on the Internet (e-business or e-commerce).

There is a "club effect" at work among the actors, thus increasing new uses.

Telephone services are developing on the Internet.

Increased productivity is linked to the circulation of information.

This decreases the price of information.

It is a tool serving research and innovation.

It is a self-fulfilling prophecy.

This facilitates the economic reach of certain regions, thus breaking down enclaves.

The younger generation is interested (an age gap may form).

It is a competitive component in the telecommunications sector.

It is a weapon in the war against illiteracy.

The second cliché off the top of the list: "Telecoms, computer and audiovisual firms will merge."

Statements that disprove...

Limits to wireless technology may slow down any attempts to merge.

Global regulation is required; an idea that does not please either the economic actors or the regulators.

Industrial logic is contradictory over the long-term, (questions of diversity and mass distribution).

In A/V, mergers might slow down the penetration of certain markets.

Statements that prove...

Technology allows for it.

There is already a convergence in the technologies involved.

The actors' strategies are heading that way.

There is a will within the industry to provide a complete offer, all around the world.

The movement has already begun.

Distributors must maximize their channels; producers must show their programs.

From Key Issues to Actor's Strategies

An initial analysis of the results from the three workshop groups reveals a high degree of similarity among participants' perspectives.

Key differences appear in the importance that they assigned to fore-seen changes or to the corresponding clichés. In this sense, the changes cited the most often by the first two groups are convergence (networks, services, sectors), the regulatory model, problems at the local level and management of "rare" (limited) resources. The main clichés or precon-ceived ideas bring out exactly the same topics. The telecom, cliché workshop is typical yet especially enriching when we look back now.

At this stage; four issues appeared:

Issue 1

Converging services, networks and markets.

Issue 2

The Evolving Regulatory Model.

Issue 3

Problems in the "Last Miles" or Local Network.

Issue 4

Management of Rare Resources at the National; Regional or Inter-national Level.

On the basis of their analysis, the working groups decided that French public authorities had a rather mediocre mastery of these issues. Yet these are key stakes which need to be monitored closely.

Workshops provide an initial image of the system, but conclusions must be translated into action. Two strategy workshops follow the "changes" and "clichés" workshops so that participants can plot possi-ble courses of action. Workshops and follow-up usually take a few meetings. In this case, two groups were formed. Half the participants worked on the analysis of actors' strategies; the other half worked on building scenarios through morphological analysis. Their results fol-low with comments.

By analyzing actors' strategies, confronting their agendas, and con-sidering the balance of power, participants can see how strategic stakes are evolving. They can then ask key questions about the future. In this instance, the group used the Mactor method to consider issues and consequences of foreseeable conflicts. (For the Mactor method, see the BASF case study, chapter 8, or *From Anticipation to Action* pub-lished by Unesco, 1994.)

The main changes identified during the previous sessions of this workshop were translated as stakes for regulation. The participants then identifed the actors associated with each "battlefield". The group thus built a list of actors who play a leading or supporting role in the telecommunication sector or whose views could fall in the balance when making certain decisions. The group then constructed a matrix "Actors x Actors" which pinpoints the powers that each actor has over the others, analyzes the balance of power associated with the stakes set out initially and then lists, as follows, the information.

This group tackled the issues through seven stakes. The actors influencing each stake were then listed in the next column.

Stakes	Associated Actors
E1: Regulation Model	European Commission, government, ART, CSA, operators, media
E2: Anti-trust Legislation	European Union, government, WCC (Geneva), Justice Dept./Min.
E3: Convergence Voice-Data	Industrials, operators
E4: Mode of Access to Subscriber	Industrials, operators, ART, government,
E5: Interoperablility/compatibility	Industrials, operators, ETSI, public authority
E6: Frequency Management	Public authority, NGOs
E7: Market	Government, consumers, operators, media

A list of actors was then drawn up as follows:
A1: Europe (standards, justice dept. EU).
A2: Government.
A3: ART.
A4: CSA.
A5: Territorial groups.
A6: Investors.
A7: Historical operator.
A8: New operators.
A9: Equipment suppliers.
A10: Distributors.
A11: Corporate customers.
A12: Private customers.
A13: Media.

With a Few Improvements for Better Thinking

First of all, the list of actors seems too limited, especially in terms of legal power. Legislation could play a key role in competition over the next ten years. Think of the AT&T case which launched the telephone wars in the United States. The State's opinion on the various law suits brought to court by local collectivities also indicates the role the legal system will have in the European telecom landscape to come. Yet, in general, the European justice system does not have the same checks and balances or self-regulating tradition as the American, and the telecommunications sector is currently regulated sectorally and controlled by public agencies.

Here the working group decided to water down the national and European judicial power potential into the actors considered public authorities. Nevertheless, a more detailed analysis will surely rank the legal system or justice as a full-fledged actor on is own.

Second, the list excludes international aspects and focuses on Europe. The surrounding world is considered benevolent, at best, and non-existent, at worst. Yet, nowadays, most battlefields are chosen by the Americans who essentially oblige the Europeans to follow along constantly. The decisions made in Asia, notably Japan, will also likely have an influence on several choices for the future. The list could be extended by taking international pressures into account.

Leading to Four Initial Scenarios

A path, in other words, a combination associating a configuration from each dimension is a scenario. Without considering the incompatibilities, the array of possible futures according to these dimensions and configurations generates $2 \times 3 \times 3 \times 3 = 54$ scenarios. By introducing limits like exclusion and preference, this "morphological space" may be reduced. Within the time allotted for this exercise, the group was able to tease out four paths without analyzing them.

The four paths or scenarios were given easy-to-understand and retain titles:
1) Much ado about nothing.
2) The Information Society.
3) Happy Few.
4) Major Trusts.

More and More Technology; Less and Less Security

This exercise helped participants map out the major forces in telecom scenarios developed by others over the previous few years. When aligned, the various scenarios reveal a few gaps. First, the technology dimension was highlighted whereas most experts agree that while technology will remain a basic tool in actors' strategies and their transactions, it is not shaping the market as much as before. Indeed from this point on, marketing and the service/product offer itself are dominating the system and from an increasingly short-term perspective. The reign of engineers has given way to that of merchants before what may be the advent of the consumer. Nevertheless, the inertia factors, considered very strong in the telecommunications sector, must be kept in mind at all times.

However, consumers are concerned about the security of their transactions as well as risks of violation of privacy. Security systems may well condition the development of new communication tools. Indeed, this dimension seems to have been glossed over in the scenarios presented.

Although catchy, the title given the first scenario should not act as a smoke screen. Even if the effects of opening up this sector to competition did not have the impact expected; even if the national champions and local monopolies have held their ground, the telecommunications sector will never be able to go back to the situation at the beginning of the information age. The behavior of both the actors and consumers has already been not only greatly but also permanently modified.

The weakness in the second scenario, "Information Society", lies in the plurality of the information society. There are many societies not one, if we take into account usage and possible changes in lifestyle as well as in products that are truly accepted. Of course, the impact of technology may be positive or negative, thus this scenario could easily be refined and subdivided.

Practical Guide for "Strategic Prospective"

First, one unofficial statistic: many futures-thinking exercises have motivated many people in a rich, collective process; whereas not too many have led to real, implemented action. Without harping, the voice of experience urges us to improve the functional side of creating futures with some practical advice.

The first condition (a *sine qua non*!) is to identify the source of the origin and the nature of the request for a futures-thinking exercise. In marketing terms, who is the client? If we continue the checklist, there are at least five key questions.

1) What position/power does the client hold within the corporate hierarchy?
2) What is the real problem or issue presented?
3) Who are the other actors involved?
4) How can they become involved in the process?
5) How does this exercise fit into the corporate culture of the client?

The most important yet often ignored condition is time. What is the timeframe or the final deadline? We have memories of major corporate clients (Renault, the Post Office, William Saurin, Péchiney) who had good intentions but a change of leadership. Many futures projects suddenly die when the pioneering executive who started the process leaves the company. Successors rarely take a shine to projects started by someone else. It is important to have corporate executives personally committed to the project and active in the steering committee. It is also important that this committee have enough time for the collective thinking activities without dragging them on for too long.

The Components and Functions of the Technical group

The mandate and tasks of each group or committee must be made clear from the start. (A checklist including request source, problem, report recipients and deadline should be given.) Intermediary documents and the final report should be the responsibility of the technical group which reports regularly to the steering committee.

Each group should have some type of leader or representative chosen by the group once it has been formed. This leader will also act as facilitator and coordinate the various tasks performed by group members. This "pilot" must be prepared to follow the course laid out and complete the mandate. In other words, the leader must set an example, monitoring activity, modifying tools but not goals, and, of course, meeting deadlines.

Launching Workshops to Initiate the Process

In our experience, a two-day, on-site seminar starts the futures process off right. Participants become group members initiated in the ways and means that may prove effective in the futures-thinking activities to follow. In this way, the group is not only consumer but also producer. The product remains the same: thought on the future. The group is ready to dive in when the workshops outlined earlier begin.

After the two days, the group is better prepared to determine the topic and define the work method jointly. The method is not fully validated until a later meeting by which time participants have had time to step back and look objectively at the process.

Organizing and Assigning Tasks

Our rule of thumb…
  - three or four meetings as the process is getting started;
  - at least three meetings annually when at "cruising speed";
  - then three to four meetings clustered near the conclusion. Again, experience shows that it is smart to set the dates of meetings and their objectives at least five to six sessions ahead of time.

Basic Housekeeping Tips

  - Always present an agenda and take the minutes at meetings.
  - During meetings every group member should give a progress report on his/her area.
  - At the end of each meeting, each participant's tasks and the agenda for the next meeting should be reviewed.

Over the course of the full futures-thinking exercise, specialists (internal or external) should be called in for advice on specific fields or applications. If possible, the expert could make a presentation, answer questions and a summary could be circulated almost immediately. If necessary, assistance or expertise may be subcontracted, e.g. in specific technical or sectoral issues.

Forming a team or working group is never easy. Group dynamics always require some effort. The hardest part is choosing an in-house leader or facilitator who can invest company and even personal time in the process. The facilitator prepares meetings, writes summaries, takes notes and encourages groups members' participation by delegating tasks. The group leader or facilitator must also foresee the various stages, problems and methods and schedule accordingly.

Here the outside consultant may prove very useful. An experienced expert not only enhances methodology but also reacts to the group's ideas, and stimulates debate. The outside expert is not needed at all meetings. The inhouse facilitator should call upon a specialist or consultant only as needed.

Choosing the Right Method: Efficiency, Motivation and Communication

No single method is imposed, but choosing a method determines how efficient the meetings will be. In other words, without a method, there is no common language, no exchange, little consistency, and few structured ideas. Nevertheless, choosing a method is not the be all and end all. We do not want to become a prisoner to the results of one method. As mentioned before, a method is a tool, among several, that helps people think better, together, about the future.

A rigorous method is a necessary factor if the group is to stick together and stay motivated. Partial results contribute to this group dynamic and should be distributed. Lastly, the choice of method must correspond to the problem(s) presented in the initial seminar, the timeframe and the way in which the results will be presented. The tools chosen must be sufficiently simple as to allow the users to appropriate them.

In the end, advice, be it on using colored pens or contractual consultants, should be taken and adapted or appropriated. The one definite obligation is preparation (agenda, objectives, method selection, proposals, etc.) Of course in the futures workshops, we use less systematic but nonetheless effective working methods e.g. imposed "time-out periods" of silence a rare feature in any group activity and a simple voting system.

A Process Rather than a Final Report

The credibility, utility and quality of a futures-thinking exercise depend on the participants' respecting certain conditions. A common breach is to subcontract thinking about the future to an outside firm or consultant. Far too many corporations and even regions have thought that hiring a well-known management consulting firm was the best idea. They missed the point. In any futures study, the final report counts for less than the process leading up to it. It is, therefore, more important to draw upon local or internal talent and use the futures-thinking exercise as a way to change the way people think and behave. The idea is to "think globally but locally" so that participants can truly be part of the creative process in a company.

6

CASE STUDIES IN INDUSTRY AND DEFENCE

The Aluminum Industry

Few cases of structural analysis applied to industrial problems are ever presented publicly. In general, such analyses can not be published because of the confidentiality risks implied. Moreover, by the time the publication embargo has been lifted, the material is usually outdated. Fortunately this is not the case for the Aluminum 2000 futures-thinking exercise, begun in 1985 on behalf of the Péchiney Group. In fact, the specialists rereading the report found that ten years later the analysis had stood the test of time and appeared almost "clairvoyant". [1]

Part of this case study was published in 1989 with Joseph Vialle, then in charge of planning at the Péchiney group. Sections of the aluminum case were presented to Petrobras executives during a conference in Brazil. The conference organizers were kind enough to grant us permission to reproduce material here.

For Péchiney, structural analysis was only the first step. Scenario building followed from 1986-1987 as a tool to shed further light on participants' strategic choices. Structural analysis proved particularly rich in that it enabled participants to sketch scenarios for the international aluminum industry. As mentioned in the first chapter, a change in corporate leadership interrupted the process, so who knows what might have happened otherwise. Nevertheless, the intellectual investment of the executives who participated was well spent. It always pays to have executives sit down occasionally and reflect upon the long-term. Interestingly enough, the decisions made later, e.g. downstream integration, with the buy-out of American Can, reflected to some extent the conclusions drawn by the Aluminum 2000 group.

A Young Metal with an Uncertain Future

The study aimed at pinpointing the key determining factors in the world aluminum industry with 2000 as a horizon. Structural analysis was the tool of choice. The aluminum system could be characterized by 75 inter-related variables.

The process of teasing out variables and reviewing the mechanisms connecting them was enriched by a series of some twenty interviews, two-thirds of which were conducted with outside experts. After the interviews, a number of the points raised could be considered probable trends or major uncertainties for the future of the aluminum industry.

---

1. Note that many of these analyses were performed under G.Y. Kerven, then president of the aluminum branch.

The Consequences of Political Uncertainty and the International Economy

Uncertainty awaits on five fronts: geopolitical (mining countries), economic (growth rates in various zones), monetary exchange (currency fluctuations), socio-economic and regulatory. As a corollary, other probable trends put forth for the year 2000, back in 1985, included international monetary instability and fluctuating growth rates. In order to adapt and survive in the face of uncertainty and change, participants saw the need to increase their vigilance and flexibility as well as diversify risks and opportunities.

Technological Explosion in Materials: Threat or Opportunity?

The raw materials sector is experiencing tremendous technological expansion, whether in composites or more traditional materials, e.g. ferrous metals, glass and wood. Why should aluminum be any different? Mixed materials are not deadly competitors and may actually represent potential markets. Everything depends on the will and strategy of the manufacturers involved.

Enlarging the Competitive and Strategic Environment of Aluminum

Manufacturers can find giant competitors along this "multi-material axis", notably international petrochemical conglomerates. One glance at the earnings of these corporations confirms how important this new challenge is to the aluminum sector.

In the eyes of many experts, strengthening the role of the London Metal Exchange (LME) seems inevitable. Nevertheless, the aluminum manufacturers may still be able to guarantee their clients stable prices. In fact, even though the LME might be called upon to play a role in generating fluctuations over the short-term, this should have little impact on the long-term competitive pricing trend in aluminum.

Recycling is a potential advantage for classic materials like aluminum. Why? The collection and disposal of composite materials may hinder further development of these materials which are at the mercy of a regulatory framework that opposes what has been called "the composite trash civilization".

Choice of Materials by Function and Service

A rapid review of the main uses of aluminum indicates that there will necessarily be a decrease if the main manufacturers limit their role to that of supplier while customers increasingly seek service (a response to a function). Service will no longer be the domain of an isolated material, given the mixes and massive choice of materials available.

Aluminum manufacturers must focus their marketing efforts on supplying a "service package". Of course this focus would affect R&D, too. Packaging is a perfect example. Here innovative materials go hand-in-hand with tooling innovations and conservation methods, hence closer links to firms downstream.

Approach and Results

In this case, structural analysis was started in May 1985 and ended in October of the same year. Drawing up the list of variables took several collective thinking sessions and involved several Péchiney executives as well as other experts. These meetings were enriched through a series of twenty-odd interviews inside and outside the Péchiney Group. During the listing, variables were divided as internal and external. Internal variables referred to the international aluminum system; external variables, to the geopolitical, social, and economic environments plus technology. By synthesizing ideas, participants succeeded in drawing up a final list of 75 variables.

The structural analysis matrix was filled in by a working committee or group created specifically for the task. Included were Messrs Bercovici, Fevre, Thomas, Vialle (Péchiney) and Messrs Barré, Chapuy and Godet as consultants. They were joined by two materials experts, Mr. Chalmin and Mr. Giraud. The group met over three days during which group members systematically asked about all the eventual interaction between variables. This group asked over 5,000 questions on the direct relationships between the variables and their intensity. The following intensities were established: strong (3), average (2), weak (1) and potential (P). Note that structural analysis also takes into account potential relations although they are practically nonexistent today. The idea is that these relationships may become probable or at least possible in a relatively distant future.

Among the variables which seem to have the most influence on the aluminum industry in the world (still horizon 2000), the following eight stand out no matter which classification method is applied. Their determining role appears firmly established.

The most influential variables are as follows:
– competitiveness of materials: this variable is fairly dependent and the most influential across the board. In other words, the future of aluminum depends on a variable with a very uncertain development/ evolution;
– financial situation of the aluminum companies: this variable appears second when ranked according to influence. Perhaps surprising, this result indicates that the future of aluminum is shaped by the financial capacity of the firms to implement their strategy and resist the ups and downs of demand and price;

– strategy of the leading clients: The position of this variable, both very influential and quite dependent, confirms the determining yet unstable nature of the main aluminum clients. Yet their choices and behavior will increasingly influence the strategy of major manufacturers;

– price stability: Here the key role of this variable can be confirmed. Its highly influential yet not very dependent nature seems to indicate that manufacturers may suffer price fluctuations;

– Alcoa, Péchiney, Alcan strategies: These three variables are the most unstable within the system. In other words, they are the most influential and the most dependent. The upshot is that the strategies of the main manufacturers are interdependent. It is worth noting that the variable "competition/cooperation among manufacturers" is ranked third in terms of potential influence whereas it ranks 41st in direct classification;

– transformers' strategies: This variable plays a vital role in the aluminum system. It is comparable to the variable "leading client strategies".

If we examine the more or less dependent nature of the variables in the aluminum system, we see that the most dependent variables are often the most influential. In fact, of the nine most dependent variables, six belong to the ten most influential. These are the actors' strategies variables already mentioned.

It is not at all surprising that strategic-technological foresight which depends on actors' strategies is also highly dependent. Among the dependent variables, we also found corporate research policy, innovation in aluminum products, recycling, competitiveness, and political corporate image. These are all closely linked.

Priority Variables Classified as Direct, Indirect or Potential

The Most Influential Variables (to be mastered)	Competitiveness of Materials Financial Situation among Aluminum Companies Leading Client Strategies Price Stability Alcoa, Péchiney, Alcan Strategies Transformer/Processor Strategies Price of Non-standard Products Management Criteria (quality, productivity, profitability)
The Most Dependent Variables (to be monitored)	Strategic and Technological Foresight (*veille* in French) Corporate Research Policy Recycling Relative Competitiveness of the Companies Political Image of the Companies Strategies of the Second-Rung Companies

Some results raise more questions than answers. It actually seems that the relative competitivity of the companies involved is far more influential and less dependent in terms of indirect and potential effects than in terms of direct effects. Should we conclude then that in the future the competitive gap between the various companies will become more determining and less "variable"?

In any event, the results concerning the demand variables are remarkable. The direct classification introduces a dichotomy between the rather dependent variables, e.g. consumption markets (packaging, construction) and demand variables that are almost independent of the system considered part of the professional markets (aeronautics, energy). In other words, part of the demand for aluminum is independent.

What surprises us should not confuse us, though. Instead some of these realizations urge us to think in a more in-depth and imaginative manner. In general, most of the results from the structural analysis confirm an initial intuition. Yet we remain on guard against the temptation of concluding that this type of analysis is unnecessary. In fact, it is always easier *ex post* to say that something was obvious than it is to reject *a priori* certain pieces of "evidence" rather than others.

Overall what surprised us was the fact that the demand variables are not very dependent. This is intriguing in that they normally should have appeared as result variables. Moreover, the variables characteristic of professional markets and mass consumption have increasingly more influence when we integrate the indirect and potential effects. This result could mean that manufacturers have less mastery of the marketplace than expected. If demand from leading clients drove the market, then the competitiveness of the materials would tip the balance.

Another interesting result drawn from structural analysis: the relatively influential character of the macroeconomic variables (monetary fluctuations, industrial production) and social variables (lifestyle and consumer habits). Most of these variables lose their relative influence on the system when the indirect and potential effects are taken into consideration.

Emerging Variables Ranked Indirect and/or Potential

Emerging Variables (Influence)	Demand Variables New Markets for Aluminum Innovation in Product and Market New Competitors in End Markets Strategy of Manufacturing States Competition-Cooperation among Manufacturers Rate of Use of Capacities (electrolysis, semi-products)
Emerging Variables (Dependence)	Free Market for Standard Products Dowstream Integration for Industrial Clients Upstream Integration for Mass Market Linkage, Networks, Partnerships

Should we conclude that the future of the international aluminum industry depends less on political, economic and social uncertainty than the strategies of the main actors within the industry and their capacity to innovate both technologically and commercially? We lean towards that general view.

Elements for Building Scenarios

Positioning variables along the influence/dependence axes and monitoring their development provides vital information that guides our thinking to possible scenarios for the future of the aluminum industry for the year 2000. (Note that although this horizon has now been reached, the material presented herein has not been changed and reveals the pertinence of the exercise.)

The structural analysis with a horizon of 2000 provided the raw data needed to analyze how the industry would develop and to highlight the relationships between groups of variables.

Yesterday, an Ideal?

The past situation is described in the following diagram which picks up the part of variable positions on the direct axis. This is an "ideal" (perhaps yesterday?) or a stable situation in which demand is dominated by the strategy of the large companies and the production context (variables 23 to 29).

The Past Situation in the Industry

PC: Production Context: Exit and entry barriers, Manufacturing flexibility, Innovation in processing, Rate of use of capacities, Recycling.

S: Strategies: Leaders' Strategies, Transformers' Strategies.

D: Demand: Professional Markets, Greater Public Markets.

Today's Ambiguous Situation

Demand is becoming independent in terms of the leaders' strategies. These strategies are less dependent on the production context than on the influence of the control variables.

The Current Situation in the Industry

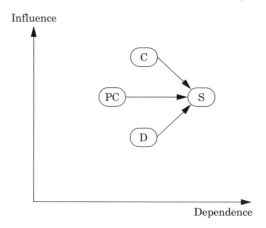

C: Control Variables: Competitiveness among Materials, Financial Situation of the Companies, Price Stability, Leading Clients' Strategies

Tomorrow's Industry: The Risk of a Separation between Manufacturing and the Market(s)?

The aluminum system is evolving in such a way that the potential indirect relations lead to the risk of a split of manufacturing and markets.

The fact that the demand is becoming independent points toward a potentially difficult situation in which the control and demand variables are influential on the strategies, thus playing more on themselves than on the production context.

Two Contrasted Strategies

The "split up" scenario envisions the manufacturers' strategy as one under the influence of both demand for the product and the control variables. The production context is no longer the determining one. In fact it has shifted into one of dependence on the system.

Strategy 1: Aluminum in either a defensive or an introverted position

Given the inertia in the aluminum industry, manufacturers adopt a stance somewhere between defensive and introverted or inward-looking. The nuance depends on whether they react or not to the influence

of the old control variables (C) and the new control variables (NC). Two new actors in particular might acquire a pivotal position and encourage this type of development, namely:
- new competitors on the end market;
- producer/source states.

Faced with this enlarged strategic environment, major aluminum manufacturers appear weak and threatened as they are divided by the strategies or actions of their traditional competition. Is this divide and conquer?

The results of strategic analysis in terms of indirect and potential relationships reveal that the system under study would tend to develop towards this strategy; i.e., between defense and introversion. Why? The demand is losing in terms of dependence and gaining in terms of influence. Domination by manufacturers thus becomes only a vague memory. Moreover, the strong increase in indirect and potential influence of new control variables confirms the above. In this strategy, manufacturers managed to cooperate and make objective alliances, a common front of sorts to face the threat of new competitors and competitive materials.

Strategy 1: Aluminum: From Defensive to Introverted Position

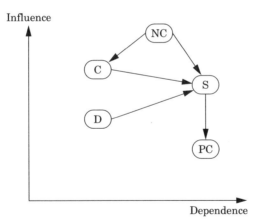

NC: New Control Variables:
- New Competitors on the end markets
- Role of manufacturer/source states
- Competition-cooperation among manufacturers

Strategy 2: Aluminum, from Innovation to Offensive

A second strategy foresees aluminum manufacturers moving into an offensive mode through product innovation. Manufacturers thus open up new markets and take control of a portion of the demand (D2). In fact, they readily adapt the production context to the development of another part of the demand (D1). The success of this market segmentation strategy depends on a fairly substantial mastery of the control variables (C + NC).

This strategy is far from being excluded by the structural analysis since the "innovation" and "cooperation among manufacturers" variables are potentially highly influential on the overall aluminum system.

In conclusion, the great disparities in material use from one country to the next can not be explained by the intrinsic performance of the materials but rather by the strategy and behavior of the main actors operating in a particular country. As a result, the aluminum industry's future depends on the manufacturers' capacity to be:

– flexible, even when facing political, economic and financial uncertainty on an international level;

– innovative, both technologically and commercially, in order to offer a broader range of mixed materials, which include aluminum, and thus meet the needs, functions, and systems. Increasingly, the client will demand that the supplier be a multi-material provider. Obviously marketing will play a pivotal role in this area.

In sum, structural analysis enabled the participants to create a hierarchy of key variables for the future of the aluminum industry by weighting the role of certain economic and financial restrictions which, after all, are the same for the competition. The ability to innovate, meet the needs of the market and create other needs will enable one aluminum manufacturer to succeed rather than another. The conflictual or cooperative nature of the actors' strategies and behavior will also play a determining role.

Strategy 2: Aluminium: From Innovation to Offensive

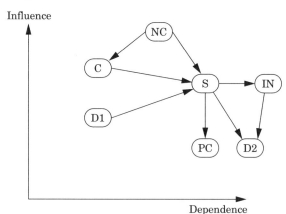

IN: Innovation:
– Production innovation
– Commercial innovation

EDF: The Utility of Futures-Thinking

This chapter section was prepared by Assaad-Émile Saab, in charge of the "Mission Prospective" at Electricité de France, in order to provide a brief history of how futures-studies exercises and strategic scenario building have evolved in a major European corporation. Rarely do we have the opportunity to reflect on how a corporation or an institution thinks about the future. The EDF case reveals just how far we have come in terms of tools, concepts and breadth of thought.

A Forecasting and Planning Tradition

Although named differently at different times, *la prospective,* foresight, or a futures-thinking process has existed at Électricité de France (EDF) since the utility's inception. This process has always been considered an integral part of forecasting and planning. Naturally accurate forecasts of future demand were essential to a company mandated to ensure the production, delivery and distribution of electricity. Beyond these basic functions, there was the need to set rates that were both fair and economically feasible. Interestingly enough, this type of forecasting at EDF also led to the development of exemplary econometric tools. Of course, in the past, the production of electricity was tremendously important for a country rebuilding and then experiencing rapid development. In fact, the magnitude of the investments required made electricity part of the national plan.

Always necessary, always present at EDF, futures-thinking has nevertheless gone through several stages.

During the 1950s and 60s, growth in electricity production remained fairly regular at 7% to 8% annually. In terms of consumption, figures doubled in one decade – a famous statistic. In those days, futures-thinking exercises were not called such and relied essentially on extrapolation. The general idea was to outline demand for electricity over the long-term, e.g. 10 to 20 years. The institutional environment was considered stable and only the economic parameters of growth were needed to generate a forecast.

Suddenly the 1970s and the oil shock hit. Futures studies or any future-thinking endeavor needed to integrate discontinuities or breaks in economic growth and consequently became more exploratory. After this watershed, it became necessary to develop different scenarios using various hypotheses on how energy prices would develop while taking into account the growing number of uncertainties.

During the 1980s, EDF was obliged to ask new questions. At this point, after the previous decades in which scenarios were based on either energy or economics, EDF had to consider the institutional and political context in which it would continue developing. Changes in this context, or environment, stemmed from the new Europe and the decentralization of the French state. Simultaneously, technology was developing at a supersonic pace while competition among different forms of energy (electricity, gas, fossil fuels) grew fiercer.

Lastly, in the 1990s, new themes became obvious priorities:
– first, the development of the institutional framework within a new European context;
– second, adoption of a European Community directive within the national electricity market;
– third, the "green wave" with sustainable development included as not only an economic but also as a social stake in terms of intranational solidarity and social justice;
– fourth, new borders of national and international development considered as specific opportunities to draw upon the competitiveness and productivity made possible through growth in multiservices and international business.

The Necessity of Futures Thinking

An exploratory procedure applied to just one company's future appears inadequate, given the need to reflect broadly on the corporate environment and to question the uncertainty affecting the institutional, economic and technological dimensions. In short, EDF needed to define its stakes in the institutional, economic and technological fields. The question was how to do it. Management wondered if the traditional forecasting and planning approach would be adequate. Jean Bergougnoux, manager of the economic research department, sought the help of Jacques Lesourne in laying down the groundwork of a futures-thinking approach. A team within the economic research department was created to work with Lesourne and to assess the results of futures-thinking exercises.

The first step involved identifying through a systemic and structural analysis the important parameters, major trends and the actors within EDF's internal and external environments. This step enables management or other participants to determine EDF's means and its margin of maneuver. The scenarios envisioned were not to focus solely on energy and economics anymore. Instead they would include social, political, technological and institutional aspects. EDF could no longer simply cross a few hypotheses and actors' strategies to define the most probable scenario. Contrasted scenarios had to be multiplied in order to see a multiple and uncertain future, as well as estimate the company's capacity to develop and adapt to that future. In response to EDF's needs, the following futures-thinking or scenario-planning method was developed from 1986 to 1987.

A New Organization: Prospective and Strategy

In 1988, the chief executive officer of EDF introduced strategic management in which futures thinking required a strategic aim and did not need to shed light on possible futures. This strategic management process followed four stages:

1) exploration of both environment and future;
2) definition of strategic axes;
3) decisionmaking in accordance with strategic orientations;
4) evaluation of the results and appropriateness of the implementation of these orientations and strategies given the initial objectives.

At this point in EDF's history, futures studies, scenario planning, or *la prospective* had to be clearly linked to strategy, hence the new term *prospective stratégique* or strategic futures thinking. Given the need to introduce change into the company itself, a "strategic economic futures research" section (DEPS in EDF's corporate organizational chart) was created. In tandem, a futures committee headed by Christian Stoffaës was set up. The "futures mission" within the DEPS was mandated to ensure that the studies produced by the various working groups would be implemented and monitored.

An Effective Program

Several studies were carried out simultaneously every year, so that some forty reports were finalized from 1988 to 1998. At the outset, Jacques Lesourne had suggested as an objective that at least half the studies started by the committee and monitored by the mission should be delivered to the strategic management committee; in other words, with the executive organ that meets with the president and CEO as well as the key managers or officers at EDF. Within the first three years, 80% of the studies were indeed sent to this decisionmaking level. This percentage serves as an indicator of the quality of these studies and the activity of the project leaders.

The futures approach also serves to initiate a collective thinking process within the various units and departments themselves during the preparation of strategic plans. Already in 1989, futures-thinking committees were struck in operations departments in order to shed more light on the decisions for which they were responsible. As a pedagogical exercise, futures thinking was thus extended to an increasingly broader circle. Futures-thinking seminars were initiated at departments in EDF-GDF (Gaz de France) for managers. In fact these seminars became part of the training program for new unit managers.

A Joint Futures-Thinking Exercise

By 1990, other French firms were expressing interest in EDF's methods. The CEO decided to launch a club called *Prospective et Entreprises* (Futures and Firms) whose members still include large public corporations like Gaz de France, France Télécom, the French railroad (SNCF), the French Post Office, and ELF (now privatized), but also other members, like L'Oréal, the Ministry of Defense and more recently, the Parisian Public Transit System (RATP).

The purpose of the club was to provide a forum where people could meet, share experiences, debate issues, and possibly undertake joint studies on the major stakes and developments affecting the member-corporations within their respective environments.

The club has carried out several timely studies over the past few years. In fact the studies have often foreseen topics of national interest. From the top of the list:
  – future of contracts between the State and public corporations;
  – French public corporations and EU law;
  – future of public utilities in Europe;
  – future of social relations within statutory companies in Europe;
  – future of retirement plans in France and Europe;
  – future of intermediary agencies;
  – future of capitalism in France.

The Futures-Thinking Philosophy at EDF

Anticipate in order to Decide

Traditional forecasting and planning methods suited an economic context of regular growth within a stable institutional framework. However, over the past three decades, companies and organizations have recognized the limits of such methods in the form of demand, global competition, industrial restructuring, geopolitical and institutional changes. In today's world, extrapolating from the past to forecast the future is no longer enough.

On the other hand, strategic decisionmaking does not only consider investment choices, the traditional domain of planning and economics. All the major choices involving the future are strategic, e.g. relationships with major partners, alliances, organizational management, investment in human resources.

In the face of uncertainty, the futures-thinking method serves to imagine hypotheses clustered around scenarios, to suggest reactions or strategic options, and to evaluate the alternatives; i.e., compare possible choices.

The First Link in the Managerial Chain

Futures-thinking activities are the first stage of integrated strategic management, as Jean Bergougnoux defined it in 1988. One should ensure that the future has been thoroughly explored before making any decisions. In this respect, a futures-thinking exercise is not a purely intellectual exercise of gathering data, and providing academic conjectures or drafting forecasts. The purpose of the futures-thinking enterprise is to provide those in charge and those making decisions with what they need to know in order to make sound decisions.

The Principles of Corporate Strategic Prospective

The systematic monitoring of developments includes detecting trends and important signals through what is traditionally called foresight in English (*veille* in French) and observation of the environment. Equally important are a follow-up of strategy and the actions of the company's major institutional, technological, and commercial partners.

The use of experts in future studies enables researchers or managers to base their work on specific analyses carried out by specialized professionals handpicked from either inside or outside the company. Besides expertise, imagination must be mobilized to shake off traditional ways of thinking and to get off the beaten track.

Reactivity and flexibility in terms of adaptation are needed because no single strategic option may be considered valid in as much as the circumstances have not changed. In other words, managers, executives, experts, and all other participants must think and reconsider the situation. Given potential threats and opportunities, futures thinking and scenario building help to imagine the possibilities and propose alarm systems.

The connection between futures thinking and strategy must be respected. They actually form a duo that is complementary yet contrary. Thinking about the future is a functional activity; in other words, an advising activity designed for decisionmakers. It must be clearly distinguished from strategic decisionmaking and its implementation, which depends upon the corporate hierarchy. Futures-thinking activities suggest open action, with a freewheeling, imaginative yet analytical spirit. Once the line between futures thinking and strategy has been drawn; however, strategy must be stable and shared by all in order to be implemented efficiently.

Organizing Futures Thinking

Organizational Principles and Structures:

Between 1988 and 1998, futures-thinking activities enjoyed a more structured framework than in the past, and dovetailed with EDF's three-level decisionmaking system, as follows:

1) The futures-thinking committee is responsible for leading and coordinating studies. It comprises the six main mangers or officers of the company (HR, economics, futures thinking and strategy, finance, legal, research, development, marketing) as well as experts from the central administration, and the individuals responsible for futures thinking within the operational departments. The futures-thinking

committee sought not to do everything alone but rather to assist EDF's experts and decisionmakers in their reflection by asking questions and providing techniques or analytical tools.

2) The strategic management committee (CGS), presided by the CEO, brings together members of the administration and the managers or officers. As the main entity mandated to define EDF's strategic orientations, this committee receives various studies from the futures-thinking committee, as well as reports from different committees within the administration. It occasionally receives studies from the operational departments themselves.

3) The economics and futures-thinking department (DEPS) unites the departments in charge of investment planning and rates, among other functions.

This organizational structure ensures the link between futures thinking and strategy by distinguishing the role of experts from that of operational decisionmakers and that of other instances within the company. It also differentiates between the futures-thinking activities of general management and that of the separate operational units.

Managers for production and transportation, for EDF-GDF services, and for equipment are called upon to develop futures thinking or futures studies in their own area. In general, each operational unit in the company is asked to develop its own futures-thinking and strategic methods as relates to a decisionmaking area considered its own within the preparation of its strategic plan.

Recent restructuring at EDF will probably lead to a revised version of the existing structure but will not likely challenge the overall spirit.

Some Methodological Tools

Most of the tools available ranging from the Delphi to the Mactor method were applied at EDF. Mentioned below are structural analysis, actor analysis, scenario building, and multicriteria analysis.

Structural analysis enables managers or any other participants to draft relevant questions as it provides a systematic panorama of the interactions and mutual dependencies of the parameters that influence the future of a company. This type of analysis also helps identify key variables according to their role as a driver or lever and their impact on the company.

Analysis of actors' strategies, that is the choice of coalitions and their contents, constitute the basic elements of strategic options. In fact, the developments are largely a function of the strategies and movements of major corporate partners.

The combination of multiple hypotheses that can be formulated for the future soon becomes a quagmire. By building coherent scenarios, as well as paths that link these scenarios, we can make contrasted futures understandable and then judge the probability of these scenarios occurring.

Strategic options constitute the choices available to a company in decisionmaking. The consequences of these alternative strategic options are assessed in light of a specific scenario being carried out. Multicriteria analysis evaluates the consequences according to the grid of objectives set by the company including the corporate mission and the company's basic interests.

Open evaluation is an essential rule in this process. A futures-thinking exercise sets its own ethics, primarily to never conclude in a definitive manner. A futures study should simply provide decision-makers with a grid for evaluation purposes plus the instruments needed to make informed strategic decisions.

Permanent Foresight at a Strategic Company

A strategic company must constantly pay attention to what is going on both inside and outside its walls. The futures-thinking committee is responsible for:

– distributing studies which may be made available to the public at large;

– holding training seminars as well as lectures/debates suitable for all those responsible for futures endeavors;

– analyzing and evaluating the current observational and monitoring structures (or creating them) in the departments within all those areas affected by corporate strategy (be it institutional, industrial, technological, commercial or social).

The above structures primarily observe the environment of the company, detect any indicators of change, alert decisionmakers to sensitive changes, and encourage strategic reactivity at the top administrative level.

A Group Learning Experience

Futures thinking at EDF was also designed as a collective pedagogical process that would prepare people to face greater uncertainty and accept the major changes ahead. For when there is a shared future vision, strategic choices virtually impose themselves.

EDF did not opt for a specialized, centralized department but rather a structure that relies upon work carried out by several pluridisciplinary teams, dialogue among various managers or directors and the breaking down of traditional barriers. The overarching goal is a permanent exchange of information and ideas as well as the creation of new ways of thinking about the future.

At EDF, studies on the future have always relied on internal expertise first. Outside opinions from universities or consulting firms are nevertheless systematically encouraged through a budget provided to project leaders.

Major Topics

Before the futures thinking committee was created, EDF had undertaken two major futures studies, "EDF and the Future" and "The Future of the Electronuclear Industry". The procedures and methods used therein contributed to the strategic themes and orientations of the initial studies carried out by the futures-thinking committee.

Since 1988, numerous subjects have been explored, thus providing background material for fifty-odd studies under the auspices of the futures-studies committee. As a result, dozens of experts and various departments within EDF worked together. These studies generated a flood of environmental scenarios, some of which did not take into account neighboring notions expressed, albeit in different terms, in other research papers. This multitude, although creative, lead to a certain opaqueness which was lifted only by ensuring that the procedures were set out and linked better. This is the price to be paid in the decentralized exploration of a multiple or pluralistic future. By summarizing the various efforts, a document called "Environmental Scenarios" was produced. It suggested five possible scenarios for the institutional development of EDF. This document provided a base for the studies that the new futures-thinking groups would produce. On the basis of that document, we could outline the following five centers of interest and five transversal themes:

Centers of Interest

The centers or poles of interest create clusters of different studies around a few major interests.

– International pole: brings together the studies related to the future in the EU electricity sector, ranging from the British to the East-European and including internationalization of electricity, the EDF's potential role as a European actor in North Africa (the Maghreb).

– The technological/economic pole directly related to electricity: includes studies on thermal decentralized production, on the partnership between EDF and basic industries, on fuel price developments, means of production, nuclear energy (irradiated fuel, technological foresight in the electronuclear sector, possible nuclear surprises). The study on global warming is also closely linked to technology, whether it focuses on the role of CO_2 or reflects upon how to avoid the freeing of carbon dioxide into the atmosphere using nuclear electricity. Lastly the effects of technology on distribution have been explored in future studies on EDF's clientele and client-computer-EDF interfaces. This is the case of the so-called "smart meters".

– The general technological pole affects EDF's situation as an actor in telecommunications or the role of EDF with regard to computerization. It also includes the future of the nuclear industry.

– The institutional pole structures EDF relationships with its various partners, e.g. public authorities, local groups, rural spaces, water legislation, and management of hydraulic resources, industries involved in changing electrical equipment and, in a slightly different register, the situation of EDF as a commercial actor and the future of the EDF-GDF mix. This pole also accounts for corporate research studies on ideological developments and changes related to electricity.

– The internal managerial and social pole covers the social future and role of managerial control as well as the future of human resources with 2010 as a horizon.

Major Transversal Themes

Five major themes stand out in almost all the futures studies:
– the powers of local groups;
– the relationships between the State and company;
– the nature and degree of European integration;
– the deregulation of the electrical system (which enters into the more general deregulation framework);
– the technological changes in electricity production and distribution.
Other key themes:
– the environment, given that EDF strategies must take into account the public's awareness and demands concerning ecology, especially water management;
– the future of irradiated fuels;
– electrical networks;
– industrial safety;
– climatic changes.

Challenges for the Years 2010-2025

EDF in the World to Come

At the dawn of the new millennium, changes appear to be occurring faster than ever before. Fifty years after its inception, EDF is now crossing the threshold into a new world in which international development, management methods, the European electricity market, restructuring of electro-technological and nuclear industries inform the corporate environment. Even if historical movements are progressive, historians like to use dates and events as hooks. After the "after-directive" context (company directive delivered June 20, 1996), the future ceased to be written in the singular. Instead scenarios became plural; the strategic options, very open.

At this point, the president of the EDF requested a futures studies along the lines of "what could EDF look like like in 2010 or 2025?"; "what are the stakes (medium-term 2010) and (long-term 2025); "what is involved in terms of preparing EDF and the next decisions to be made?"

Three major themes stand out as priorities in the medium-term: development of the institutional framework in terms of European Union dynamics; renovation of the social; and new frontiers in development. The technological theme should be envisaged as long-term, given the uncertainties surrounding the horizon of technological ruptures (breakdowns or breakthroughs) and the relative weight of the demand for energy and the environmental pressure on technology. The future of the nuclear energy industry is a special case to be considered when reflecting on the future of technology. The absence of CO_2 emissions tips the scales in favor of nuclear energy or balances out the implied waste disposal problem.

Institutional Framework and the European Union

The European community directive on electricity has already changed certain aspects of the EDF's institutional structure, legally established in 1946. Yet still other changes may be expected, especially at the executive level and in the roles played by the respective regulatory agencies at the local, national and European levels.

It will also be necessary to work on the notion of "industrial and financial group" since the EDF group's development should be considered in terms of "maintaining the status of an EPIC" (Public Company of an Industrial and Commercial Nature). Also at stake here is the principle of specialization which becomes an issue of limiting our sphere of activities to our core competencies and developing some room to maneuver with Europe.

Equally important in terms of the institutional framework will be:
– monitoring the process of restructuring in the electricity industry in Europe and the world;
– keeping a clear vision of the legal and economic stakes for the EDF group at a national and European level;
– promoting active strategies that mobilize staff and encourage initiative in terms of dealing with current or potential competitors.

Social Renewal

Beyond problems in changing working relationships, the fundamental question is: What should be done now to keep the social component integrated in EDF's desirable futures? EDF feels that it has time but not much and should act soon!

Without further delay, EDF must outline its paradigm for the company's development in order to guide the various actors involved. Otherwise, there is a real yet underestimated risk that changes and decisions will be postponed and the potential or opportunities afforded by changes in EDF's environment will be jeopardized.

In order to flesh out the key long-term questions on national and international development, the following elements of a long-term policy should be considered:

– the international sector offers tremendous opportunities. EDF should seize well targeted opportunities in order to benefit from its sources both in terms of the competitivity and productivity inherent in international growth;

– downstream development is not an end in itself but rather a means of reinforcing EDF's positions and of preparing for the competition's attack;

– EDF's durability lies in lasting alliances with local groups. This solid foundation should be consolidated and supported in both qualitative and quantitative terms.

Technological Challenges and Sustainable Development

Visibility right up to the horizon 2025 remains high. Although during this period the world demand for energy should double, the primary source of energy and the conversion methods are ostensibly the same. The foundation of electricity production will remain fossil fuels, existing nuclear energy, increased hydroelectric equipment, and the development of renewable energy, where possible. The main uncertainties will come from environmentalist pressures. Here the overarching question is whether sustainable development is possible in both the developed and developing worlds.

Will we see harmonious use of the earth's resources in the upcoming thirty years? Will regional imbalances grow? Will we rise to the challenge of paying the ecological price of growth?

Strategy and Futures

Perhaps more than in other large companies, EDF's futures-thinking and scenario-building procedures are organically and institutionally tied to strategic decisionmaking. It is not enough to supply decisionmakers with a backdrop for global scenarios or to draw their attention to one particular eventuality. The idea is to define, evaluate and provide probability rates for a limited number of strategic options. From this perspective, penetration of the futures-thinking process throughout the organization is essential even beyond the pedagogical goal of making people aware of the future. Assessing *a posteriori* the results of futures-thinking studies when confronted with both reality and the strategic options that those studies inspired thus becomes extremely important.

Futures thinking, strategy and operational decisionmaking must interact while remaining distinct. In this way, the strategic company can succeed in acting not only on the current "front" but also on uncertain futures which yield both threats and opportunities.

ICW 2010: Looking for a New Individual Combat Weapon

This case study, part of a project code-named ICW 2010, includes information from research carried out on behalf of the French Ministry of Defense, Armed Forces (DGA), in 1989. In fact, we thank Mr. Michel de Lagarde of the DGA for his kind permission to publish this remarkable example.

The ICW 2010 exercise was supported methodologically by Michel Godet, who was assisted by Pierre Chapuy and Isabelle Menant of the Groupe d'Etudes Ressources Prospective Aménagement (Gerpa). With the help of complementary studies, the ICW exercise led to the design of a prototype "multi-arm-multi-projectile" weapon, abbreviated as PAPOP in French. It is an individual combat weapon (ICW) with indirect aiming that enables an infantry soldier to fire upon stationary, armored or moving targets with specific projectiles.

The ICW 2010 remains remarkable as one of the rare published cases in which a futures-thinking exercise led to concrete action. What makes this case all the more fascinating in terms of futures-thinking endeavors is the rediscovery of morphological analysis. Somehow morphological analysis had been ignored since the late 1970s. Since then, however, scenario building "by method" has become almost systematic, be it for partial or full scenarios. Perhaps the inventor of morphological analysis, Fritz Zwicky, did indeed succeed in making invention a routine!

Actually this case also reminds us why morphological analysis was forgotten. The method quickly leads to a morphological space rich in scenarios and technologically possible solutions. So the quandary becomes choosing only a handful. The famous, out-of-print book by Eric Jantsch (1967) on the topic developed the selection process at length; however, microcomputing, notably the Morphol software package, has helped in navigating through morphological spaces. In this instance, computers also enabled us to develop Multipol, a simple and appropriable multicriteria selection method for uncertain futures.

How to Define a New ICW?

The mandate from Armed Forces Headquarters was for a "brains trust", or expert panel, including representatives from the Infantry Center for Tactical Studies and Experimentation, the army's technology department and the DGA. The objective was to carry out a study that would define and design a system for future individual weaponry. Participants included Lt. Col. Fluhr, Lt. Col. Navec, ICETA (chief engineer) Durand, Messrs Dupuy, de Lagarde, Rouger, and Senior Medical Officer Gorzerino.

The initial idea was a study on what this weapon could be in terms of tactical use of the infantry, the potential of various types of technology, as well as the ICW's technological and industrial limitations (horizon 2010). The objective was to highlight the most promising techniques and technologies which could then be acquired or developed to meet the specifications determined for this new weapon.

This pre-feasibility study was designed to define a weapon corresponding to NATO's specifications for an individual combat weapon (ICW). These included the following:
– incapacitation of targets that are heavily protected and invisible behind a mask or in a shelter;
– increase in the area of engagement and efficiency of the grenadier-infantry soldier;
– incapacitate moving targets from a specific distance.

If the last two can be achieved by improving classic weapons firing small caliber ammunition with kinetic energy, the first specification would impose a radically new design.

Approach Adopted

With a view to organizing their reflection, participants (the brains trust) decided to use structural analysis to highlight key variables likely to affect this future weapon. Why structural analysis? The simple answer is that the method was very frequently used at that time and was found in the first chapters of my book.

Yet three years down the road, the group had not reached any satisfactory conclusions. Some of the difficulties encountered stemmed from the French army's rotation system at headquarters. For example, the futures-thinking group included officers from across the country, named to posts in different places and at different times. Over three years, the constant turnover had affected the quality of the exercise. Another problem was the seemingly innocent shortcut that the participants discovered. They used to fill out the structural analysis matrix individually rather than collectively in a workshop. At the risk of being redundant, we emphasize here that this type of activity must be a structured group effort.

As a result of the problems outlined above, the DGA contacted us to help pick up the pace. We can not really say whether or not the tool already chosen was the most appropriate; however, it was most important for the group's self-confidence and faith in futures-thinking tools to demonstrate how to carry out a successful structural analysis.

We advised the group to employ the following futures tools:
– strategic futures workshops, anticipate missions, capacities and equipment with a horizon 2010;

– structural analysis and Micmac to pinpoint key variables in the strategic environment, ICW military effects, limitations and specifications;

– morphological analysis to scan the field of possibilities and find practical solutions in order to profile the ICW;

– Multipol method for multicriteria analysis in an uncertain future to select the most interesting solutions.

The work really consisted in drawing up a list based partially on workshop results. This voluntarily limited list would, nevertheless, represent the system variables for the future ICW and enable us to construct a structural analysis matrix. Filling out and processing this matrix allowed participants to position these variables on planes, along axes, according to their influence and relative dependence. Analysis of the variables led to a graph and the selection of key variables used in the study of four technical components and six essential selection criteria. On the basis of these elements, the futures-thinking group carried out a morphological analysis. Using the Multipol method, participants could trace the most compelling configurations of the ICW in terms of strategy, technology and economics with the horizon 2010.

Structural Analysis and Key Variables

The futures-thinking circle was reinvigorated through workshops and opened slightly to include new participants. Members of the working committee led a collective session on the following:

– the future environment, in order to identify the stakes and threats. Each group member was asked as an individual (silently) and then collectively to list strategic, technological, economic, and socio-organizational changes, as well as determine desirable, feared, and anticipated consequences. They also were asked to identify the actors involved and the stakes;

– the armed forces' missions, capabilities and equipment adapted to this environment. This dimension would allow participants to see which capacities needed to be adapted. Again individual and collective reflection focused on the characteristics required according to capability and equipment.

Also on the agenda, a hunt for clichés, organized by the armed forces, again with a 2010 horizon. Here each participant was asked to list individually then collectively the clichés or conventional wisdom "out there" on the army, its missions, capabilities, equipment, and relations with NATO partners, in 1989 and from then to 2010. Lastly, the group proved or disproved each of the main clichés presented.

The List of 57 Variables

The structural analysis method seeks to highlight key variables, hidden or not, in order to ask the right questions and encourage participants to think about counter-intuitive aspects or behavior within the system. In this instance, structural analysis was enriched by the use of the Micmac approach. (Note: Micmac is the French acronym for Matrix of Crossed Impact Multiplications Applied to a Classification.)

What is surprising does not have to be confusing but should incite serious thinking and trigger extra imagination. For example, structural analysis aims to assist futures-thinking groups, but it does not replace them. The method does not detail systemic operations but rather highlights the main characteristics of the system's organization.

This particular structural analysis ran for three months. The working group drew up a list of variables following the workshops. These 57 varieties were then classified in different groups: environmental variables (Friend/Enemy, Combat, Technico-political); effect variables (Negative for Enemy (ENI) and positive for Friend); restriction and quality variables (ICW use).

Using variable "index cards", each variable on the list was defined completely by the members of the working group, and then validated collectively. Participants took an initial census, per variable studied, of the relations of influence and dependence with the other elements on the list and then ferreted out the technological elements, with possible configurations, as seen below.

Structural Analysis and Key Variables

The direct influence of each variable on the set of other variables are illustrated in matrix form. Each element of the matrix represents an influence (0 = no direct relationship of influence on the two variables considered; 1 = a direct relationship of influence). We also took into account the level of influence between two variables. The following convention was used: 1 = low relationship; 2 = average; 3 = strong; P = potential relationship. Note that P may indicate what is now a nonexistent or almost nonexistent relationship, but the system may make it probable or at least possible in a relatively distant future. P levels were also given 0-3 ratings.

The working group filled in the matrix during a three-day meeting. Participants systematically considered all the eventual relations between variables.

Some 3,249 relationships; i.e., 57×57, were considered direct influence given priority status. For example, direct influence i on j or direct influence j on i, by excluding the indirect influences, those which pass by an intermediary variable. Obviously it is important to distinguish the direct influence relationships from those that are not! In our experience, a good matrix rating would reveal 15% to 25% direct influences, according to the dimensions of the matrix. The rate reached here (23%) thus seems correct.

List of Variables (A): Environment

Variable Category	N°	Variables Retained
Friend	1	Characteristics inherent to soldier bearing ICW
	2	State of soldier bearing ICW in combat
	3	Individual equipment of basic unit
	4	Group equipment of basic unit (Friend)
	5	Organic arms of basic unit (Friend)
	6	Firing support possessed by basic unit (Friend)
	7	Basic unit's actions (Friend)
	8	Operational capability of the basic unit (Friend)
Enemy	9	Characteristics inherent to eneny soldier
	10	State of enemy soldier in combat
	11	Individual weapons and equipment of enemy soldier
	12	Group equipment of the basic unit (Enemy)
	13	Organic arms of the basic unit (Enemy)
	14	Firing support that the basic unit possesses (Enemy)
	15	Concept of enemy force use (Enemy unit action)
	16	Characteristics of enemy's modes of action in combat
	17	Operational capability of the basic unit (Enemy)
Combat	18	Priority enemy targets for the ICW (Enemy soldier on foot)
	19	Secondary enemy targets for the ICW
	20	Numeric balance of power
	21	Theater of war
	22	Conditions of operations
Technical-Economic Aspects	23	Technical changes affecting the IWC 2010
	24	Interoperability/Functionality of ICW
	25	Political image of a French ICW
	26	Army's budgetary limits
	27	French industrial policy
	28	Industrial policies of Frace's partners

List of Variables (B): Effects to Be Produced

Variable Category	N°	Variables Retained
Negative Effects on Enemy	29	Pinpoint antipersonnel effect sought
	30	Area antipersonnel effect sought
	31	Antivehicle and anti-light-armored vehicle effet
	32	Antitank effect sought (degradation, firing function, mobility function
	33	Antihelicopter effect sought (dissusion)
	34	Antimine effect sought (detection, forward release)
	35	Degradation of the enemy's means of firing assistance
Positive Effects on Friend	36	Detection acquisition and localization of enemy
	37	Continuous all-weather combat
	38	Symbolic nature of ICW

List of Variables (C): Restrictions & Qualities

Variable Category		Variables Retained
Concept	39	Concept of dependability of the arms system
	40	Functional organization of the arms system
	41	Power source
	42	Mass of arms system with initial issue
Technical	43	Nature of projectile
	44	Aiming
	45	External ballistics
	46	Terminal ballistics
	47	Fire power
Use	48	Ease of use in peace time
	49	Ease of use of ICW in approach-march combat situation
	50	Minimal amount of prepartion time to fire ICW
	51	Ease of use of ICW in firing
	52	Discretion and invulnerability of ICW
	53	Overall tactical efficiency of antipersonnel (Friend)
	54	Appropriateness of ICW to threat
$	55	Cost of ICW possession over 25 years
	56	Competitiveness
	57	Distribution of ICW

ICW Variable Card n°29

VARIABLE CATEGORY	:	Type B – Negative effects to be produced on ENI (Enemy).
TITLE	:	Effect sought : timely anti-personnel at a set distance (imperative).
DEFINITION	:	PIncapacitate an enemy solider, in the open at a set distance. ✓ Once hit, the enemy soldier must not be able to use a weapon (return of fire prohibited) and must be back in battle within 7 days. ✓ Being incapacitated means: – definitive destruction (death); – long-term suppression (7 days). Lethality must be preferred over suppression.
KEY POINTS	:	✓ Incapacitate an enemy solider at specific distance? ✓ Immediate or temporary incapacitation? ✓ Immediate of temporary suppression?
INFLUENTIAL VARIABLES	:	18, 30 à 36, 54, 55.
INFLUENCED VARIABLES	:	2, 5, 7, 10, 11, 23, 30 à 33, 35, 38 à 40, 42 à 47, 53 à 56.

Participants should always keep in mind the limits of structural analysis. The first limit stems from the subjective nature of the list of variables. Caution has, of course, been exercised in that information has been gathered and condensed in the "variable cards". Moreover, given the logistics involved, the number of variables can not exceed a few dozen. An arbitrary regrouping of the subvariables is the next necessary step. This is both the advantage and disadvantage of the method.

The second limitation stems from the subjective nature of filling in a matrix. A matrix is never reality. It is a means of looking at reality, like a snapshot. To use the photograph analogy, structural analysis reveals things that translate part of reality, as well as the talent of the photographer and quality of the photographic equipment. In fact, examples from a French governmental commission (Commission Boissonnat) on labor have shown that structural analysis may actually reveal group subjectivity, lead participants to hold their reactions in check to encourage consistency in the group or challenge certain clichés.

With the limits of structural analysis in mind, we can review the results obtained and their essential contribution. The method serves to structure ideas around a problem systematically. The obligation to ask thousands of questions prompts participants to discover relationships that would never have been considered otherwise. Overall, the structural analysis matrix serves as a probe and provides the futures group with a shared language.

The more a variable has an effect on other variables, the more influential it is. The same applies if that variable is influenced by others more than it depends on them. In the end, each variable is matched with an influence indicator (°/000 of the total influences normed for the system) and a direct dependence indicator for the entire system.

By reading the matrix, we can classify the variables by their

– level of direct influence: importance of influence of a variable on the whole system, obtained through the total of links created per line;

– level of direct dependence: degree of dependence of a variable, obtained by the total of links created per column.

Plan Influence/dependence

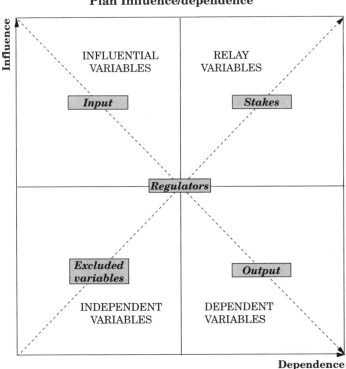

The full set of variables may thus be positioned in °/000 within the plane of influence (ordinate) and the plane of dependence (coordinate) since the values of influence and dependence are normed.

Secondly, if we take into account the feedback effect in which each variable is involved, we can hierarchize the variables according to

ICW 20100 Structural Analysis Matrix

	N°	Variables Retained	1	2	3	4	5	6	7	8	9	10	11	12	13	14	15	16	17
VARIABLES A		**ENVIRONMENT**																	
FRIEND	1	Characteristics inherent to soldier bearing ICW	0	3															
	2	State of soldier bearing ICW in combat		0				2	2										
	3	Individual equipment of basic unit(Friend)	2	1	0					1									
	4	Group equipment of basic unit	2		1	0				2									
	5	Organic arms of basic unit (Friend)	1			1	0	2	2										
	6	Firing support possessed by basic unit (Friend)	1					0	2			1							1
	7	Basic unit's actions (Friend)	1	1				1	0			1							
	8	Operational capability of the basic unit (Friend)	2						3	0									
ENEMY	9	Characteristics inherent to enemy soldier									0	3							
	10	State of enemy soldier in combat									0								3
	11	Individual weapons and equipment of enemy soldier		1	2						2	0							1
	12	Group equipement of basic unit (Enemy)									2	1	0						2
	13	Organic arms of basic unit (Friend)				1					1		1	0		2			2
	14	Firing support that the basic unit possesses (Enemy)	2								1				0				
	15	Concept of enemy force use (Enemy unit action)	2	1	1	1	1	3	1		1	3	3	3	3	0		2	2
	16	Characteristics of enemy's mode of action in combat	3					1								1	0		
	17	Operational capability of the basic unit (Enemy)									2						3	0	
COMBAT	18	Priority enemy targets for the ICW (Enemy soldier on foot)			2	1	3	1	2										
	19	Secondary enemy targets for the ICW			1	2	2	P	1										
	20	Numeric balance of power	3				3	3	3		2								
	21	Theater of war	2	3	3	2	2	3	2		2	2	2	3	2	2		3	
	22	Conditions of operations	3	2	2			3	3	1	3	1	2			3	3	2	1
TECHNICAL-ECONOMIC ASPECTS	23	Technical changes affecting the ICW 2010				2	2	2	1			2	2	2	1				
	24	Interoperability/Functionality of ICW																	
	25	Political image of a French ICW	1																
	26	Army's budgetary limits				1	1	1											
	27	French industrial policy																	
	28	Industrial policies of France's partners																	
VARIABLES B		**EFFECTS EXPECTED**																	
NEGATIVE EFFECTS ON ENEMY	29	Pinpoint antipersonnel effect sought		1			1		1			3	P						
	30	Area antipersonnel effect sought		1			2		1			3	P						
	31	Antivehicle and anti-light-armored vehicle effect		1			1					1							
	32	Antitank effect sought (degradation, firing function, mobility funtion)		1			1					1							
	33	Antihelicopter effect sought (dissuasion)		1			1					1							
	34	Antimine effect sought (detection, forward release)		1						1									
	35	Degradation of the enemy's means of firing assistance		1			1	1				1							
POSITIVE EFFECTS ON FRIEND	36	Detection acquisition and localization of enemy		1		1	1			1									
	37	Continuous all-weather combat		1				2	2			1							
	38	Symbolic nature of IWC		3						1									
VARIABLES C		**RESTRICTIONS & QUALITIES**																	
CONCEPT	39	Concept of dependability of the arms system		1															
	40	Functional organization of the arms system																	
	41	Power source																	
	42	Mass of arms system with initial issue	2	1															
TECHNICAL	43	Nature of projectile			2							1	2						
	44	Aiming		1															
	45	External ballistics																	
	46	Terminal ballistics			P							2	2						
	47	Fire power	2				1	1											
USE	48	Ease of use in peace time		1						1									
	49	Ease of use of ICW in approach-march combat situation		1				1											
	50	Minimal amount of prepartion time to fire ICW																	
	51	Ease of use of ICW in firing		1															
	52	Discretion and invulnerability of ICW				P													
	53	Overall tactical efficiency of antipersonnel (Friend)					1	1											
	54	Appropriateness of ICW to threat		1			1	1											
ECONOMIC	55	Cost of ICW possession over 25 years																	
	56	Competitiveness																	
	57	Distribution of ICW	1									P							

18	19	20	21	22	23	24	25	26	27	28	29	30	31	32	33	34	35	36	37	38	39	40	41	42	43	44	45	46	47	48	49	50	51	52	53	54	55	56	57
																		1	1		3			1	2						1	2	2		3	1	1		
																		1			2			2	3						1	2	2		3	1			
		P																1	1					1	1						2	2	1		1				
																		2										1					1					
			1																															2					
																					2	2	1	1	1	1	1	1	2		1	1	1	1					
																													1			1		2				

Plan Influence × Dependence : Micmac

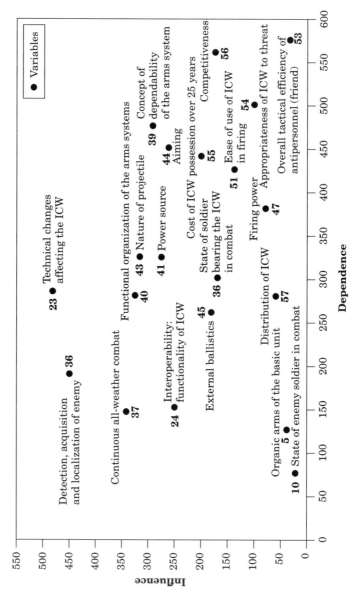

influence and dependence. In effect, the Micmac method does allow participants to see the influence that one variable exercises on another through a third, a fourth, even a fifth. The direct and indirect influences of the variable represent the system the most realistically. Highlighted are the determining factors (main determinants) of the situation under investigation. The input variables and result or output variables help participants understand the organization and structuring of the system under the microscope.

The Micmac grid or plane follows in a simplified form; i.e., it does not retain the ICW external variables, which are essentially input variables, and the excluded variables. According to the working committee, the so-called key variables which have an above-average influence are also essentially relay variables. The variables with above-average dependence are output variables

What to Do with the Key Variables?

True confessions from an expert consulting team: after structural analysis, we felt a bit sheepish. How could we use these results to look for new technological solutions for the ICW? This question seemed unanswerable, an intellectual roadblock of sorts, until the umpteenth rereading of the variables reminded us of morphological analysis, as invented by Fritz Zwicky in the 1940s for American military applications.

In concrete terms, we simply needed to recognize that nine of the key variables were technological components of the ICW and that six were evaluation criteria, e.g. continuous all-weather combat, pinpoint antipersonnel effects, side effects, possession costs, competitiveness, ease of use in peace time. The last criteria were put aside initially.

These nine technological components of the ICW (functional organization of the weapon and projectile, energy sources, type of projectile, aiming, materials, etc.) may lead to several configurations, possible technical answers, which may have already been at least partially listed through the "variable cards". Although the numbers may still boggle some, the next steps are simpler, so to speak. There were thousands of possible technological solutions so that the question was where to start and how to decide on a limited number of new solutions that meet the objectives set out.

The ICW's Morphological Space or 1001 Solutions

The ICW was considered a nine-component system in which each component can take a specific number of configurations. In the example given here, the source of energy may take the following configurations: solid, liquid, gaseous or electric. Here are a few other configurations as defined during this exercise:

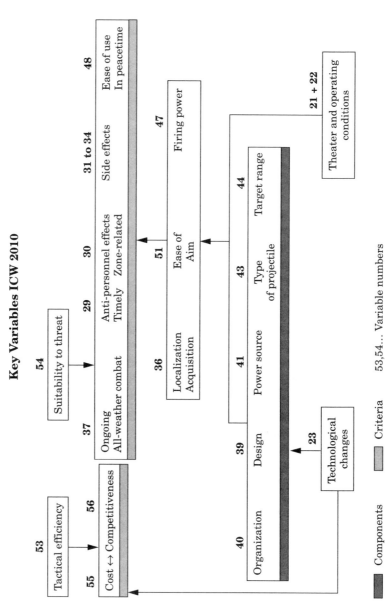

Key Variables ICW 2010

- Monoarm, or one type of launcher (e.g. FAMAS);
- Polyarm, or several type of launchers (e.g. M16);
- Single (mono) projectile, or the firing of one projectile of one type only, at a time;
- Polyprojectile, or the simultaneous firing of several projectiles identical (or not) or the successive firing of different types of projectiles.

The array of technological solutions identified through this decomposition is called "morphological space". Each solution corresponds to a path in the morphological space. This path links the configurations of each component at a rate of one configuration per component. The ICW morphological space represents 15,552 combinations, or nine components with respectively 2,3,6,3,6,3,2,2, and 2 configurations.

Using this method raises several issues related to the limits and the illusion of massive mathematics. First, the selection of components is delicate and requires serious, in-depth thinking like that also carried out in this study using structural analysis. Actually the number of components and configurations multiplies quickly so that the system soon becomes unwieldy. On the other hand, an overly limited number of components would impoverish the system, so there is a need to find a compromise like the one adopted in the AIF case. The compromise always implies retaining those components which are the most determining. It is important to pay attention to the independence of the components, also called dimensions, and not confuse them with configurations, also called hypotheses.

This scan of possible solutions within today's imagined field may appear exhaustive because of the exponential mathematics. Yet the field has not been definitively surveyed because it evolves over time. By omitting one component or simply one configuration essential to the future, we run the risk of ignoring a facet of the field of possible futures.

To prove our point, let us switch to a hypothetical past case, if this method had been applied to the function "knowing what time it is" in the early 1950s or 1960s participants would have imagined everything except the quartz watch!

Lastly, the user or participant can end up drowning in numbers. The very stating of solutions becomes difficult once up in the hundreds. For a system with four components and four configurations, we start with 256 possible combinations already. How can we outline the useful morphological subspace, or subset of useful solutions, under these conditions?

A Vast Morphological Space: Fifty Solutions Selected

Reducing the morphological space is not only desirable but also necessary because the human brain can not explore one by one the possible paths generated and it is futile to identify combinations which will be

ICW Morphological Space

Compnent		N°	Configurations					
Functions	ARM	40	mono-arm 1	poly-arm 2				
Organization	PROJECTILE		none 1	monoprojectile 2	polyprojectile 3			
Type of projectile		43	kinetic 1	explosive 2	incendiary 3	chemical 4 biological	rays 5	multiple-effects 6
Aiming		44	direct visual 1 (market, optical, line of fire no target device)	indirect visual 2 (sreen)	non-visual 3 (radar IR, laser)			
Power source		41	solid 1	liquid 2	gas 3	electricity 4	nuclear 5	mechanical 6
WEAPON DESIGN								
Maintenance			modular 1	non-modular 2	consumable 3			
Functions		39	functional chain 1	fonctional bloc 2				
Internal kinetic of ICW			moving parts 1	non-moving parts 2				
Materials			classic materials 1	non-classic materials 2				

rejected once the selection criteria (technical, economic, etc.) are taken into account. Some choices have to be made in order to identify the fundamental components with regard to the criteria. In the case of ICW, we opted to follow a four-part procedure.

Selection Criteria and Policies

Here participants had to identify the economic, technological and tactical selection criteria that would enable them to evaluate and pick out the best paths (technological solutions) from the array of possible paths (morphological space) prior to morphological analysis. The following criteria were retained from the structural analysis: continuous all-weather combat, pinpoint antipersonnel effects, side effects, possession costs, competitiveness, ease of use in peace time

Different weighting systems for the criteria defined the various policies. In this respect, two policies were defined: economic and military in accordance with the principle that participants had to retain solutions corresponding to all the military objectives and economic restrictions. The economic policy successfully integrates the cost of owning the weapon over a 25-year period and competitivity but also covers the continuous combat or side effects; whereas the military policy favors something suitable to the threat, e.g. continuous combat, antipersonnel effects and side effects, but also considers competitiveness.

Weighting Criteria for Each Policy

Criteria	Policies	
	« Economic »	« Military »
❶ Cost	6	1
❷ Competitiveness	4	3
❸ Continuous, all-weather combat	3	5
❹ Anti-personnel effects	1	5
❺ Side effects	2	3
❻ Ease of use in peace time	2	1

Pinpointing the Main Components and Technological Incompatibilities

Prior to assessing the solutions, we believed some pruning was needed. It was decided that an initial reduction of the morphological space would mean keeping only those components, among the nine key variables identified, which seemed to be the most determining given the criteria already mentioned and the policies defined using these criteria. For this to work, the components were classified according to the criteria. To determine the main components, each one was graded on a scale of 0 to 5 in terms of impact on the criteria, e.g., none, very weak, average, strong, very strong.

After working individually, group members reached a strong consensus that enabled them to retain the following four components:
- organization of the weapon;
- organization of the projectile;
- nature of the projectile;
- aiming.

The result applied to both policies considered, the economic and military, after a weighting of the coefficients per policy.

This procedure enabled us to examine, as a priority, four main components out of the nine initially considered. The original morphological space of 15,552 possibilities was thus reduced to a useful subspace of some one-hundred solutions. In other words, the group was able to reduce the space by a factor of 150.

A review of technical incompatibilities then enabled participants to eliminate a healthy 50% of the solutions.

From Evaluating Solutions to Choosing the PAPOP

We then evaluated the various remaining solutions according to each economic and military policy; in other words, for each weighting of the criteria. Our assessment enabled us to set up a classification of these fifty-odd solutions. (The Multipol software classifies this type of data quickly.) To do so, we graded each solution according to the six criteria retained. By applying the corresponding weight to each policy, we got two grades for each solution. Two classification systems were thus created, as the following diagram shows. When compared, we could discern the hard core 22 solutions which included:
- best solutions for the overall set of criteria and the policies (in top ten classification);
- average ranking solutions or those with one grade in one classification system and rising in the other classification system (from tenth to twentieth position);
- excellent solutions in terms of certain criteria only and maintained by a particular member of the working committee.

According to the chart, the combination 2363 is classified first, according to military policy and fifteenth according to economic policy.

The twenty-two solutions were found in the deep core of the useful morphological space and then regrouped by family. In other words, they appeared according to their similarity or identical solutions to one of two configurations.

Each of these families and the twenty-two solutions was analyzed and evaluated in detail with special attention paid to the configurations linked to the five secondary components.

ICW Morphological Space with Four Key Components

Component	N°	Configurations					
ARM	40	mono-arm 1			poly-arm 2	polyprojectile 3	
PROJECTILE		none 1	monoprojectile 2				multiple-effects 6
Type of projectile	43	kinetic 1	explosive 2	incendiary 3	chemical biological 4	rays 5	
Aiming	44	direct visual 1		indirect visual 2		non-visual 3	

TECHNICAL SOLUTIONS		FR.F2 or PM (1,2,1,1)	FAMAS (1,3,6,1)	PAPOP (2,3,6,2)

Wrap-up and Comparison of Economic and Military Rankings (Extracts)

Solutions				Military Policy Ranking	Economic Policy Ranking
OA	OP	P	V		
2	3	6	3	1	15
1	3	6	3	2	4
2	3	6	2	3	9
2	1	5	3	4	18
1	2	6	3	5	5
1	3	2	3	6	13
1	2	2	3	7	8
2	3	2	3	8	35
2	3	6	1	9	13
1	3	6	2	10	6
1	3	6	1	11	1
2	3	1	3	11	34
1	2	6	2	13	3
1	3	1	3	14	22
2	1	5	2	15	20
1	1	5	3	16	23
2	3	2	2	17	33
1	2	6	1	18	2
1	3	2	2	19	20
1	2	1	3	20	12
2	3	2	1	21	27

Abbreviations: OA: Organization Arm; OP: Organization Projectile; P: Profile of projectile; V: Aiming.

This last phase enabled the group to advance the following conclusions:

– analysis and reflection on the different components of the arms system, so that the nature of the projectile plays a determining role in defining the ICW;

– given the horizon, the concept of the radiation of an arms system was excluded for considerations related essentially to the battlefield environment. (Note that the concept of a biochemical warfare system was also excluded);

– the four remaining concepts could be classified in two categories: innovative concpets with multi-effect, explosive or incendiary projectiles, a classic concept using kinetic projectiles which would be an improvement on existing systems.

The study also revealed a certain number of conclusions considered transversal:
- interest in a single-arm weapon for mass use;
- ease of use and cost;
- key role of fire-control in continuous all-weather combat;
- advantage of a single projectile weapon being multi-effect and the innovation of a "polyarm multiprojectile" weapon of less complexity yet high performance overall in terms of the evaluation criteria.

After these additional studies, the PAPOP was designed. The "infantryman's weapon for the 21st century", it is original as a multi-arm-multiprojectile weapon that uses an explosive ammunition launcher and a kinetic ammunition launcher. The PAPOP met the needs expressed in terms of the following essential criteria:
- explosive ammunitions set to triggering device programed to follow a path to achieve a high probability of hitting the camouflaged targets;
- high caliber, which, combined with strong initial strength, leads to a strong, specific impulsion. The idea being to obtain a high probability that the target will be incapacitated with its NATO protection;
- effective fire-control, assistance in programing for the soldier firing and indirect aiming will allow the soldier to fire from a sheltered spot.

At this juncture, two lessons in morphological analysis should be reviewed. First, morphological analysis imposes a structured form of thinking about the components and configurations to be considered and allows for a systematic scanning of the field of possible futures. Although perhaps initially overwhelming, the mathematical formulae must not paralyze the thinking process in some form of "analsis paralysis". The useful morphological subspace can be reduced to one-tenth or one one-hundredth of its original size. To do so, selection criteria are introduced. For example, the multicriteria method Multipol, plus the restrictions of exclusion or preference. The Smic-Prob-Expert method allows for the probabilization of the combinations of configurations.

Lastly, after this exercise, the group declared that the use of the various methods had been a productive "detour" in structuring and organizing its thoughts, especially on the definition of ICW key variables using structural analysis to unearth the technological components and selection criteria as well as to analyze and evaluate the concepts of weapons systems using morphological analysis and multicriteria evaluation. The participants also emphasized how much more useful these methods were when the user remains aware of the inherent limits and respects certain conditions for their application.

CASE STUDIES IN SERVICE SECTOR

IT5: Global Scenarios

In May 1992, the ECRC (European Computer-Industry Research Center) embarked on a futures or foresight study of the European IT industry with the year 2000 as a horizon. Entitled "Information Technology in the year Two Thousand Think Tank" the code name soon became IT5 for obvious reasons. Michel Godet and Pierre Chapuy helped the IT5 group of economists and researchers from Bull, ICL, Siemens and the ECRC pool examine the impact of new technology, regulation, and globalization. Structural and morphological analysis, cross impact analysis plus global scenario building were the key tools used by the group. In fact this case study develops the scenarios drafted by the IT5 group for the international environment. With hindsight, we can appreciate the group's perspicacity and effective use of futures tools.

Only four possible scenarios were selected out of the dozen suggested. Note that the content of the other subsystems has been kept confidential due to its strategic nature. Part of this case was published in an article co-authored with Gérard Comyn, Managing Director (ECRC) in *Futures,* April 1994.

The group started its activities with a structural analysis where the interrelationships between some 60 key variables of the system were studied. These key variables were grouped into five subsystems:
1) international (geopolitical and economic) context of the 1990s;
2) autonomous technological determining factors;
3) infrastructures of the IT and communication systems;
4) strategies and actors' games;
5) market trends.

Each of these subsystems led to a morphological analysis seeking to identify the various possible states or configurations for each variable or component of each subsystem. The possible scenarios correspond to combinations of possible states. This case study presents the scenarios built by the IT5 group for the international context (first subsystem) only.

Scanning Global Scenarios

It is important not to confuse the dimensions or key components of the scenarios (demographic, technological, economic political, social...) with the configurations that each of these components can present. This is where morphological analysis works wonders.

There is only one initial hurdle: A system made up of four components, each having four configurations, will in principle have 256 ($4 \times 4 \times 4 \times 4$) possible states. How can we steer through this morphological space without being swamped by the sheer number of possible combinations? One answer is provided by the combined utilization of morphological analysis and probabilization of combinations of configurations (interplay of hypotheses) through the Smic-Prob-Expert method.

The originator of the morphological method, F. Zwicky, envisaged a method would turn invention into routine, that commonplace procedure. Morphological analysis often proves useful in stimulating the imagination, helping to identify hitherto unknown products or processes, and scanning the field of possible futures scenarios. The principle underlying the method is extremely straightforward. The system or function under study is broken down into sub-systems or components. These components must be as independent as possible and yet listed as exhaustively as possible to represent the totality of the system. This field of possible combinations is called the "morphological space". (See case studies in chapters six and seven for examples.) Naturally there are constraints, e.g. technical incompatibility, which make several families of solutions unworkable, thus reducing the morphological space. It is also possible to give preference to those combinations of configurations which appear more propitious than others, in terms of such criteria as development costs, safety factors, feasibility, etc.

The Geopolitical Context of the 1990s

IT5 participants stated the obvious: the world is changing. The geopolitical, monetary, energy, technological, economic and social environment around us, will undergo profound upheaval in the next ten to fifteen years. By definition, futures-thinking activities with a time horizon of 2000 are easier to run than up to the year 2010. In particular, the horizon 2000 enables us to disregard the consequences of the main change to occur in the coming decades, a major demographic change.

The Seven Components from A to G

We try to identify these earth-shaking changes through various components:

    A.   Demography and its imbalances
    B, C. Geopolitical context and the role of the Eastern countries
    D.   European uncertainty
    E, F. Conditions of globalization and trade
    G.   Perspective of growth.

A. Demographic Imbalances and the South-North and East-West Migratory Flows

The demographic explosion of the poorest countries and demographic decline of the richest countries is a heavy trend which, if maintained for two or three decades, will modify the situation worldwide and disrupt our societies. For instance, the population of Europe in 2020 will be comparable to that of Nigeria or Brazil. In 1990, the population of the southern shore of the Mediterranean exceeded the population of the northern shore. If the current trend were to continue, by 2030 the southern shore would be twice as populous as the northern shore.

The apparent demographic stagnation in developed countries stems from their slowing birth rate, a trend which started in the mid-1960s in both Western and Eastern industrial countries. The United States, Japan and Europe are no longer able to ensure the replacement of current generations. Moreover, in terms of age, third world countries have increasingly larger and younger populations. The perspective of migratory flows from eastern countries will certainly raise pressure to introduce controls and limit the immigration flows, which will inevitably engender new problems in East-West relationships.

Of course these projections are not forecasts and will probably not correspond to the future reality, especially given migratory pressures. By the year 2030 some of today's minorities could represent 20% of the total population in countries like Germany, France or England.

Three configurations are taken into account for the demographic trends in the Western countries:

A1. Aging of the population, immigration control, ethnic conflicts.

A2. Migratory flows from the eastern and southern countries to the West, with the corresponding integration problems.

A3. New babyboom in the West and acceptable migratory flows.

B, C. Uncertainties due to the Lack of a Regulator

The absolute value of a power does not prevent its relative decline. The United States currently represents only 22% of the world's GNP, as compared to 40% in 1955. The USA may no longer be powerful enough to impose itself as regulator (as in a bipolar world), but it is still powerful enough to play a disruptive role, since it retains a minority freeze on the world system and is thus capable of preventing any other regulator from taking its place in a multipolar world.

In other words, fluctuations in American economic policy could themselves raise inflation rates around the globe. In the meantime, we share the hypothesis presented by certain economists about the uncertainty over exchange rates, with the dollar between 4 FF and 10 FF. Although the scale of this uncertainty may be hard to accept, it would be irresponsible not to take it into account.

On the other hand, Japan, which may have approximately 10% of the worldwide GNP, has no vocation for becoming the center of a new « Economic World ». Japan is politically isolated in its zone, but has always been turned to the West, be it nineteenth-century Europe or contemporary America. The popular myth of Japan as the hub of a pacific zone, which would relegate the old "Atlantic World" to its periphery and, as a result Europe, remains a myth.

The absence of a regulating force is all the more critical, since in the heart of third world countries internal social explosions are to be expected as well as a multiplication of regional and local conflicts. The seed of tomorrow's social explosions lies in today's trends: Galloping demographic rates, flagrant inequality (i.e. luxury rubbing elbows with extreme poverty), massive urbanization in gigantic megacities that resemble shanty-towns more than cities.

Beyond the multiple uncertainties of the international imbalanced and turbulent environment, two permanent factors may be stressed:

– international monetary instability (the monetary system is a reflection of the geopolitical system) and, in particular, the persistence of heavy fluctuations of the dollar in comparison with other currencies;

– "self-centered" development of developed countries on their own, e.g., for most of the products and services, four-fifths of the solvent markets will remain in the USA-Europe-Japan triad.

Relatively speaking, certain strategic and military giants are economic dwarfs (Russia) whereas economic giants (Japan, Germany) are military dwarfs. This lack of balance is a source of tension. Obviously the bipolar "Cold War" world no longer exists, but can the multipolar world succeed without major upheavals?

Indeed, demographic and political shocks, irregular development, reinforced nationalism plus the absence of a regulator could combine to generate conflict and breed a climate of international insecurity. Unfortunately, In these conditions, management of an increasingly interdependent world has little chance of working by means of dialogue, foresight and concerted policy.

Defence issues are central. Will the East and West ally their forces to become the police of the United Nations? Will Europe remain "Atlantic" (NATO) with regard to defense, yet part of the European Community with regard to economy? The Eastern countries shift to a free market economy will not work right in the beginning. A possible failure of internal reforms in Russia and the new republics in the East could represent a threat to Europe. History tells us that an external war frequently played the role of an outlet to internal contradictions of countries; the Russian military potential remains colossal and Europe must not decrease its defence.

Let us make an intermediate conjecture: Instead of accepting ever increasing help from the West, Russia could refocus on the internal problems of its split empire and leave to the United States and its allies the task of defusing the time bombs which are bound to explode in third world countries.

Three configurations were taken into account with regard to the geopolitical context:

B1. Tensions and conflicts, without regulation of interdependence.

B2. Limited conflicts in the countries of the South and the East, uncertainties in the West.

B3. New international order and emergence of an interdependent, multipolar world.

Finally, the role of Eastern Europe seems very uncertain. Three configurations will be taken into account:

C1. Splitting, regional wars and a significant flow of refugees.

C2. Unequal development, social and regional tensions.

C3. Economic convergence and integration of the East and the West.

D. Europe's Uncertain Future: Division or Integration

Europe, the greatest solvent market in the world, constituted the new commercial El dorado of the 1990s. Europessimism, which prevailed up until the mid-1980s, fell out of fashion. The effect of the announcement of the great domestic market and the perspective of monetary integration played a positive and stimulating role and acted as an effective mobilizer. In short, the Old World has gained confidence in itself.

The history of European integration and union, its successes and crises, has been marked by the permanent confrontation of the Community's desire for economic and political integration and the States' preoccupation with safeguarding their national sovereignty.

The overall impression is that the road to a united Europe is narrower than ever. The easiest part has been accomplished, but to go further, the States will have to strip off layers of national sovereignty at the monetary, fiscal and social level. Many states are simply not prepared to do so. In addition, the enlargement of Europe with new countries remains a risk that renders the laudable objectives of coherence and political cohesion among member countries even more difficult.

The expansion of economies to a world scale will entail new restructuring and painful delocalization on the social level; in other words, lost jobs. The risks of fragmentation in Europe, such as divergence in the capacity to adapt to economic globalization, are considerable as well as the risks of reinforced regional protectionism.

Three configurations will be taken into account for the level of European integration:

D1. Failure of the Europe of Twelve and a return to the national scale.

D2. Europe of Twelve, stable but only by economic integration.

D3. Political integration of Europe of Twelve and enlargement to include new members;

E, F. Conditions of Competitiveness, Exchange and Globalization

Technological, industrial, and relentless commercial competition between companies for market share in what has become a global marketplace will persist. Transnational space remains the arena of this competition among the large multinationals which have a tendency to create worldwide oligopolies with large sectors of activity. This competition is heightened by cooperation and strategic alliances, notably in the technological field, which tends to further reinforce the entry barriers for firms which are not co-opted in the oligopoly.

New production and organization techniques bring hope (increased productivity, new products and services) but also threats (jobs, liberties). Everything will depend on the political and social choices made in connection with the new technologies and the rate of their diffusion. Note this issue reappears in a more developed form later on as it constitutes a major uncertainty.

The differentials of competitiveness among companies will increasingly be based on the quality of the organization and mastery of information systems surrounding the new technologies. After hardware and software, the so-called "orgiware" will be a determining factor in productivity within competitive situations.

Five major trends are at work for the years to come:
– mass production of variety by small scale production systems;
– comparative advantage of low salaries, less relevant than automation processes and the development of communications;
– flexibility of the production machinery, which is indispensable for adapting to fluctuations characterizing the markets in renewal;
– need for alliance and cooperation with other companies at the level of precompetitive research, or development and industrialization due to the globalization of markets which alone will enable expenditure on technology to be profitable;
– reinforced coupling of scientific research and marketing within an effective strategy for the administration of the technological resources of companies.

At the European level, the regulation and introduction of norms will be a factor that reduces uncertainties with regard to the rules of the game. However, this factor will also generate new areas of competition, hence turbulence. International competition experienced mainly by the manufacturing industry, until now, will spread to activities which thus far have usually been "protected", e.g. banking and insurance.

Lastly, the very conditions for the establishment of these new regulations are evolving: more and more frequently, the CEC and international organisms such as the WTO or even the American Congress will become strategic sites for decisions.

Between transnational and regional, the national range provides comparative advantages which frequently are extremely diversified through three distinct mechanisms. In the first place, public policies of States with regard to matters of education, norms and public markets will define the technical environment of companies. In the second place, social and national dynamics will determine collective attitudes with regard to the division of added-value, the rules of the game between social groups and the relationship of individuals to their work and to the company.

All these trends are heading toward an extension of free trade and Europe's opening up to international competition. Nevertheless, the question of massive delocalization looms in the industrial sector, and now also in the service sector. These areas require information processing with repercussions on employment, especially in Europe, which is less protected than its partners. Overall delocalization will make protectionist maneuvers most probable by one country or by groups of countries.

Three configurations may be considered in terms of the conditions of exchange and competition:

E1. National protectionism (end of GATT).

E2. Regional protectionism (regional barriers and free exchange between regional blocs).

E3. Extension of GATT and free trade, fierce competition between enterprises.

The following configurations will also be taken into account for the globalization of economies:

F1. Reduced.

F2. Variable, according to regions and sectors of activity.

F3. Intensive.

A Key Question: Will the New Technologies Spread as Fast as Planned?

Overall, progress will probably remain slow due to the power of inertia, an inherent force in productive and social systems. Indeed, numerous points of resistance to the effective introduction of the new technologies can be observed.

Resistance is, without doubt, stronger in the tertiary sector in that this sector has temporarily been subjected less to the pressure of international competition. At the end of the 1970s, it was understood that within only a few years, office automation would invade a full range of services, especially banks and insurance companies. Yet if we look around today, office automation did not eliminate many administrative jobs. Numerous factors concur to explain this slower-than-expected penetration. In the first place, we have to deal with managing the time made available by the latest technology; i.e., production management. What would be the purpose of investing to obtain greater productivity, if it could not be converted into expanded production or into decreased manpower? Think of the situation of saturated markets or weak growth or idle personnel. A reduction of working hours can only be progressive if it remains distributed fairly among the sectors.

Moreover, the generalization of office automation brings relative transparency to the working world, something that flies in the face of established hierarchies. Consider for a moment that computer technologies are not neutral towards power structures. We really should not be surprised then that certain actors (frequently executives) deep in the heart of a corporation, feel jeopardized, and resist innovation.

Also, we have to remember that what is technologically feasible is neither necessarily economically profitable nor socially desirable. One concrete example is telecommuting or working from a home office. It is very unlikely that work at home will develop to such an extent that a large percentage of office jobs will disappear. Several factors work against this maximal hypothesis. First, the current conditions of urban living: close quarters, an ill-suited apartment environment render a full working day unpleasant. Second, people are people, and work represents a socialization process corresponding to needs less and less satisfied otherwise.

G. Slow, Irregular, Unequal and Interdependent Growth

Interdependence is more than a trend or fiction; it is a measurable reality. Indeed it may be quantified through multiple indicators, as the share of ever increasing national productions dedicated to export. This greater opening up to the outside world means that no nation can claim to control its proper growth alone. If we return to the traditional car analogy: the accelerator is international, only the brakes are national.

It is now impossible to introduce structures and rules for the international and national game which has been adapted to the new context of interdependence and technical and economic changes. A general and concerted economic revival hardly seems possible. In passing, it should be noted that growth will not be stimulated by aging populations, either.

Irregularity more than sluggishness will seriously impact investment decisions and entail forecasting errors and sudden sways in attitude, swinging from optimism to pessimism. Periods of recession will be followed by periods of recovery, as if compensatory forces were at work to keep growth at a weak average of 2%. Historically, if we take levels of development into account, the result is surprising at four to five times more in absolute value than an average year drawn from the nineteenth century.

However, neither the GNP nor GDP is the only indicator that should be taken into account. One must not confuse the rhythm of growth (a flux) with the level of development (a stock). GNP is a flux which renews itself each year. Also, the quality content of this growth flux is far more important than its actual annual increase. Our aging populations will definitely be more vulnerable than ever before to such aspects as quality of environment and living conditions.

The majority of experts have made conjectures for the upcoming years which would have seemed improbable only a few years ago, e.g. a rate of inflation below 5%, positive, realistic interest rates, plus a very weak and irregular growth.

Yet their hypotheses are not solid. It is to be expected that there will be new oil shocks from now on up to 2005, which would destroy growth, assuming it should start off again in a strong and lasting manner. However, this perspective of new oil shocks fades farther away, the farther growth is out of sight. In fact, as in 1988-1990, sustained growth for two to three years could occur by means of the compensatory force of the recession of the preceding years. Basically, conditions for the return to strong and durable growth still need to be met. In an increasingly interdependent world, the absence of an international regulatory force is cruelly felt. If there is no alternative by the year 2000, eighty percent of the solvent world's demand will still be addressed to the developed countries of the triad. In other words, the solvent world's demand will not increase on account of the population's aging and it runs the risk of fluctuating more and more in accordance with the rhythm of optimistic or pessimistic cycles of anticipation.

The gap between North and South, East and West will continue widening. This lopsided development would become an additional source of tension among neighbors who are developing fast and are moderately populated versus those subjected to the struggle of underdevelopment and overpopulation. Consider the example of Haiti and the Dominican Republic, two very different countries on the same island.

At this point, four configurations were taken into account for GNP, the average growth rate of the 90s:

G1. The recession (less than 0.5% of growth).
G2. A weak and fluctuating GNP (1.5% on average).
G3. An average growth (2.5%).
G4. Strong growth (over 3%).

The combinatory analysis resulting from the high number of components and configurations seems inevitable. Initially there were a considerable number of possible scenarios, 2,916, or the product of $3 \times 3 \times 3 \times 3 \times 3 \times 4$, the number of configurations. This number, however, may be reduced through morphological analysis. Here, the most *a priori* relevant and coherent ways have been retained by the group which extracted four of them, each of them being represented by a color: black, gray, blue and pink.

A1 B1 C1 D1 E1 F1 G1:Black scenario
A2 B1 C1 D2 E2 F2 G2:Gray scenario
A3 B2 C2 D3 E2 F2 G3:Blue scenario
A3 B3 C3 D3 E3 F3 G4:Pink scenario

IT5, International Context Morphological Analysis

Demographic Trends in Western Countries	A1 Aging of populations Migrants control ethnic conflicts	A2 Migrant flows from east and south to western countries Integration problems	A3 New baby-boom in Western countries and acceptable migration flows
Geographical and Geopolitical Context	B1 Tensions and conflicts No regulator of interdependence	B2 Limited conflicts in the south and eastern countries Uncertainties in western countries	B3 New international order of a multipolar, interdependent world
Role of Eastern Europe	C1 Disintegration regional wars refugees .	C2 Unequal development Social ad regional tensions	C3 Economic convergence and integration of the countries (east and west)
European Integration	D1 Failure of the Europe of 12 Come back of smaller Europe	D2 Stable Europe of 12. Integration of markets only	D3 Political integration of Europe of 12 Extension to new members
Conditions of Trade and Competition	E1 National protectionism (end of GATT)	E2 Regional protectionism (regional barriers and free trade within the block)	E3 GATT extension free trade Strong competition between firms
Globalisation of Economy	F1 Reduced	F2 Variable according to the regions and sectors	F3 Intensive
Annual rate of growth of the GNP	G1 Recession Less than 0.5%	G2 Low with fluctuations 1.5%	G3 Medium trend based 2.5%	G4 Strong More than 3%

However, relevance and coherence do not necessarily mean likelihood.

Likelihood of the Global Scenarios

The diversity of scenarios (black, gray, blue and pink) does not prejudice their individual and overall likelihood. In other words, do these scenarios include the majority of the most probable ones? To answer this question, the SMIC method and the Prob-Expert software were used. In effect this method actually assigns probabilities to the scenarios; i.e., combinations of realized or unrealized hypotheses, from information on individual probabilities of these hypotheses and conditional probabilities. Nevertheless, the transition from morphological analysis to cross-impact requires further explanation.

In order to find the most probable scenarios, the IT5 experts met in London on May 7, 1993. This was an opportunity for them to give their opinions on the proposed configurations and the probability of their occurrence. For instance, the configurations of the component European integration; i.e., D1 = failure, D2 = stability, D3 = integration, were estimated on average with the following probabilities: P(D1) = 0.4; P(D2) = 0.4; P(D3) = 0.2

As the configurations are assumed to be exhaustive and exclusive, the total probability is one. This assumption of exhaustiveness is often questionable. Hence we recommend adding a new configuration per component. This new configuration was simply called "Others". In this sense, we have exhaustiveness by definition.

In this case study, the group of experts considered the probabilities of "other configurations" as negligible and did not add any new configurations to the following five subsystems:

1) international (geopolitical and economic) context of the 1990s;
2) autonomous technological determining factors;
3) infrastructures of the IT and communications systems;
4) strategies and actors games;
5) market trends.

Moreover, for several reasons, the use of the SMIC-Prob-Expert software is restricted to six fundamental hypotheses. Therefore, it is not possible to consider all the components and combinations. We can only rely on some of them.

Six hypotheses which characterize the various subsystems were considered:

H1: Political integration of Europe (D3).

H2: Extension of free trade (E3).

H3: Low and irregular growth (G1 or G2, i.e. less than 1.5%).

These first three belong to the international context.

H4: Integration with telecoms (this hypothesis comes from the subsystem called "Information and communication infrastructures" which envisages situations like access from home to optical fiber facilities).

H5: Active support to R&D (This hypothesis comes from the subsystem "strategy and actors game').

H6: Slowing down of the IT market increase: This hypothesis of an average increase of less than 8% in turnover comes from the subsystem "market trends".

The efficient use of this method requires that the number of hypotheses and consequently the number of variables which describe the scenarios be limited to five or six. The experts cannot assign a probability to the full set of thinkable scenarios (which means 64 scenarios for 6 hypotheses). Of course the total of the probablility of these 64 possible scenarios is equal to one as these scenarios (combinations of hypotheses) are exclusive and as it is sure that one of them will occur.

The Smic provides a direct response to this problem. In fact, with this method it is only necessary to know:
– the simple probability of the realization of a hypothesis within a given period of time; take $P(i)$ as the probability for the hypothesis i to be realized;
– conditional probabilities of realization of pairs of hypotheses; take $P(i/j)$ as the probability of the hypothesis i occurring, knowing that the hypothesis j occurs and $P(i/\text{not } j)$ is the probability of i occurring, knowing that the hypothesis j has not occurred.

The Smic method corrects the raw probabilities given by the experts to obtain coherent results, i.e. results which satisfy the classical equations of conditional probabilities. In any case the experts cannot give coherent answers, i.e. answers which verify the classical rules of probabilities:

$$P(i) = P(i/j)P(j) + P(i/\text{not } j)\,(1 - P(j))$$
$$P(ij) = P(i/j)P(j) = P(j/i)P(i).$$

At the same time, the Prob-Expert software calculates the probabilities of the scenarios. As the system cannot be fully determined – there are more unknown variables than independent equations –, there is an infinity of vector solutions for the scenarios. Using the SIMPLEX method allows the extreme solutions for each scenario to be selected. Usually the "Max of Max" solution is preferred; i.e., the solution which gives the highest value to the most probable scenario.

The experts' skepticism regarding European unification appears immediately. Hypothesis H2 gets a probability of only 0.2 for the advancement of political integration. That corresponds to the D3 configuration in the morphological analysis. The same experts have then assigned a 0.5 probability to the D2 configuration (stability of Europe limited to market integration) and 0.3 to the configuration D1; i.e., the break-up of Europe and the return to national states.

Another indicator of the coherence of the experts' answers is the quadratic remainder resulting from the optimization done by the Prob-Expert software. As for linear regression, it is best to minimize the difference between the initial information and the data which verify the probabilities axioms. The lack of coherence in the data would be shown by a remainder greater than 0.2; whereas in the current study its value is only 0.102, which proves the data's coherence.

The scenarios generated by the 6 hypotheses (H1 to H6) are classified by decreasing order of probability. The cumulated probability of the 64 possible scenarios is equal to 1 (by definition, as an exhaustive set of exclusive situations). The equiprobability is around 1.5% (1/64).

Usually the probability of the most probable scenario is about 15% and one third of the set of scenarios covers 80% of the total of the probable scenarios. In this case the result is exceptional as the solution which maximizes the most probable scenario assigns the value 0.40 to the so called S28 scenario (001001), which means more than four chances out of ten. This corresponds to the unfavorable situation which extends the current situation with:

not H1: The political integration of Europe is not realized.

not H2: The expansion of free trade does not work.

H3: Slow and irregular growth (less than 1.5%).

not H4: The integration with telecoms does not work.

not H5: R&D is not actively supported.

H6: The development of the IT market is slowing down.

The other scenarios are much less probable. In fact, the following four scenarios teased out of the group are five to six times less probable but maintain a certain likelihood.

Group 1: Recessive set back; almost 6 chances out of 10. This group corresponds to the gray and black scenarios previously envisaged.

The overall probability of this group is 57%. The group is characterized by 001... as answers to H1, H2 and H3, which means a context with the withdrawal of the aging Europe turning in on itself, or even the breaking up of the European Community with likely limitations to free trade, all these events leading to low or very low growth. This recessive setback is not favorable to the IT markets, since integration with the telecoms could not be achieved, maybe due to the resulting lack of support in R&D.

Group 2: Recession and incomplete opening up (less than 1 chance in 10).

This group of two scenarios has less than one chance in ten to succeed. The weak growth or even recession is very likely due to an incomplete opening up; i.e., only from the economic point of view within one particular scenario which outlines a Europe broken up by free trade and the recession; or only from the political point of view with S43: Europe as a political fortress without a firm free trade agreement, or even with a breaking up of GATT (now WTO).

In a recessionary context Europe's opening outward cannot be complete and it becomes impossible to achieve the political integration of Europe simultaneously with the extension of free trade. The support of R&D does not help avoid a slowdown in the IT markets, especially since the integration of IT with the telecoms has not been achieved (idea of "not H4").

Group 3: Growth by the opening up of Europe
(less than two chances in ten)

This group of seven is characterized by sustained economic growth and it is the most heterogeneous. If the opening up is incomplete (four scenarios) the IT markets can remain dynamic assuming successful integration with the telecoms. If the opening up is complete (political integration of Europe with extension of free trade) as in the three scenarios, the evolution of the IT markets is uncertain and does not depend on either R&D support or on the integration with telecoms but seems to be dependent on the political and economic success of Europe. This complete openness corresponds to the pink scenario from the morphological analysis and has fewer than seven chances in a hundred to succeed.

Group 4: Self-centered development
(more than 15 chances in 100)

This group is characterized by regained growth (idea of "not H3"), the non-extension of GATT or even a decline in free trade and by a freezing or even an explosion of European unification. The development of the IT markets is rather favorable except in the case of one scenario only where the conjunction of R&D support and integration with telecoms cannot prevent the IT markets from decline possibly due to the regionalization of trade.

This group of four scenarios is close to the blue scenario which is characterized by average growth, by a maintained "economic Europe" but without extension of free trade. The likelihood of this blue scenario is then about 10%.

In sum, the black and gray scenarios (recessive setback) are unfortunately the most probable, with more than 60 chances in a hundred. The blue scenario (self-centered development) has only 15 chances in 100 to succeed. The pink scenario (growth by opening up) is far less likely to happen (7 chances in100). It is as likely as S42, or the scenario in which Europe exploded by free trade and the recession and twice as likely as S43 in which Europe is a political fortress with an exploding GATT due to the recession).

It should be noted that the following hypotheses, – political expansion and economic closure of Europe –, increased economic openness raising the possibility of a setback in European construction, had been rejected *a priori* as they did not appear in any of the initial scenarios (black, gray, pink or blue) selected in the initial table of the morphological analysis.

Scenario S37 (110110) is in principle the most desirable (a triumphant Europe from both the political and economic points of view, in an expanding economy, with integration achieved with the telecoms, sustained support of R&D and recovery of the IT markets). It is assigned a null probability. The same situation applies in most of the international context scenarios with a profile starting at 110. It seems that the extension of free trade is almost incompatible with the political unification of Europe, and vice versa. This result is interesting in the current context of European doubts.

It is necessary to contextualize this conclusion. It is only the result of a collective vision in May 1993, as expressed by a set of European IT industry experts being questioned on the international context up to the year 2000. This vision can be seen as pessimistic. However, let us remember that a comparable exercise on the prospects of the steel industry in France by the year 2005 was done in 1990 and 1991. The hypotheses about growth were almost as pessimistic as in the current case (for instance the probability of keeping growth at less than 1.8% per year was 0.6).

In the current case the probability analysis with the Prob-Expert software confirmed the coherence and pertinence of the choice of the 4 scenarios (black, gray, blue and pink) elaborated in the morphological analysis. Nevertheless not all have the same likelihood to succeed; in addition, other scenarios on international evolution have been identified whereas the morphological analysis phase did not reveal them.

Scenario Building at Axa France [1]

The futures-thinking exercise and strategic scenario building was carried out in France from March 1994 to December 1995, under the direction of Planning and the leadership of Professor Michel Godet.

Until recently scenario planning was restricted, albeit unofficially, to a few specific sectors where long-term heavy investment was the norm, e.g. air and rail transportation, electricity, aluminium and petroleum production. In fact most service companies did not see the need to hold futures-thinking exercises.

Gradually, however, interest arose in the telecommunications and computer sectors. Soon areas like finance and tourism joined in because they too experienced growing uncertainty about the future given the threefold bind of deregulation, economic problems, and market globalization.

Certain forward-looking pioneers stood out from the start. One was Axa France, a leader in insurance. Axa France is actually an umbrella company for all the French subsidiaries of the Axa insurance group. In the early 1990s, the French entities had decided to look to the future in order to prepare the traditional four-year plan (1996-2000). The previ-

---

1. Part of this case study first appeared in the international journal *Futuribles*, (Issue 203, November 1995). It was written by Paul Benassouli, Director of Planning, and Régine Monti, research-fellow.

ous plan (1992-1996) had focused exclusively on greater rationaliza-
tion of resources and the reorganization of the new Axa, which had
expanded through many buy-outs.

Given the company's objectives and focus on distribution, Axa's
1992-1996 plan had not taken into account how the general or competitive environment would evolve. The new plan (1996-2000) would,
however, take into account the international objectives of Axa, its
quality and profitability directives. Moreover, with a ten-year future
horizon, the plan would integrate external challenges more readily
and set the strategic course for the five years immediately following
(1996-2000). Note that the futures-thinking exercise took place two
years before Axa and UAP (Union des assurances de Paris) merged.

A Pragmatic Approach

The procedure that Axa France adopted reflects how futures-thinking
exercises have evolved and been applied to planning within major corporations. Today's companies have less time to think and feel an
almost urgent need to act. Hence our mandate sounds increasingly
like a bad self-help book – "how to conduct a meaningful exercise with
managers on major future trends and uncertainties that is both coherent and realistic". In other words, what can we really achieve in six
working meetings?

Axa France, a relatively recently established group known for its
rapid integration of numerous acquisitions as well as its mobile and
highly decentralized structure, could not consider anything time- or
labor-intensive, like a specialized department that would require
divesting and reallocating directors from various subsidiaries to take
part in the process. On the contrary, the idea was to encourage the
company's general managers to work together. The overall goal was to
look to the future with a shared vision as they identified threats,
opportunities and potential bifurcations thus preparing for expected
changes and hopefully fostering desirable changes while fighting
feared changes. In short, participants would have to identify possible
futures and pinpoint which of these would be the most probable. The
horizon adopted was 2005.

Given the nine-month deadline, we opted for efficiency and selected
two main tools from the futures toolbox, structural analysis to find key
variables and actors' strategies to explore possible changes. Three
other methods mentioned in earlier chapters were also used, namely
the futures workshops, morphological analysis and the Smic-Prob-
Expert.

As emphasized earlier, selecting a methodology (workshops or
structural analysis) to determine key variables is not a goal in itself.
The first objective is to encourage participants to express their vision
of the future. Otherwise this underlying future vision remains

Environmental scenarios were built following the ten-step schedule listed below:

1. Futures seminar: acquisition of analytical methods, identification and hierarchization of the factors of change affecting Axa, choice of the most pivotal environmental components for Axa in France (mid-March 1994).
2. Small group sessions: drafting of scenarios grouped into broad fields (April-June 1994).
3. Joint sessions: presentation of results from various groups and the construction of environmental scenarios (June 1994).
4. Survey on the future of insurance in France (July-September 1994).
5. Probabilization, selection and analysis of scenarios (October 1994).
6. Selection of one main scenario and identification of alternative hypotheses (November 1994).
7. Presentation of the main scenario and the alternative hypotheses to the various subsidiaries (December 1994).
8. Appropriation and integration of the main scenario and hypotheses in the plans of the different subsidiaries (January 1995).
9. Drafting of a plan in each subsidiary (February-June 1995).
10. "Arbitration" and allocation of resources (4th term 1995).

implicit. It is only by verbalizing that vision that the group can gain greater insight into certain member's stances or disagreements. Obviously having some idea of a future vision makes corporate decision-making more efficient.

Exploring Futuribles through Morphological Analysis

Once the key dimensions of the scenarios are set out, three or four scenarios must be drafted per component. These scenarios should be pertinent, coherent, realistic, and likely to occur within the horizon selected.

Morphological analysis was applied for each key area during a half-day meeting of a sub-committee composed of the three managers most affected. Preparatory work had been carried out, e.g. consultation of experts, documentation, interviews, etc. Once again it is a constant juggling act to get the management committee involved while taking up as little time as possible.

As we have seen, the principle of morphological analysis is simple: break the system under study down into sub-systems, components or fields, and then identify the resulting configurations. For example, the dimension, or key field, "demography and society", highlighted in the Axa France scenario-building sessions, may be broken down into components. In fact these components were identified during the futures workshops. In Axa's case, these are also the main factors of demographic and social change likely to have a major influence on the com-

---

Eleven Key Components

1. Demography and society.
2. European construction/structure.
3. Real interest rates.
4. Growth rates.
5. State interventionism.
6. Retirement system.
7. Taxation and life insurance.
8. Health system.
9. Demand for insurance.
10. Technology.
11. Distribution channels/means of distribution.

Note: In accordance with confidentiality agreements, only the first five may be detailed here.

---

pany's very future. These factors appear in the graphics that follow. They include aging, migratory flows, worksharing, plus taxation and work. Each of these components may take several possible shapes, commonly called configurations. If we take the horizon 2005 as an example, the migratory flows might be comparable to today's at 100,000 annually or they could rise sharply to 300,000 a year. Another possibility would be an even balance between immigration and emigration. If we keep these three configurations separately, we could say that we had explored the set of possible futures, at least quantitatively. This type of thinking was applied to each subcomponent. Highlights of the results follow as a diagram showing morphological analysis: of the component "Demography and Society".

In Axa's case, the group decided, whether right or wrong, that the following were not realistic:
- a drop in the French fertility rate to 1.4 children per woman;
- massive immigration;
- a net balance through emigration.

All the combinations with these configurations (18 scenarios) were thus eliminated. Certain paths were considered unrealistic. For example, the group did not envisage a worksharing program or system that excluded a section of the labor force and the development of family-related jobs.

After excluding these, only three scenarios for the component "demography and society" were retained in Axa's overall scenario-building process. (See broken, thin and solid lines within the diagram.)

The three scenarios read roughly as:

1) "Rigidity and Extended Duality"
This is a straight scenario with no social innovation or questioning of the limits weighing on the job market. Two worlds coexist: the offi-

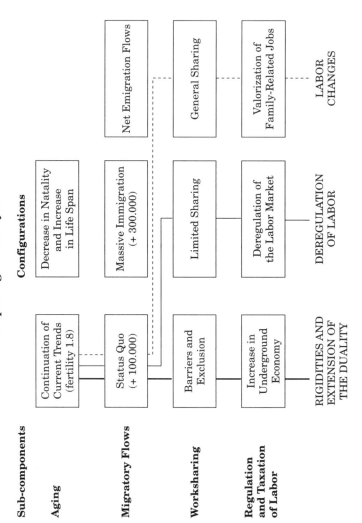

**Demography and Society Component
Morphological Analysis**

cial work world, as regulated as ever and very traditional in terms of shifts and working hours; the underground economy in which a growing segment of the population gets by through under-the-table payment for small jobs.

2) "Deregulated Labor"

The name says it all. It is the "American plan" or a more flexible labor market where innovation remains localized in certain fields or regions.

3) "Changes in Working"

This is a scenario of collective voluntary efforts which leads to the recognition, organization and development of new types of jobs. There is also a serious reconsideration of social life, e.g. greater leisure time and different lifestyles.

Each of the components of Axa France's future scenarios was analyzed morphologically. The following outline summarizes the environmental scenarios foreseen by restricted groups of experts during April and May 1994. Note that use of the box "Others" is not only an attempt at exhaustive research but a reminder not to forget what may otherwise easily be forgotten. When determining probability for the configurations, we check to see whether the "Others" box is indeed unrealistic.

Outline of Environmental Scenarios for AXA France

Demographic and Society	Rigidity and Extended Duality	Deregulation of Labor	Labor changes	Others
European Construction	Reinforced Convergence	Chaotic Convergence	Others	
Economic Growth	Growth Rate Above 2%	Growth Rate Below 2%		
Interest/ Inflation Rates	Real Interest Rate Above 4%	Real Interest Rate Below 4%		
State Intervention	Reinforced State Intervention	Stable State Intervention	Decrease in State Intervention	Others

In June of 1994, the management committee of Axa France collectively approved this outline of scenarios with a 2005 horizon.

Determining Probable Futures

The objective of Axa's management committee was to pinpoint uncertainties and major future trends as part of the 1995-2000 planning exercise. Naturally they wanted to go further in order to retain a limited number of scenarios with high probability ratings.

Construction of the Questionnaire (Scenario Probabilization)

The crossed-impact method consists of asking questions with simple and conditional probability on a limited number of hypotheses. Use of these methods means exploring possible futures across a restricted number of main hypotheses (5-6 binary hypotheses).

One of the main problems in using these approaches is determining the few hypotheses which represent the key components and subsequent configurations. Hypotheses are selected on the basis of the scenario outlines. One hypothesis per component is retained. This becomes the most probable configuration. The configuration is identified by an initial probabilization performed quickly by asking each expert his/her opinion. An average of these simple probabilities attributed to each configuration is then calculated. Let us take the component "demography and society" as an example. The highest average attributed by group members was that for the configuration "rigidity and extended duality" at 35%. This hypothesis was therefore retained as the main one.

**Probability Attributed to the Configurations
of the "Demography and Society" Component**

Component	*Configurations*			
Demography and society	Rigidity and extension of the duality	Deregulation of labor	Labor changes	Others
	35%	28%	27%	10%

*Average Simple Probability Rates
Attribued by Experts*

Main Hypothesis Retained :
Labor : Rigidity and Extension of the Duality

All the main hypotheses for Axa France were determined on the basis of the most probable configurations for each component. The list of hypotheses follows:

H1. In terms of aging (fertility rate of 1.8); migratory flows of one million more in the upcoming ten years; inequitable worksharing which leads to more and more exclusion, barriers or ceilings, and an extended underground economy.

H2. Reinforced Convergence for Europe. The Europe of Maastricht is effective and the single market becomes a reality. Member states respect the economic and financial criteria, e.g. low inflation, low interest rates, budgetary rigor.

H3. Sustained growth rate (above 2.2%).

H4. High real interest rates (above 4%).

H5. Reinforced state interventionism in France, e.g. predominance of a strong state. The French State increases its hold on the economy through organizations managed by its social partners. Social budgets are better mastered and labor regulations are reinforced.

H6. Retirement: budgeting maintains the distribution. The end of indexed pensions. Moreover, the level of contributions deducted from salaries remains constant. There is partial "budgetization". There is no sign of implementing a capitalization system using a tax incentive program.

H7. Tax advantages of life insurance are maintained.

H8. Health system continues to flounder. Technological progress spreads rapidly. Yet in parallel, the growing medical demand is a heavy trend (or megatrend). Professional expenditures in the health system continue rising at the current rate. The State can no longer meet its obligations and withdraws.

H9. Unchanged demand in terms of clients. Expectations about prices (best value for the dollar), services (simplicity) and client needs do not really change.

H10. The traditional insurance distribution system continues to be eaten away on the edges.

Given the restriction on the number of hypotheses (maximum 5 or 6), it was impossible to probabilize in one questionnaire the full slate of Axa France scenarios using the Smic Prob-Expert method. Two questionnaires were needed: one on the social and economic environment; the other on the insurance context (H7, H8, H9, H10). Both questionnaires shared one hypothesis, H5, which was used to link identified changes and build the full scenarios with the 2005 horizon. However this part of the case study is not presented here.

The two questionnaires were circulated among members of the company's management committee during the summer of 1994. They were questioned in writing on the simple probabilities of each hypothesis (P(i): probability that the hypothesis i occurs, as well as on the conditional probabilities of the hypotheses taken in pairs (P(i/j): probability that hypothesis i occurs when hypothesis j occurs or P(i/not j) and probability that hypothesis i occurs while knowing that hypothesis j has not occurred.

A sample questionnaire page follows.

Processing the Results with the Smic-Prob-Expert Software

We used the Prob-Expert software to process the two questionnaires and then probabilize the various environmental scenarios for Axa France with a horizon of 2005. The data were determined by taking an average of the answers provided by Axa France's management committee in the summer of 1994.

Questionnaire

Simple Probability
Question: **What is the probability that the hypothesis
H3. Continued Growth from now until 2005 will occur?**

**Signification: I consider that it is probable that in ten years, the growth
rate will remain the same.**
These hypotheses are evaluated with the following probability scale:
1) Very improbable event.
2) Improbable event.
3) Moderately probable event.
4) Probable event.
5) Very probable event.

Conditional Probabilities
Question: **Knowing that Hypothesis H3 (Continued Growth from now
until 2005) has occurred**, what do you think the probability is that each of
the following four hypotheses will occur?

	Improbable			Probable		
H1. Work World: rigidity and extended duality	1	2	3	4	5	Ind*
H2. Reinforced convergence in Europe	1	2	3	4	5	Ind
H3. High real interest rates	1	2	3	4	5	Ind
H4. Reinforced State intervention	1	2	3	4	5	Ind

* Independent.

Probabilization of the Hypotheses using Smic Prob-Expert

The initial result of processing is an average net probability and the
standard deviation, taking into account the correction indicated in the
diagram, attributed to each hypothesis by the experts.

Probability Rates and Scenario Selection

The beauty of the Smic Prob-Expert method is that it reveals the probability attributed to each of the 32 scenarios by each expert. These are
the 32 scenarios generated from the combinations of five hypotheses

Positioning of the Economic and Social Environmental Hypotheses according to their Average Probability and Standard Deviation

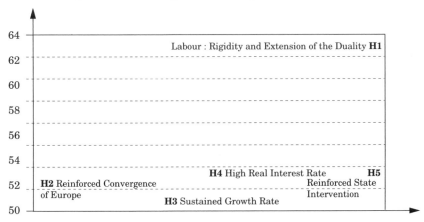

Legend:
H1. "Rigidity and Extension of the Duality" is the most probable hypothesis on average but the experts remain divided on this one. (high standard deviation).
H2. "Reinforced convergence of Europe". This is hypothesis is probable on average; i.e., one chance in two that it will occur. The expert opinions converge on this result (weak standard deviation).

on the social and economic environment of Axa France, horizon 2005. The most probable scenarios stand out, thus revealing the future visions of the various experts. We also calculate an average probability per scenario for the group itself. On the basis of this calculation, the most probable scenarios are selected.

The selection process seeks out combinations of two and then three hypotheses that group a minimum number of scenarios which represent the largest share of the field of possible futures. Here we find the greatest probability. In the case of Axa France, we found that four combinations of three hypotheses brought together 16 scenarios in four groups that indeed represented 70% of the possible futures. In concrete terms, according to the expert participants, we have more than two out of three chances of ending up in one of these combinations in 2005.

From each of these four groups, the most probable scenario was selected. As a result, we went from 16 to 4 scenarios.

Axa's four social and economic environmental scenarios with a horizon of 2005 appear in the following diagram. The first one, "Managed Crisis", represents 25% of the possible futures. This is a rare case. The probability rating for the other three scenarios is almost the same at 15% each.

It is also possible to identify, for each expert, the proximity of the various scenarios. The more probable the scenario, the closer it is and vice-versa. We end up with a fine snapshot of the different future visions of the experts surveyed.

Culling the Social and Economic Environmental Scenario Groups

E1. Managed Crisis (26%)
Work World: Rigidity and Extended Duality
High Real Interest Rates (above 4%)
Reinforced State Interventionism

E2. Inflationary Front (14%)
Work World: Rigidity and Extended Duality
Low Real Interest Rates (below 4%)
Reinforced State Interventionism

E3. Europe Embroiled in Social Tension (15%)
Work World: Rigidity and Extended Duality
High Real Interest Rates (above 4%)
No Reinforced State Interventionism

E4. Organized Liberalism (17%)
Work World: No Rigidity
Low Real Interest Rates (below 4%)
No Reinforced State Interventionism

Environmental Scenarios for AXA France

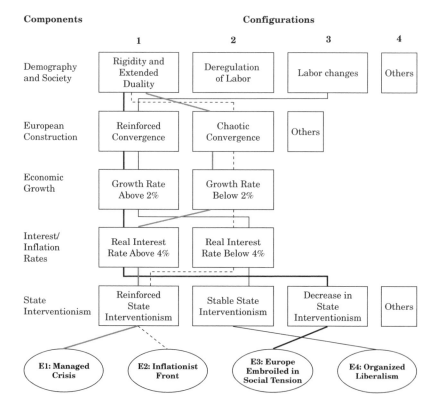

Environmental Scenarios for AXA France

E1. Managed Crisis: Here there is no consensus on main issues among the various European countries. The dream of a union fades. The French State faces an economic slowdown aggravated by social rigidity. It is the State putting out fires again. This context presents high real interest rates which are favorable to the insurance industry.

E2. Inflationary Front: The French government tries to jumpstart the economy through increased consumer spending. Social conflicts are temporarily avoided through wage increases which have disastrous effects on inflation. Real interest rates fall. The idea of European convergence fades. The State intervenes step by step in both the social and economic sphere.

E3. Europe Embroiled in Social Tension: In this instance, European convergence becomes an economic priority. France maintains high real interest rates; Brussels' power grows. Economically, Europe is a success. Growth rates exceed 2%. However, social crises, especially in the labor market, intensify. Europe does not implement reforms.

E4. Organized Liberalism: The social and economic context improves. Reforms succeed in promoting employment and battling other social ills without State intervention. A social hiatus seems to be taking shape. At the same time, the low real interest rates encourage productive investments. This healthy step can be seen in a growth rate higher than 2% and in an attenuation of previously seen social rigidities.

Analysis of Corresponding Visions
The Expert's Postions according to Scenario Probability

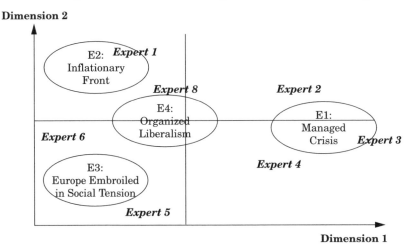

The Axa France 2005 scenarios were generated by crossing the four social and economic environmental scenarios and the five insurance industry scenarios (drawn from a questionnaire not presented here). Interestingly enough, by uniting these two scenario groupings, the participants found one shared hypothesis, H5 "Reinforced State Interventionism". Among the twenty possible scenarios, nine were selected, the others were eliminated because of incompatibility in terms of H5, e.g. H5 = 0 in one case and H5 = 1 in another.

The pure futures-thinking stage ends with the selection of nine scenarios that represent a significant portion of Axa's possible futures for the year 2005. Once the field of possibles is reduced to what is probable, we turn to what is desirable. This is the start of the planning stage.

From Scenario Building to Planning

The shift from scenario building to planning is never easy. It is already no mean feat to select only one scenario that clarifies the array of possible futures. We understand just how confusing planners find working from several possible environmental scenarios. What can be done to retain the richness of the results of scenario building while remaining functional? The solution in the Axa France case consisted in keeping the most probable of the probable scenarios as the basis for the plan. This scenario became known as the "main scenario". This socio-economic environmental scenario "Managed Crisis" showed a probability rating of 25% and brought to the plan the risks and breaks (bifurcations) corresponding to the alternatives envisaged in the other scenarios considered highly probable and thus retained.

Some may object that this choice of a main scenario (the most probable of the probable) is simplistic in terms of the ambitions expressed at the offset of the exercise. However in terms of operationalizing a strategic plan, exploring the possible futures and pinpointing the probable ones is not a waste of time. In fact the participants became well aware of the risks of breaks or bifurcations in the trends that might affect their choices and cause them to rethink their course of action. The strategic plan will only become stronger in this sense.

The main scenario is used in two ways to build the plan. First, the scenario serves as the basis for environmental hypotheses that provide a backdrop to the plan itself. Some hypotheses are directly integrated into the plan, e.g. the real interest rates. Other elements are studied more, in a traditional fashion, to quantify the consequences of various combinations of hypotheses on the company's markets or market segments. In this sense, the main scenario can become a shared reference point that all the subsidiaries may use.

Afterward, with the main scenario in mind, each entity works toward its own strategic choices by asking the following two questions:
 – what to do to reach our objectives, given our strengths and weaknesses and the conditions set by the main scenario? (In short, what to do to achieve x?);
 – which moves should be made to prepare for possible breaks/bifurcations? (In other words, what to do if xyz?)

The first question leads to acting on the future environment and reflects a proactive attitude; whereas the second question requires adapting to an expected future environment and is a preactive attitude.

Of course it would be foolhardy to decide upon a strategy for the next five years on the basis of one main scenario. In fact, even if it is the most probable scenario, (25% in Axa's case), it remains not very likely since for Axa there are three out of four chances that the company will end up in another situation.

At this stage of making strategic choices, participants or managers must take into account the possible breaks or bifurcations that might occur given the situation described in the main scenario. Participants have to ponder each bifurcation highlighted in the analysis of the other highly probable scenarios and how that break or bifurcation would affect the conditions chosen within the hypotheses attached to the main scenario. Here, on the basis of the information provided, the tremendous uncertainty weighing on the industry in terms of developing trends was pinpointed for each hypothesis. For example, if the main scenario foresaw developing a certain market by making a heavy investment in computer technology then envisaging that market's disappearance for regulatory reasons, it would encourage participants to opt for a more rustic solutions that would be easier to reconsider. (We might even ignore the fact that operating costs would be higher.) The decisions are made within the framework of the main scenario but they take into account the notion of breaks, or ruptures. The decisions may thus speed up achievement of objectives or reevaluation of those objectives.

The virtual obligation to evaluate the consequences of these breaks or bifurcation points sheds new light on investment choices. In fact, occasionally the process may be halted to avoid exposing "irretrievable" costs. "Solid" solutions are thus preferred; in other words, solutions adapted to the contexts outlined by the most probable or most "flexible" scenarios, which can easily be revisited or challenged if there is a change in context. As a result, the company can better integrate uncertainty into its decisionmaking process.

Each subsidiary took the main scenario and probable bifurcations, or breaks, into account. Working groups were set up, again, to encourage that participants share their vision of the future.

The last stage, planning by scenario, or scenario planning, took place at the end of 1995. At this point, discussion turned to the plans presented by each subsidiary and the necessary resources for their projects. We were reminded that another contribution of the initial futures-thinking seminar is that it provides the criteria and weighting system (arbitration) used in this decisive stage.

All in all, what remains etched in the memories of the people in charge of corporate strategy and operations is the maturity gained through a futures-thinking exercise. Under fire, this "intellectual cross-training" will translate to strategic reflexes far sharper than those produced by a classical planning process with no prior reflection on the future.

Will Paris Need a Third Airport in 2030? If So, Where?

Site selection and scenarios seem particularly well-suited. However, choosing where to build a new airport for a large city, be it Athens, Paris or Montréal, raises many pertinent issues.

Over the past 25 years, we have been asked six times by various actors in government, the transportation sector, as well as the airport authority (Aéroports de Paris, or ADP) to consider the future air traffic situation in the Parisian region. The question boiled down to whether or not air traffic would make a new Paris airport necessary in the next few decades.

Each time the question came up, the reply was more negative, given the capacities of the provincial airports, e.g. Lille. It is worth noting here that regional hubs are underdeveloped in France, in comparison with other European countries. Nevertheless, the government mandate given to Jacques Douffiagues, former transportation minister, included a second, new question: Where should this hypothetical airport be built? The precautionary principle requires that appropriate, thinly populated land be selected, rezoned and expropriated for an airport. Otherwise, uncontrolled urban development may rob future generations of their choices. The following section presents extracts from Jacques Douffiagues' report to which we officially contributed.

The French ministries for supply and services, transportation and tourism created the Douffiagues Commission to study the air transportation situation in the greater Parisian area with the year 2030 as a horizon.

The commission's work followed two distinct yet equally necessary phases:

Phase 1: draft various scenarios and suggest that the seemingly indispensable measures be immediately implemented. The Commission proudly pointed out that almost all the measures had been enshrined by the French government during a ministerial council meeting in October 1995;

Phase 2: prepare an orientation document, primarily for the ministers, to guide them in the choice of a site for the new international platform which would be created outside the Ile de France or Parisian region yet be designed primarily to serve that region.

The Third Airport Paradigm

After the first phase, the commission did not favor the idea of a third international platform. The commission's research over 15 months led the participants to confirm that current traffic conditions, and even the predicted conditions whether short-, medium- or long-term, indicated that the needs of the greater Parisian region would be amply met by

– coordination and moderate development of Charles-de-Gaulle Roissy Airport, as part of the scenario with the least noise impact;

– release of a portion of the traffic (mail and commercial) to other platforms in the region or bordering regions, e.g. Beauvais, Reims, Pontoise;

– redirection of a significant percentage of the medium and long-distance carriers to the major provincial platforms, e.g. Lyon-Satolas, Lille-Lesquin, and even possibly, Nantes-Notre-Dame-des-Landes (intermodal technique).

Potential Traffic for Provincial Airports in France

In 1995, one-third of the current traffic at Orly and Roissy airports was comprised of provincial residents in transit. The traffic at the second largest French airport (Nice) equals 10% of that of the first (ADP). Note that the second British airport, Manchester, enjoys traffic equal to 20% of the London airports.

The potential of Lille in terms of passenger handling is great (7 million passengers rather than today's 1 million); whereas the Satolas airport has a potential capacity of 15.5 million rather that the current 4.5 million.

On November 17, 1995, the ministers of supply and services, transportation and tourism, as well as the secretary of state for transportation, confirmed by letter their decision to move on to the second phase. Here the focus was on selecting sites within the greater Parisian region, but beyond the core. Given the situation, selecting a site was a major issue in regional development policy.

The initial goal was to analyze sites according to specific evaluation criteria including:

– quality of access by land and air;
– environmental impact;
– investment cost;
– regional characteristics;
– level of social risk associated with location.

The commission worked according to instructions within a strict timeframe. In order to structure their thinking, the participants used Multipol, a multicriteria selection method useful when the future is uncertain. The following pages trace how the group applied Multipol to a problematic and public choice.

A Wager and Its Risks

Choosing a better site for an airport that will open at the earliest in 2020 or 2030 is an especially difficult task. In 25 to 30 years, the basic elements at the heart of any choice will be considerably different. Technology will have evolved, as well as the European and international supply and demand. The very face of air transportation will have changed along with airport systems, urbanization around the French capital, road networks, lifestyles, even public awareness of risks and disturbances. Futures-thinking efforts may well have been launched but they only quantify on the basis of various hypotheses, the market demand with horizons of 2015 or 2030. No one can guess what aircraft capacity or performance will be at that point. No one can be sure of the disturbances new aircraft may cause, just as we do not know about the precision, navigational power or control of new vehicles.

Forecasted Passenger Traffic and Flow Movements

1980-1990 Change in number of passengers
ORLY: 4.4% per year
ROISSY: 8.1% per year

Traffic in millions (PAX)	1995	2015	2030
Orly *(capacity)*	26.7	24-30	27
Roissy *(capacity)*	28.4	50-60	63-80
Demand	55.3	64-95	90-124

Movements	1995	2015	2030
Orly *(capacity)*	239 000	250 000	250 000
Roissy *(capacity)*	331 000	350 to 520 000	400 to 540 000
Demand	570 000	600 to 770 000	650 to 900 000

N.B. Hypothesis based on a simple average: 140 passengers rather than the current 120.

Even after the decision has been made, one of the main difficulties in this type of situation lies in the uncertainty created by the 15- to 20-year period required to set up the logistics of a new airport system. This uncertainty should be seriously considered when selecting a site. However, the context in which the new airport will develop can only be known when that decision is made and announced.

Developing a new airport outside a known region is a gamble in unsure future territory. It is not a classical case of a major project, like a container with a known content, e.g. large commercial stadium or an industrial plant relocation. Nor is it even an irreversible decision, a

> ### A Deficit of 250,000 Movements or Surplus of 140,000 for the year 2030?
>
> With this horizon, predicted traffic varies between 90 to 124 million passengers and 650,000 to 900,000 for the main centers. Just how relevant a new airport would be depends on how much air traffic grows during the period 2015 to 2030 and not the period 1995 to 2015. Obviously in the hypotheses that use low growth, a third airport would be totally unjustified, even in 2030. Given this highly uncertain context, the long-term must be kept foremost in mind. Actually, as we approach 2030, we can no longer exclude an increase in the demand higher than today's forecast, nor can we exclude a major technological or structural change in transportation or the impact of factors related to the environment or regional development that would make new air transportation facilities necessary even sooner.

single major expenditure. Instead this decision requires reserving a site for an eventual air transportation center. The nature of this venture is not so readily defined and can not be evaluated for another ten years. It will not even start operations until 2020.

The Procedure Adopted

The Douffiagues Commission developed its own procedure designed to take into account the inherent uncertainty. The commission began a "multicriteria analysis" comparing only the potential sites presented by the regions concerned. There were 13 sites spread over three regions. This study was carried out using the same questionnaire designed according to the needs of the commission and informed by the regions and analyzed by the appropriate departments of the federal ministries of supply and services, housing, transportation, tourism and the environment. On the basis of these elements, the commission proceeded to three successive screenings so that no site presented any major flaw and so that there was some basic hierarchy among the sites according to the objectives already given.

The first screening relied on technical feasibility criteria, in other words:

– basic data like soil, real estate and property values;

– quality of the air space in terms of weather patterns, obstacles, current and future route compatibility and approach paths;

– environmental impacts such as population, noise levels, natural and constructed historical or heritage sites, sensitive areas, etc.

The second screening used adaptation to the regional clientele as a criterion. Here the issues were ground access, employable population, commercial zoning. The main task here was to analyze the conditions for eventually developing an airport in terms of passenger or customer service while keeping the characteristics of the region in mind. The list included road systems, rail service, population served, commercial/ shipping zones, regional characteristics, employment, and urban structure.

The third screening used the "demand scenarios" and airport operations. The objective was always to identify the most flexible sites in terms of airport infrastructure, e.g. support or satellite role, bipolar operations with an existing airport or an independent airport. At this stage participants also had to consider the consequences of reserving a site should the new project not materialize. The paradigm is essentially limited to the direct and indirect costs implied in merely reserving a site. It soon became apparent that the stakes are lower economically in this case than the cost of an airport or the cost of a poorly selected site. We are talking about investments of approximately 1 billion French francs in the first case versus 20 to 50 billion francs in the second. This aspect did not seem discriminatory to the commission.

The commission asked territorial or regional organizations and consular groups who had an interest in the greater Parisian region to provide data related to the technical-economic feasibility criteria for each site. These data were sent through the regional governmental offices.

The Regional Partners

Three regions submitted files which met the objectives of the commission; i.e., create a new large, international airport in the greater Parisian area, outside of Ile de France.
The Regions were as follows:
Centre: seven sites; three near Paris at Sainville, Santeuil and Beauvilliers along the ultrarapid Atlantic train route; four distant sites at Marboué, Bonneval, Arrou, Crucey-Senonches.
Haute-Normandie: two sites along the Seine, on the Vexin Plateau and the sother plateau of the Eure River.
Picardy: three sites along the northern ultrarapid train route, in other words, Hangest-en-Santerre and Vermandovillers between Amiens and Saint-Quentin and Rouvillers, a site near Compiègne. The regional management of the supply and services ministry identifies a possibility at Fouquescourt, not far from Hangest and Vermandovillers.

Evaluation and Multicriteria Choice using Multipol

The commission realized that any examination of the sites presented would be imperfect from the start and that further studies would be necessary. The specific location, for example, could always be optimized, but only through deeper analysis. The idea of picking two or three sites came up, in the case of a tie or some instability in terms of their advantages or, more likely, a feeling of comparing apples and oranges.

Within this context, it became important to present the actors (regional groups, etc) with the full set of elements behind the commission's rationale, e.g. criteria, files presented plus technical estimates, and also to develop a method that was sufficiently simple and convivial that people could appropriate it. Given the motives and context, the Multipol method was chosen.

Each site was evaluated by the commission in terms of the five main dimensions: quality of air space, ground accessibility, environmental impact, clientele and employable local population, with several criteria, also defined by the commission.

The evaluation relied on a simple, familiar 1-5 scale ranging from 1, which meant highly insufficient or highly incompatible with the dimension considered, to 5, which meant very good or completely compatible. Note that 0 was not used since no site was excluded on the basis of one single criterion.

Moreover, the sites were not judged in a uniform fashion. Participants had to consider the various contexts related to the very objective of the study. With this in mind, the commission proceeded to judge the pertinence of the structures and corresponding sites according to the short-, medium- and long-term demand, the positioning of the Parisian region within Europe, the Paris-province relationship, the economy of the supply and the positioning of the French airline industry, the coherence and efficiency of the overall structure in serving the greater Parisian region, and lastly, the inherent costs and associated risks.

For the aspects related to the selection of a site based on feasibility and adaptability criteria, excluding an evaluation of airport structures, the variety of regional and economic development policies translated into a weighted system, with coefficients applied to the dimensions of the crtieria thus enabling participants to set up a hierarchy of sites according to possible policies.

Commission members distributed a weight of 15 points on five dimensions and again for four political orientations, or possible value systems. The four types of weighting criteria were as follows:
 – weighting criteria to make air transportation a priority;
 – weighting criteria to make regional development a priority;
 – weighting criteria to make the environment a priority;
 – weighting criteria with no differentiation of criteria (weighted average).

Multipol calculates the weighted score for each site for each set of criteria. As a result, we can draw up a chart and graph of the comparative profiles of the sites according to the weight given the criteria.

Macrocriteria and Corresponding Sub-criteria

Macrocriterion 0.   Basic data, ground accessibility
Subcriteria:
– soil and subsoil;
– real estate and property matters.
Subcriteria for ground access:
– current distance by road from center of Paris;
– access time for the A 86 highway;
– the combining indicator for the commission related to the proximity of
  the sites;
– in terms of the A86 and the existing railroad network.

Macrocriterion 1.   Quality of Air Space
Subcriteria:
– meteorological conditions, geographical characteristics and obstacles;
– overall reorganization of the structure;
– available air space;
– airline routes;
– approach procedures;
– combined evaluation indicator for the commission.

Macrocriterion 2.   Environmental Aspects
Subcriteria:
– residents affected (a 40 to 8 km zone);
– residential areas affected;
– noise level per residential area;
– natural and manmade heritage sites;
– commission's combined evaluation indicator – environmental effects.

Macrocriterion 3.   Clientele and Site Region
Subcriteria:
– road access for the Ile de France region within a radius of 30, 45, 60, or
  75 minutes (1995 or 2015);
– road access for the greater Parisian region outside Ile de France within
  a radius of 30, 45, 60, or 75 minutes (1995 or 2015);
– road access for those outside the greater Parisian region within a
  radius of 30, 45, 60, or 75 feet minutes (1995 or 2015);
– population 2015 greater Parisian area at 60 and 75 minutes;
– ratio between the potential market in term of the 60-minute zone
  around the greater Parisian area;
– commission's combined evaluation indicator.
Subcriteria for the region selected:
– employment within a radius of 30 to 45 minutes in 1995;
– commission's combined evaluation indicator;
– accounting issues, employment, urbanization, activities.

Given the risk, the uncertainty surrounding the policies, a stability
plan is carried out. Two dimensions are used: the average scores and
standard deviations.

Multicriteria Analysis Grid

Regions	Sites	Macro Criteria Dimensions				
		Quality of Air Space	Quality of Ground Access	Environmental Impact	Clientele Base	Regional Employable Population
Upper Normandy	Plateau du Vexin normand	1	2	4.5	4.5	4.5
	Plateau sud de l'Eure	1	2	4.5	3.5	4
Center	Sainville	3	4	4	5	5
	Beauvilliers	3	4	5	5	5
	Santeuil	3	4	4	5	5
	Bonneval	4	1.5	2	2	2
	Marboué	4	1.5	2	2	2
	Arrou	4	1.5	4.5	1.5	2
	Crucey-senonches	1	2	4	3	4
Picardy	Vermando-villers	1.5	1.5	2.5	1.5	2
	Fouquescourt	1.5	1.5	4.5	1.5	2
	Hangest en Santerre	1.5	1.5	2	1.5	2
	Rouvillers	2	3.5	1.5	4.5	4

Chart of Weighted Criteria (or Coefficients)

	Quality of Air Space	Ground Access	Environment	Clientele Base	Employable Population	Sum of Weights
Air Transport Priority	4	3	1	4	3	15
Regional Management Priority	1	4	3	3	4	15
Enviromental priority	1	3	6	2	3	15
Undifferentiated	3	3	3	3	3	15

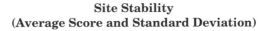

Site Stability
(Average Score and Standard Deviation)

The analyses reveal that a major international airport is technically possible at any of the sites proposed. No differentiating element is politically insurpassable. Yet to commission members, certain sites appear better located than others. Any conclusion is obviously simplistic and any decision frustrating, but the wager – and it is a real gamble –, is not a sure thing. Producing a proposal is in the commission's mandate; however, the decision belongs politically and exclusively to the political powers involved. The commission proposes; the government disposes.

The air traffic criteria lend a significant advantage to sites in the central region (exception: Crucey-Senonches) rather than those in Upper Normandy or Picardy. In these two regions, there is some risk of traffic problems, to varying degrees, with existing airports.

The criteria related to ground service do not favor sites like Upper Normandy and Crucey-Senonches in the central region. These sites do not have a new ultra-rapid (TGV) rail line.

Most of all, the commission believed that the basic choice, in terms of geographic position, should be founded on a market demand strategy and not on the supply side. One, the market demand strategy appears more coherent with the political will to follow market laws within the European context, an idea expressed repeatedly by successive administrations. Two, the supply strategy corresponds better to emerging sectors whereas the market demand strategy suits mature sectors. This would seem to be the case for air transportation (horizon 2015-2030).

Given these views, and on the basis of the elements available, the commission concluded that the best sites in terms of the clientele were the residents of the Beauce, the region closest to Paris. According to this hypothesis, the choice should be based on site optimization without any bias toward one region or another, as was the case with the commission and Beauvilliers. The commission defended its choice by pointing out that the classification process using most of the other criteria pointed in the same direction.

Distance to Sites from Paris Notre-Dame
(as the crow flies)

Sainville	64 km
Rouvillers	67 km
Santeuil	71 km
Beauvilliers	78 km
Vexin Normand	80 km
Bonneval	92 km
Plateau sud de l'Eure	92 km
Crucey-Senonches	94 km
Hangest-en-Santerre	100 km
Fouquescourt	106 km
Marboue	106 km
Arrou	113 km
Vermandovillers	114 km
Vatry	135 km

The commission recommended that the hypothesis of reserving the Beauvilliers site in Eure-et-Loire be validated and further developed by the appropriate goverment departments.

Actually, in each exercise using weighted criteria, the Beauvilliers site ended up on top. Sainville and Santeuil always followed. The Plateau du Vexin in Normandy and the Rouvillers site fought for the next rung on the ladder depending on policies (as seen in the weighting of the criteria).

This summary proposal had more nuances, implied certain limits and came with comments. The proposal must be understood within the context of "suggested sites". Deadlines limited the commission's choice of method and it could only call upon regional entities for lists of sites. Obviously this method does not claim to be exhaustive.

Another point to keep in mind, the conclusion is the result of a choice and weighting of criteria. These are the choices and weighting of the commission. The government will prove or disprove these choices and possibly substitute them with others. The method proposed will facilitate matters, should this be the case.

Ultimately the supply side of air transportation depends on how attractive the site is for airlines. This point can not be stressed enough and the market alone will decide on this point. Realistically, operators always prefer the closest site rather than the farthest, especially for short flights and medium-sized carriers. Experience in air transportation shows that it is difficult to nurture an airport designed for long flights without the support of a short- and medium-distance network. The conditions for a site far away thus remain doubtful and the possibility of operating three airports remains problematic.

The second airport in Montréal, Québec, reveals a great deal on this topic. The division of flights between the original airport (Dorval, 25 km from the city) and Mirabel (60 km) led to economic decline in the Montréal region as a number of operators turned to Toronto or northern US cities, especially New York. Openly declared a white elephant in the press, Mirabel never managed to gain a strong foothold in the world of air transportation. After February 20, 1996, however Mirabel became an airport for cargo, charter or night flights. The 1996 decision followed several in-depth studies which confirmed that maintaining intercontinental flights at a distant facility made Montréal vulnerable to the American hubs and its traditional Canadian rival, Toronto. The loss of more than half its intercontinental flights would have had an extremely negative impact on development in the greater Montréal region. Of course the Mirabel airport chapter also reflects the history of federal-provincial politics in Canada. Nevertheless, when the ADM, or Montréal airport authority, decided to bring transatlantic or international flights back to Dorval after twenty years, we were reminded that a problem can not be put aside easily.

The main advantage of this multicriteria analysis was that it imposed a systematic gathering of information and a collective thinking process that was far more rigorous than what could have been achieved without this logical framework (identification of sites, Defined criteria, Evaluation of sites by criteria, Testing sensitivity of results against the possible policies). Note that the overranking of the Beauvilliers site was such that no better classified site could be found regardless of the policy tested, as seen through the weighting of criteria.

In the end, although the Beauvilliers site was finally selected by the government, it may never really become the third airport of the Parisian region. Yet someday on the horizon, Beauvilliers might stand out as a necessity if Orly were submitted to more drastic restrictions than today's. For instance, if a major crash occurred then the situation might change dramatically. However Beauvilliers as site is a conjecture among other possibilities in what are fortunately still the "open skies" of airport transportation.

Five years later (2000) when annual growth in air traffic volume reached 7 percent and more for the Paris airports, the question of a

Site Ranking According to Policies

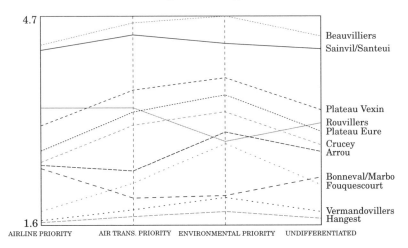

third airport reared its head once more. This time, we were called upon to ensure the methodological transfer of the scenario techniques previously employed. In the context of what is popularly called the new economy, the prospects for air traffic are more optimistic for the upcoming decades. The question now is clearly where to locate this third airport and perhaps even a fourth airport devoted exclusively to freight shipments.

8

BASF FACING AGRI-FOOD AND ENVIRONMENTAL CHALLENGES

The BASF case study shows how the future of agri-food and environmental challenges can be considered by the main stakeholders (corporations, farmers, consumer groups, etc.) over a long period (3 years). This innovative approach was initiated by one the former directors of BASF France, Bernard Lafourcade with methodological advice from Michel Godet (Cnam), and Pierre Chapuy (Gerpa). Of particular technical interest here was the use of the Mactor method. [1]

The Full Futures Process from Upstream to Downstream

Agricultural products occupy a significant rank among BASF's many sectors. In fact agricultural products represent over 15% of the BASF Group's overall activities. BASF manufactures ammoniac-based fertilizers, phytosanitary products utilised to protect crops, and food additives, including vitamins used in animal feed.

Within the European context, BASF's priority market is the French agricultural sector. The BASF Group currently leads the French market, which comes second to the American market worldwide. As a result, the agricultural products division at BASF France enjoys a certain independence and defines its own strategy.

Upheaval in the French agricultural sector in the early 1990s, caused by a redrafted joint agricultural policy and the shift from GATT agreements to the new World Trade Organisation led BASF France to rethink its strategy, especially product merchandising.

Relations between BASF and farmers follow the pattern of a traditional merchandising infrastructure – agricultural cooperatives, retailers and wholesalers – and require joint initiatives to supply the market better. Eager to consolidate its position on the French market, BASF sought to strengthen relations with the operations managers or officers of distribution companies in a lasting way. This step marked a break from the past when the focus was on purchasing managers.

Instead of offering some form of incentive travel (a common practice in this sector) and instead of drafting the umpteenth quality pledge, BASF decided to offer these small-to-medium-size business managers, who are usually caught up in day-to-day matters, an opportunity to reflect upon the future and the stakes which would determine their commercial success or failure.

---

1. This case study was prepared as a report, published in full as a Lips Working Paper (n°11) and developed in the article "Scenarios and Actors' Strategies: The Case of the Agri-Foodstuff Sector" by Bernard Lafourcade and Pierre Chapuy in *Technological Forecasting and Social Change*, vol. 65, n°1, September 2000.

A Participatory Futures-Thinking Exercise

Initially, a two-day seminar for training and futures exercises was offered to distribution managers. They were asked to consider as a group (suppliers and clients) the factors of both change and inertia that would affect the sector from 1997 to the year 2005, plus any pre-conceived notions on these two topics. After this exploratory phase, yet still within a workshop setting, participants identified the measures they would need to take to control some of the major stakes identified during the previous phase.

After the two-day event, participants had made enough progress to realise how effective this type of futures exercise can be. Yet they remained aware of the need to develop several themes, all of crucial importance for their own future. They also asked that the futures-thinking process continue under the auspices of BASF.

A summary of the two-day meeting was written up 1) to enable participants to repeat the process or something comparable in their own company and 2) to highlight priority topics for futures-thinking exercises. On the basis of these topics, working groups were set up including BASF operations executives and managers attending voluntarily from BASF client companies. This last group made up over 80% of the audience at the preliminary seminar in Venice.

Six meetings were scheduled over the following year so that each topic could be explored. The schedule allowed for the use of futures techniques (environmental scenario building, actor analysis, analysis of competence trees, etc.) in order to investigate possible futures in the agricultural channel, [1] winning strategies for distributors and, lastly, common goals on which both distributors and suppliers would do well to agree.

As part of the wrap-up stage, a seminar was held in Lisbon, in June 1996. Most of the participants from the Venice seminar attended as well as some important clients whose awareness of the exercise and its results was considered appropriate.

After the first phase, participants wanted to continue the collective thinking process by integrating new partners and by focusing on other major themes. As a result, the topics listed below were studied over the following two years:
  – changes in the distribution profession;

---

1. Channel, sector, channel, chain, stream... depending on the context any one of these three words may be used to translate the French word *filière*. Sector is broader whereas chain reflects the interrelatedness of the actors, or stakeholders. Channel evokes the flow of goods and services. For the broadest, general sense, the *food* or *agri-food industry* has been used.

– impact of new environmental demands on the profession within the agricultural channel;

– consumer expectations in food security and how these influence future behavior of players in the sector.

A steering committee made up of volunteers from the sector carried out most of the studies. The topics were presented during seminars which brought together approximately fifty distributors each time. The research or results were then published in different formats in different collections, *Futuribles International* and the Lips Working Papers and also in the journal *Technological Forecasting and Social Change*. Professor Michel Godet and the Gerpa consulting team provided the steering committee with methodological support.

The past three years of futures-thinking exercises, led by BASF Agriculture with the participation of its clients, may be broken down into three phases according to the following four principles:

1) choose procedures that will specifically answer distribution questions;

2) use methods adapted to the time and means available;

3) select simple, concrete, appropriable tools that encourage reflection and group expertise;

4) enlarge the circle of individuals involved gradually as the themes develop.

The Future: What Stakes? Which Actors? What Are the Key Questions?

This particular process stemmed from BASF's openness to using "strategic prospective" methods and tools to answer the questions really asked by real agricultural distributors, who are also BASF Agriculture France's clients.

Three main questions came out of the studies based on the intial seminar which had brought together forty-odd managers from agricultural distribution firms in the spring of 1995. The following three questions led to the first phase (1995-1996):

– what are the possible medium-term developments (horizon line 2005) in terms of farmers' expectations? *(N.B. these are the direct customers of agricultural distributors)*;

– given these expectations, what skills can distributors offer and in which areas should they develop?;

– more generally, what are the stakes for agricultural distribution in the ten-year period (1995-2005)? who are the main players on the field and what important conflicts can we expect?

After the first phase, the distributors wanted to consider the environmental factor and how both consumers' and citizens' demands related to environmental issues are evolving. Throughout the first phase during the spring of 1996, Mad Cow Disease [1] stole the spotlight from the environment and food safety in the collective thinking exercise.

The second phase included a futures-thinking exercise with the year 2010 as a horizon line. This phase was designed to enable participants to understand in detail how the environment [2] interacted with the various components of the agricultural sector in order to anticipate what would be at stake in this sector and to suggest possible medium-term answers.

Future visions developed during this phase also enabled the group to build three contrastive scenarios according to major issues.

Once again, the importance of food safety and the demands of actors downstream (agri-food, or agro-alimentary, industries and retail commercial distribution, especially mass distribution) in the agricultural channel became evident. Hence during the third phase in 1998, the steering committee decided to focus on actor analysis for the issues of food safety and the environment.

Methods Adapted to the Time and Means Available

The studies and methods chosen enabled participants to find answers to the questions raised within four to five group or steering committee meetings over five or six months of work. Whereas the initial two-day seminar used the workshop format so that forty agricultural distribution managers could all participate. After this seminar, thirty managers agreed to continue working as a group for four days staggered over six months.

The Delphi technique, based on three rounds of surveys, and the Régnier Abacus, based on a color-coded voting system, were used in the second futures-thinking phase. Some fifty agricultural distribution managers and forty BASF technical-marketing staff members were thus able to participate. The second phase was led by the steering committee which included fifteen people who met for four half-days over six months.

In the third phase, fifteen actors in the agricultural and agri-food sector spent four days carrying out actor anaysis on the topic of food safety.

---

1. The Mad Cow frenzy was not an environmental problem as such. It was the problem of a dysfunctional industrial channel and its control. Nevertheless, the Mad Cow Crisis revealed with particular clarity the notion of risk associated with agricultural and agri-food channels: food safety, conservation of the "environmentalized" production chains.

2. In terms of the struggle against pollution and harmful substances, nature conservation and protection of natural resources, preservation and enhancement of quality of life.

Simple and Appropriable Tools Reflect Group Expertise

The methodological procedures – especially the tools used – enabled groups of managers in distribution firms to work as a group by exchanging opinions, sharing information within a common framework and encouraging reflection through their professional expertise and that of other actors in the sector.

These thirty agricultural distribution managers built competence trees for their own companies according to type. The participants then profiled different types of farmers or growers, and detailed their expectations for technical areas, services or financing.

During phase 2, approximately 100 managers were polled. They gave their vision of the limits and opportunities created by the environment within their sector and of the development of these limits in the future. They also described the policies and courses of action that they envisaged adopting to meet the challenges on the horizon.

Similarly, professionals in the agricultural and agri-food sectors identified the food safety "battlegrounds". They also pinpointed the most important actors involved and the goals each one was pursuing. They created two synoptic tables that represent the influence capacity of the actors among themselves and the positions of the actors on each of the goals (see two matrices: actors/actors and actors/goals).

Lastly, after each of the three phases, forty-odd distribution managers and a few other participants (internal or external in terms of agriculture) attended a wrap-up seminar. This occasion enabled participants to present results plus test and complete the data. Joint working sesions have also helped group members to pinpoint pertinent areas for action in terms of relevence according to the stakes already identified.

Enlarging the Circle Downstream

Although futures thinking began with only agricultural distribution managers (co-ops and companies) and BASF Agriculture staff attending seminars, it gradually spread within the sector so that:

– a greater number (up to 100) of agricultural distribution managers could take part using the combined Delphi-Abacus technique during the second phase;

– farmers could be integrated as of the second phase;

– representatives from agri-food industrial groups (downstream) could join the steering committee during the third phase.

Fuller discussions were also held upstream, and representatives of several actors from outside the agricultural sector (e.g. consumer groups, public authorities, mass distributors...) were invited to react and participate during the wrap-up seminars.

The Future of the Agricultural Channel by BASF and Its Clients: the Three Stages of Futures-Thinking

Phase 1 (*) : BASF and Its Distributors: A Shared Future (1995-1996)
- Identify ongoing changes and the stakes implied for agricultrual distribution, e.g., technical factors, economics, and training.
Clientele
- 3 working groups made up of distribution managers; 4 one-day meetings over six months.
Tools
- Understand the current demands of farmers and anticipate their future needs: *morphological analysis*.
- Analyse the distributor's profession, strengths and weaknesses: construct *competence trees* (both future and present) of the distributors' offering.
- Detail the main battlefields of the future, inventory the goals of the actors involved, understand alliances et opposing interests: *analysis of the actors' game* inside and outside the agricultural channel.

Phase 2: Agriculture and environment with the horizon line 2010, "futures consultation" (1997)
- Understand the interfaces between agriculture and the environment now and in the past.
- Anticipate changes to the horizon 2010, reflect on measures that distribution can take.
Clientele
- A panel of a hundred-odd distribution managers (response rate 48 to 58%).
- An internal panel of 40 technical-sales representatives at BASF.
- A steering committee that unites distributors and farmers and experts at the wrap-up seminar.
Tools
- *Delphi-Régnier Abacus*: a Delphi questionnaire over three rounds (past, present, future) staggered over 5 months (votes and explanations), plus and efficient voting mechanism: the Régnier Abacus.
- A *morphological analysis* to construct *contrasted scenarios* of the relationship between agriculture and the environment, horizon line 2010.

Phase 3: Food Security and Environment, Analysis of the Actors (1998)
- Identify the battlefields related to food safety and the environment.
- Understand the manoeouvres of all the actors involved, analyse the forces active in the situation, pick out major conflicts, identify necessary or possible alliances.
Clientele
• A Futures-Thinking Group including industrial suppliers, distributors and farmers that expanded to include downstream players, e.g. independent farmers.
• The other actors: mass distributors, public authorities and consumer associations brought together by:
- agreements as to fostering thought;
- the wrap-up seminar to comment, criticise, complete the data.
Tools
Actor analysis (stakes, battlefields, actors present, goals pursued) using the Mactor method.

(*) Preceded by a seminar that brought together some 40 managers.

Environmental Issues (Horizon 2010)

As a result of Phase 1, environmental restrictions were pinpointed as one of the major threats in the agricultural sector. The regulatory agencies, e.g. Brussels, ministries, various boards or lobbies, and the agricultural sector itself, all of whom are in favor of the development of environmental demands, do indeed seem to be the most powerful actors.

Now more than ever, distributors must focus specifically on the environment. Of course the entire agricultural channel must pay attention, given that the environment, if not previously ignored, has only recently became an issue for many. Given the "recentness" of the issue, futures techniques were chosen accordingly.

The second futures-thinking phase for BASF and its clients ran from October 1996 to May 1997. Their objectives were the following:
– identify the main aspects of development for the medium term in the environment as a field;
  – evaluate potential consequences for the agricultural sector;
  – envisage possible measures to be taken.

In order to include a large number of distributors in this phase, the Delphi-Régnier Abacus was used. It combines the Delphi format in which a panel of experts answer and mail in a questionnaire with the Régnier Abacus, an expert consulting technique in which votes are color-coded and debated.

Later, on the basis of this analysis, which was complemented by contributions from experts and debates during the wrap-up seminar, three scenarios related to "agriculture and the environment, horizon line 2010" were generated. They present three possible interfaces between the agricultural sector and the environment, according to future visions of the profession.

Two Expert Panels

A hundred general managers of distribution firms (cooperative or commercial) considered representative of the diversity of French agriculture comprised the first panel. Categories included: major grain growers, specialized farmers, intensive or extensive breeders, arboriculturalists, vintners, and mixed-crop farmers... to name a few. The questionnaire was sent to a named addressee and the follow-up process handled by BASF's sales representatives/commercial agents in the various regions. The rate of return was high: 55%, 48% and 58% for the first, second and third rounds. [1]

The second panel comprised forty BASF Agriculture commercial technicians. They answered the same questionnaire, however, this

---

1. Some seventy percent of the managers polled answered at least one of the three rounds. Slightly more than thirty percent answered all three.

internal consultation allowed the company to develop the thinking process within its own walls, thus improving mutual understanding of the problems and enhancing the possibility of dialogue between BASF and its clients. [1]

The two panels were polled three times on a series of 22 questions presented as statements, for a total of 66 subjects consulted. [2] Ideas covered the past, present and future of the interface between agriculture and the environment, as well as the actions to be implemented. It was also requested that participants explain their choice briefly so that the problematique of the two populations surveyed could be detailed.

Questions were developed for the second and third rounds on the basis of the previous round. The following five themes were highlighted:

- general, social, economic and environmental context;
- overall development of the agricultural channel, and subsequent impact on interfaces with the environment;
- restrictions related to the environment imposed on the channel;
- external actors and their roles or actions in terms of the enviroment;
- behavior and any measures related to the environment within the sector.

Future Visions of Agricultural Distribution

The medium- or long-term visions held by agricultural distribution managers reveal a certain degree of consensus in their votes and explanations. As the following examples illustrate:

- by the horizon line 2010, distributors expect (read hope for) a return in public trust in agriculture. They also believe that accountability (trackability) will play a vital role in regaining the public's confidence;
- overall they do not believe that reinforced environmental restrictions by the year 2010 could challenge the paths and trend-based growth of agriculture; however, they believe in limiting the most harmful forms of restrictions;
- they do think that environmental restrictions will have a major impact on agricultural trades or professions by the year 2010 (e.g. generalization of expenses, statements of requirements, or bids tendered, subcontracting/contractualization, safety goals, etc.).

Through the futures-thinking process, it became obvious that the year 2010 held several major areas of uncertainty in which develop-

---

1. For this panel response rates obviously reached almost 100 percent.
2. For the second and third rounds, questions took into account previous answers.

ment of the system remains open and the distributors' opinions diverge on the following aspects:
   – societal agreement to pay for environmental quality;
   – importance and clout of the environment in international trade legislation, especially in WTO regulations;
   – development of specific areas of technology in the sector and the possibility that the technology will be implemented and accepted (especially in terms of genetically manipulated food processing).

This uncertainty also affects the behaviour of actors in the sector. Questions may be raised as to:
   – the sectorial capacity to develop agriculture that remains intensive and productive but is much cleaner than it is today;
   – the sectorial capacity to act as a coordinated unit in environmental measures and actions – obviously this implies significant and coordinated effort in terms of training and developing skills at the local level.

Building "Agriculture/Environment" Scenarios with the Year 2010 as a Horizon

On the basis of participants' visions of the future (either consensus or dissension) morphological analysis was used to draft full scenarios about relations between the agricultural sector and the environment up to the year 2010. Eight building blocks laid the foundation of these scenarios including major arbitration cases involving the economy, social demand, and environmental restrictions, e.g., regulation, commercial skill, demand, and their impact on agriculture, and farmers' taking the environment into account, possibly in their choice of agricultural techniques.

Three scenarios followed: the first is dark; the second, rosy; the third, considered trend-based by many.
   – 2010 "conflictual relations" between "agriculture" and the "environment": the relations remain conflictual. Public trust in the sector did not come back, partly because the agricultural sector did not become sufficiently committed to environmental protection, e.g. water and chemical use. Also the sector failed to respond to public concerns about food safety;
   – 2010 "rise of logical agriculture" ("integrated farming"): the profession and entire agricultural channel became strictly committed to taking back the environment and meeting society's expectations. The consumer's and citizen's confidence did return. This confidence is based primarily on contractualisation which became commonplace throughout the channel, and on professionalism among those active in the sector plus pertinent, broadly shared information;
   – 2010, "plurality and discomfort": Through the efforts of a large segment of the sector, consumers were reassured, however their trust remains shaky. The environment is still perceived as a growing restric-

tion by the majority in the channel. Some are still uneasy about any improvement in terms of the environment.

The first scenario looks black, while the second seems rosy. The third scenario, according to current dynamics, might be considered the trend-based scenario.

Mobilize Actors on Environmental Challenges

The BASF-client futures process was carried out in a very decentralized way. Several dozen distribution managers as well as BASF employees took part, thus the group could build and refine reference points and ideas which favored integrating the environment into their commercial activities. The Delphi-Abacus method further contributed to the collective learning process. Indeed, often questionnaire answers were developed during real working meetings at the distributors'.

The questions were ordered so that participants were surveyed in a manner conducive to "prospective" and strategy. The following questions exemplify this approach:

– What can happen in the future? Why would the system develop in one way or another?

– What could the impact be on my own activities?

– What could I do to prepare for expected developments or to anticpate them?

– What could I do to make the system head in a direction beneficial to me?

Results of the exercises, especially the scenarios for 2010, were presented several times to general meetings of cooperative or commerical groups, to boards of directors, or to technical/financial staff at training seminars. These presentations further contributed to making actors aware of the importance of the environment among the actors.

Mactor Analysis Applied to Food Safety

Given the tremendous impact of food safety issues and links with environmental problems, e.g. chemicals, pollution, new technology like genetic manipulation, the steering committee decided at the third phase (1997-8) to continue with agricultural distributors on the theme "food safety and the environment".

The objectives were the following:

– analyse the stakes, short and long term, in food safety and the environment plus pinpoint the consequences in terms of either demands or opportunities for the sector;

– know well the downstream situation in both food safety and the environment;

– make downstream segments aware of the upstream situation;
– find possible short-term action to take in conjunction with downstream actors.

The thinking exercises revolved around actor analysis, using the Mactor method.

Make the Entire Agri-food and Agricultural Channel Think Together

Given the significant role played by actors upstream in this channel, the steering committee decided to integrate actors from the agricultural sector as well as consumers and public authorities. Two methods were used:
– interviews with some twenty people during the initial survey;
– participation of representatives from agri-food industries in the Group.

The Circle comprised some fifteen people:
– distributors (half downstream in the agri-food channel);
– farmers;
– representatives from large food industrial groups;
– BASF members.

A smaller group within BASF worked in close cooperation with the Gerpa consulting group to prepare the meetings and prepare reports in between each meeting. Professor Michel Godet supervised the process.

Other actors, such as public authorities, consumers' groups and distributors were met during the initial questionnaire stage and became involved in the process during the intitial seminar and during the debate over the results in the fall of 1998.

The Four stages of the Mactor Method

The Futures Studies Group analysed strategies regarding food safety and the environment using the Mactor method. This method is structured around several components, which are described here as four distinct stages.

The first stage seek to identify the different dimensions of the problem, e.g. the issues at stake and potential battlegrounds, the main actors, and their objectives as they engage on the battlegrounds identified.

In this case, a detailed survey was conducted among all the actors (including industrial suppliers, agricultural distributors, farmers, representatives of the agri-foodstuffs industry and the mass marketing sector plus consumers). The Futures Studies Group then analysed and summarized survey findings.

The second stage involved analysing and describing the strategies identified, in two ways:

i) identifying the direct influences exerted by the actors on each other ("actors/actors" matrix), and;

ii) describing and measuring the position of each actor in relation to each objective ("actors/objectives" matrix).

This second stage was carried out as a joint effort by the Futures Studies Group, during two meetings lasting about ten hours altogether.

In the third stage, the two matrices are fed into the Mactor software for processing. The result helps us provide a more detailed picture of the relative positions of all the actors (dominant or dominated by others), to identify the objectives for which they feel the most concern, those which are controversial or not, and to highlight the diverging and converging interests reflected in the various positions.

Results are interpreted during the fourth stage. After this, of course, the results are made available to all the actors so that they can analyse them in the light of their specific situation or their own ideas on the issues involved, and draw out conclusions for their corporate strategies.

Ten Issues, Eighteen Actors, and Twenty-One Objectives

The basic construct for this analysis of strategies on food safety and the environment was built up in two stages.

First, some fifteen interviews were conducted with representatives from all segments, from industrial suppliers upstream right through to the mass marketing industry and consumers.

Interviews were thus conducted with farmers, representatives from agricultural cooperatives (with or without downstream activities), agri-foodstuffs manufacturers, representatives from mass marketing corporations and consumer observers.

In addition, documents were compiled to ascertain and include the positions of various other parties interested in the debate on food safety and the environment (conference reports, interviews in specialised journals, etc.), together with the results of opinion polls conducted among the general public and agricultural community.

The Top Ten Issues

Using these interviews as a basis, the Futures Studies Group identified the major areas where food safety and environmental issues emerge. These areas make up the "battlegrounds" where the future of the food system will be played out around the theme of food safety.

Depending on which way the stakes are played out, the story of the food chain will be very different. The same issues polarize the various actors as they take up their positions on a series of objectives and as they seek to protect their interests and achieve certain results.

Although the identification of the issues at stake is not used as direct input in the Mactor procedure, this is the foundation on which the two essential components of the method are established; i.e., the list of actors and the list of objectives.

The final list of issues identified by the Futures Studies Group included the following:
1. Consumer confidence in food products.
2. Consumer arbitration/participation on food quality and safety as well as on environmental protection.
3. Relevance and quality of consumer information.
4. Changing environmental and health standards.
5. Impact of new technologies (products and processes).
6. Degree of control over the system – or leadership – exerted by the mass marketing sector.
7. Upstream/downstream integration and increasingly frequent contractual arrangements in agricultural production.
8. Distribution of costs and added value within the system.
9. Overall competitiveness of French agri-foodstuffs (including environmental protection and food safety aspects).
10. Distribution of (legal) responsibility for food safety.

Eighteen Actors

Using the list of ten main issues, together with research data from previous years and findings from the interviews conducted in the first phase, the Futures Studies Group drew up a final list of eighteen actors who were considered key actors in terms of the future of food safety.

These actors were identified and differentiated in particular through the convergence or divergence of their positions with regard to the main battleground areas.

Two types of actors in agricultural distribution (cooperatives or commercial enterprises) were identified in this way, those with and those without activities which would therefore integrate them within downstream segments. It was considered that those with experience and responsibilities in the manufacture of processed products, and especially in marketing them directly to the public, played a different role from that of distributors who are only involved in supplying products or collecting them from farmers.

Similarly, the Futures Studies Group made a distinction between consumer associations and environmental protection associations. Although some of their concerns lie in the same areas, e.g. the use of plant protection products or pollutant discharges into water, their behavior patterns and objectives are not quite identical. In addition, they do not initially place the same emphasis on some food safety objectives.

The final list of actors identified by the Group was as follows:
 1. Industrial suppliers not involved in R&D.
 2. Industrial suppliers involved in R&D.
 3. Agricultural distribution (supply and collection only).
 4. Agricultural distribution with downstream integration in agri-food-stuffs.
 5. Farmers under contract to downstream agri-foodstuffs manufacturers.
 6. Independent (non-integrated) farmers.
 7. Large agri-foodstuffs companies.
 8. Small agri-foodstuffs companies.
 9. Mass marketing (including "deep", or "hard" discount).
10. Specialized distribution and retailing.
11. Catering.
12. National agricultural organisations (including advisory bodies).
13. National government (ministries).
14. Regional authorities (devolved State authorities, local government).
15. Supranational organisations (European Union) and international organisations (WHO – World Health Organization, WTO, FAO, etc.).
16. The media.
17. Consumer associations.
18. Environmental protection associations.

It should be remembered that this list, like the list of objectives further on, was drawn up by a Futures Studies Group in which the upstream segments of the system were represented only by the agro-chemicals and agro-pharmaceuticals industries through to the agri-foodstuffs industry. Neither the mass marketing sector nor consumers were directly represented. Both lists may therefore be slightly biased.

Nevertheless, these downstream actors were fairly widely interviewed during the initial survey. Moreover, the upstream actors represented in the Forward Studies group – especially the agri-foodstuffs industrialists – are in daily contact with those not involved in the Committee's discussions and are well acquainted with their positions and strategies.

Twenty-One Objectives

As representatives of their category within the system, members of the Futures Studies Group identified objectives by describing their aims on the various "battlegrounds".

On the basis of this initial material (about fifty objectives identified during the workshops), the group drew up a final list of twenty-one objectives. These were the objectives that it considered were being pursued by the eighteen actors identified above, within the major issues at stake where the future of food safety will be determined.

The wording of these objectives needed to be formalized as much as possible. Because the method involves positioning each actor according to whether they are very *much in favor, in favor, indifferent, not in favor* or *very much against*, the objective have to be formalized as specifically as possible to allow the position of each actor to be assessed correctly.

The final list of twenty-one objectives identified by the Committee was as follows:

1. Ensure that all products supplied by the system are harmless to public health.
2. Ensure adequate transparency (good practice report, traceability).
3. Make continuous objective assessments of the "household shopping basket" to check on food safety and environmental compatibility "from table back to stable".
4. Educate and inform the public on the issues at stake in the food system, especially technological issues.
5. Protect brand name image (especially as regards product safety, "tradition" and environmental compatibility).
6. Promote the "environmental and safety" content of distributor brands.
7. Shorten supply channels (from farms to consumers).
   [Reduce the number of intermediaries (processing, transport, retail outlets, etc.) between producers and consumers. In other words, "cut out the middleman".]
8. Develop quality labelling and promote local specialities.
9. Inform public debate, even by "fostering controversies" over new technologies.
10. Restore confidence in institutions as well as in health and environmental monitoring procedures.
11. Ensure both nutritional quality and flavor in products.
12. Introduce new and rational regulations.
    [Which must be well founded scientifically as well as politically and socially applicable and economically sound.]
13. Focus on new technologies to enhance competitiveness through innovation.
14. Ensure that added value accrues to upstream segments (primary production and processing).
    [Added value to be shared in such a way as to ensure the survival of upstream segments, especially by justly rewarding their services.]
15. Reflect competitive sales prices downstream in purchase prices upstream.
    [Ensure that downstream competition or lower consumer prices are paid for by all those involved in the system.]
16. Develop contract-based arrangements between responsible partners
17. Develop integration from downstream segments (distribution).
    [For mass marketing corporations, to acquire or develop the means to integrate food production or processing with its suppliers upstream.]
18. Implement incentives and eco-taxes for the agri-foodstuffs sector.
19. Clarify the legal responsibilities of each level in the system and provide information on these responsibilities.
20. Avoid maximizing the use of the precautionary principle.
21. Maintain control over the environmental impacts of the system.

Four Main Types of Objectives

Most of the twenty-one objectives may be grouped into four main categories:
- protection of the public interest;
- internal system operation;
- information for citizens and users, and public debate;
- the "rules of the game" for the future.

Public interest objectives

Some objectives are fairly general and relate to the public or collective interest. These include objective n°1 *[Ensure that all products supplied by the system are harmless to health]*, n°3 *[Make continuous objective assessments of the "household shopping basket"...]*, or n°21 *[Maintain control over the environmental impacts of the system]*.

Objectives concerning internal system operation

Other objectives relate more to the way the system operates. These include competition or internal technical or economic cooperation within the system, and include n°14 *[Ensure that added value accrues to upstream segments (primary production and processing)]*, or n°16 *[Develop contract-based arrangements between responsible partners]*.

Objectives concerning information and public debate

Several objectives involve education, information and awareness issues and public debate. Naturally they are important in confrontations between actors over the issue of food safety.

For example, objectives n°4 *[Educate and inform the public on the issues at stake in the food supply system, especially technological issues]*, n°9 *[Inform public debate, including by "fostering controversies" on new technologies]*, or n°19 *[Clarify the legal and penal responsibilities of each level in the system and provide information on these responsibilities]* all belong to this group.

The fact that several objectives of this type exist demonstrates the importance given by the Forecasting Group to public awareness in strategic interplay among actors, both today and in the years to come.

Objectives likely to determine the rules of the game in the future

In the end, a number of objectives will determine how food safety "battlegrounds" are likely to evolve in the future. The battles taking place around these objectives and the way conflicts of interest are resolved will contribute to the laying down of new rules, which – depending on the direction taken by the system – will be more or less favorable to food safety, to maintaining control over risks to consumers, and to technical innovation.

These same objectives will affect how the future of food safety plays out.

Examples of these key objectives are n°10 *[Restore confidence in institutions and in health and environmental monitoring procedures]*, n°18 *[Develop incentives and eco-taxes for the agri-foodstuffs sector]* and n°20 *[Avoid maximizing the use of the precautionary principle]*.

Two Input Matrices: "Actors/Actors"; "Actors/Objectives"

Professionals Exchanging Views to Fill In the Two Input Data Tables

How strategies on food safety and the environment are carried out will depend not only on the positions each one adopts for or against the various objectives, but also on the strengths of each actor, on the influence they have on each other and on the pressure they are capable of exerting on the system.

Two types of relationships therefore needed to be documented: the position of each actor with regard to the objectives, and the influence exerted by the actors on each other.

Two Mactor input data tables were filled in to obtain:
– the "actors/actors" matrix shows the direct influence each actor is capable of exerting on each of the others;
– the "actors/objectives" matrix shows the position (for or against) of each actor in relation to each objective.

These two matrices (see input data conventions below) were built up by the Futures Studies Group in the course of two working sessions, representing a total of about ten hours of discussion.

The discussions which took place among the members of the Futures Studies Group (upstream industrialists, agricultural distributors, agri-foodstuffs manufacturers) were extremely fruitful. All those taking part were able to explain clearly how they saw each issue, so that the discussions led all of them, as representatives of their "category", to give an accurate idea of their position regarding each of the objectives identified by the group.

By formalizing this input in table form after all the questions had been put systematically to all actors, on all topics, or objectives, the Futures Studies Group was able to build up a picture of the system and a jointly agreed "starting position".

This starting point, or common view, was reflected in the two matrices and subsequently used as input data for the Mactor processing package. This package not only provides different synoptic pictures, but also brings out various hidden parameters, which are otherwise masked by the complexities of the system (18 different actors and 21 different objectives, i.e. total of some 700 possible intersections between actors and between actors and objectives).

Conventions used to fill in the "actors/actors" matrix

The table showing the relative powers of influence of actors on each other was filled in using the following scale:

4: "i" is capable of jeopardizing the very existence of "j" is vital to the existence of "j";

3: "i" is capable of preventing "j" from carrying out his missions;

2: "i" is capable of jeopardizing the success of projects undertaken by "j";

1: "i" is capable of jeopardizing the management processes of "j" to some extent in time and space;

0: "i" has little influence on "j".

Conventions used to fill in the "actors/objectives" matrix

The table showing positions with regard to objectives specifies:

a) agreement or disagreement on the objectives, using the following conventions:

   (+) if actor "i" is in favour of objective "j";

   (–) if "i" is not in favour of objective "j";

   (0) if "i" has a neutral or indifferent position regarding "j";

b) four different levels of agreement or disagreement, revealing the degree of priority given to each objective:

4: the objective jeopardizes the actor's very existence/is vital to the actor's existence;

3: the objective jeopardizes the fulfilment of the actor's missions/is vital to the actor's missions;

2: the objective jeopardizes the success of the actor's plans/is vital to the actor's plans;

1: the objective jeopardizes the actor's operational processes (management etc.)/is vital to the actor's operational processes.

Highly Uneven Powers of Influence

Outline of the Methodology

The following table ("actors/actors" matrix) showing the direct influence of each actor on one another gives the total "influence" (horizontal sum of indice in the matrix) and total "dependence" (vertical sum) of each actor on the system. This makes it possible to calculate the indicators which position each actor in terms of "influence/dependence", thus showing their relative positions.

Influence may be exerted directly by one actor on another, but also indirectly through a third. These indirect influences (and dependencies) can be accounted for through a simple calculation to give a more exact picture of reciprocal influence.

Both the degree of influence and dependence of each actor and the feedback reactions that can affect them can be integrated in a single synoptic parameter expressing the balance of power. The more favorable this is to a given actor, the more power he has to influence both the way the system evolves and the other actors, and the less subject he is to the influence of others.

Actors × Actors Matrix

Actors	Suppliers with no R&D	Suppliers with R&D	Agricultural distribution with no downstream integration	Agricultural distribution with downstream integration	Integrated farmers	Non-integrated farmers	Large agri-foodstuffs Co.	Small agri-foodstuffs Co.	Mass marketing	Other distributors	Catering	Agricultural professional bodies	National authorities	Regional authorities	International organisations	Media	Consumer associations	Environmental protection associations
Suppliers with no R&D	0	2	1	1	0	1	0	0	0	0	0	1	1	1	0	1	0	0
Suppliers with R&D	2	0	2	3	1	1	0	0	0	0	0	1	1	2	1	1	1	1
Agricultural distribution with no downstream integration	3	2	0	1	2	1	0	1	0	0	0	2	0	1	0	1	0	1
Agricultural distribution with downstream integration	3	3	1	0	3	1	1	2	0	1	0	3	1	2	0	1	1	1
Integrated farmers	2	2	3	3	0	1	0	1	1	1	0	3	2	2	0	0	0	0
Non-integrated farmers	2	2	3	3	1	0	0	0	1	1	0	3	1	1	0	0	0	0
Large agri-foodstuffs Co.	3	2	3	3	3	1	0	1	3	3	3	1	2	2	2	2	1	1
Small agri-foodstuffs Co.	2	2	2	2	1	0	1	0	1	2	1	0	1	2	1	1	0	0
Mass marketing	1	1	1	3	3	1	3	4	0	2	1	1	2	2	1	2	1	1
Other distributors	0	0	1	3	1	1	1	2	1	0	0	0	1	2	0	1	0	0
Catering	0	0	0	1	0	0	2	2	0	1	0	0	0	1	0	0	0	0
Agricultural professional bodies	2	2	2	2	3	2	1	1	1	1	0	0	2	2	1	1	1	1
National authorities	3	3	3	3	4	4	3	4	3	3	3	3	0	2	2	2	1	1
Regional authorities	2	2	3	3	3	3	3	3	2	2	3	3	2	0	0	2	1	1
International organisations	3	3	3	3	4	3	3	3	2	3	3	2	3	3	0	1	1	1
Media	2	2	2	2	2	2	2	3	2	3	3	1	3	3	1	0	3	2
Consumer associations	2	2	2	2	2	2	3	2	3	2	2	1	2	3	2	2	0	1
Environmental protection associations	2	2	2	2	2	2	3	2	2	1	0	1	3	3	2	2	1	0

MACTOR

Actors × Objectives Matrix

Actors	Ensure health and safety	Ensure required transparency	Shopping basket assessments	Educate and inform the public	Protect brand name image	Promote distributor brand content	Shorten channels	Develop quality labels enhance local specialities	Inform public debate, foster controversies	Restore confidence in institutions	Ensure nutritional quality and flavour	Introduce new and rational regulations	Increase competitiveness through techn. innovation	Ensure added value upstream	Reflect downstream competitive pricing in upstream prices	Develop contracts and partenerships	Develop integration from downstream	Develop incentives and eco-taxes	Clarify legal and penal responsabilities	Avoid maximising the use of the precautionary principle	Control environmental impacts
Suppliers with no R&D	1	-2	0	-2	0	0	0	-2	-3	2	0	-2	0	3	0	0	-1	0	-2	3	0
Suppliers with R&D	3	3	1	2	0	0	0	2	-3	3	2	3	3	3	-3	2	1	1	3	3	3
Agricultural distribution with no downstream integration	2	2	1	1	1	1	-3	2	-3	3	2	3	2	3	-3	2	-3	-2	2	3	2
Agricultural distribution with downstream integration	3	3	2	2	2	2	-3	2	-3	3	3	3	3	3	-3	3	-3	-2	3	3	2
Integrated farmers	3	3	2	1	2	1	2	3	-3	3	2	2	2	4	-4	3	-2	-3	2	3	2
Non-integrated farmers	2	1	0	1	0	0	3	3	-3	2	2	1	2	4	-4	1	-4	-3	1	3	1
Large agri-foodstuffs Co.	4	3	3	3	4	-1	-2	0	-3	3	4	3	3	4	-4	3	-3	1	3	3	2
Small agri-foodstuffs Co.	4	3	3	2	4	0	0	2	-3	3	4	3	3	4	-4	3	-3	-1	3	3	1
Mass marketing	4	3	3	2	1	3	2	3	2	2	3	2	2	0	4	3	2	0	3	3	1
Other distributors	4	3	3	2	2	-3	2	3	0	2	3	1	1	0	4	2	0	0	3	0	1
Catering	4	2	3	1	2	0	0	1	-3	2	4	3	2	0	4	1	-3	-1	3	1	1
Agricultural professional bodies	2	2	0	1	0	0	1	3	2	2	0	1	2	4	-4	2	-3	-2	0	3	2
National authorities	4	3	2	1	0	0	0	3	-3	4	1	3	1	2	1	0	0	2	2	-2	3
Regional authorities	4	3	2	1	0	0	1	3	-3	4	1	2	2	3	1	1	-1	2	2	-3	3
International organisations	4	2	0	0	0	0	0	1	-2	3	1	2	1	1	0	0	0	1	2	-2	2
Media	0	0	1	0	0	0	0	1	4	-1	0	0	0	0	0	0	0	0	2	0	0
Consumer associations	4	3	3	3	0	0	3	2	3	3	3	2	2	0	0	1	0	2	3	-3	2
Environmental protection associations	3	3	2	2	0	0	1	2	4	2	1	1	-1	0	0	0	0	3	2	-3	4

MACTOR

The following diagram shows how influence and dependence can be mapped as a diagram.

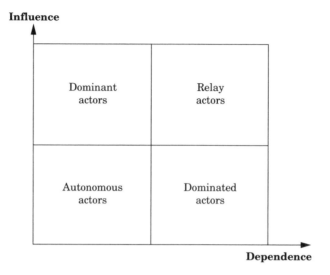

Dominant, Relay and Dominated Actors

This diagram, based directly on the input data compiled by the Futures Studies Group, shows the following:

– dominant actors, i.e. those who are capable of exerting strong pressures on the others without being subject to strong pressures themselves. These are primarily external to the system and include international organisations, the media and consumer or environmental organisations;

– relay actors, who are both highly influential and subject to strong pressures themselves: these are the other external actors (national and regional authorities) and, internally, the agricultural professional bodies, large agri-foodstuffs industries and mass marketing corporations;

– dominated actors, who have little influence on the others but are subject to strong pressures themselves. These include all upstream actors except the large agri-foodstuffs industries and distributors other than mass marketing corporations.

Only one actor, representing "catering", seems relatively autonomous (exerts little influence, but not much subject to pressure).

Which shows the indirect influence and dependence of actors on each other, is closer to the actual pattern of interplay. Here, three others have joined the group of dominant actors: national authorities, large agri-foodstuffs industries and mass marketing corporations.

Apart from the large agri-foodstuffs (AF) industries, all other actors in the upstream food economy are in a position of dependence within the system.

As both highly influential and highly dependent, the regional authorities and agricultural professional bodies (APB) are in an intermediate position. Either by virtue of their position as spokesmen for their profession at national level, or as public bodies with strong regional attachments, both play an essential role as relays in the system.

By comparing intersecting positions as represented by each pair in the analysis – such as industrialists, farmers and distributors – we can discern differences in their positions on the "playing field". Involvement in R&D (as in the case of industrial suppliers), integration with downstream segments (as in the case of agricultural distributors) and – to a lesser extent – integration within a sector of the system (farmers) increases potential influence within the system.

Relative Powers of Influence

The six influential or highly influential actors are mostly external to the system. These are the international organizations and national authorities, associations and the media, to which may be added the large agri-foodstuffs manufacturers and mass marketing corporations.

Two of the actors have average powers of influence: the agricultural professional bodies and the regional authorities.

In all the others, powers of influence are moderate to low; i.e. well below 1, or even very low as in non-integrated agricultural distribution, catering, suppliers not involved in R&D.

Taking average powers of influence as equal to 1, the figure for suppliers involved in R&D is 0.48; whereas integrated farmers stand at 0.53, and agricultural distributors with downstream integration at 0.61.

Involvement in R&D (distributors), downstream integration (distributors) and – to a lesser extent – integration within a sector of the system (farmers) increases powers of influence and therefore the actor's ability to exert pressure on the system.

The leading distribution companies score 1.39 and the major agri-foodstuffs industries 1.49. At the top of the power of influence league, the associations stand at around 1.9 and international organisations at 2.

Relative Influence and Dependence

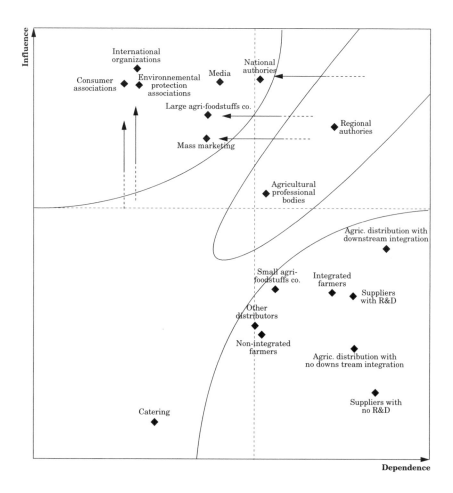

The arrows show the main directions in which secondary influences are exerted between actors. They show, for example, how national authorities and leading agri-foodstuffs and mass marketing corporations become part of the dominant group.

Relative Powers of Influence among Actors

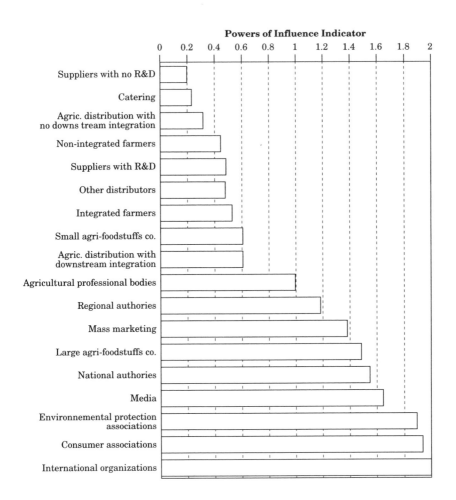

Example:
Consumer associations or environmental protection organisations have practically twice as much power of influence as agricultural professional bodies and three times as much as agricultural distributors.

Ambivalent Positions

One actor's position may converge with another's regarding specific objectives, while diverging from the latter on a different objective. If the same actor demonstrates similar ambiguity in relation to all the others, then he may be considered as highly ambivalent, and, preferably, should not be actively sought as a partner.

Overall ambivalence among the various actors was fairly moderate, with scores ranging from 0.18 to 0.72.

The least ambivalent, and therefore the most "dependable" as allies, include distributors other than mass marketing, international organisations and the small agri-foodstuffs manufacturers. At the other end of the scale, the most ambivalent, and therefore the least dependable, are suppliers not involved in R&D, the media, and environmental protection associations.

Ambivalence Ratings

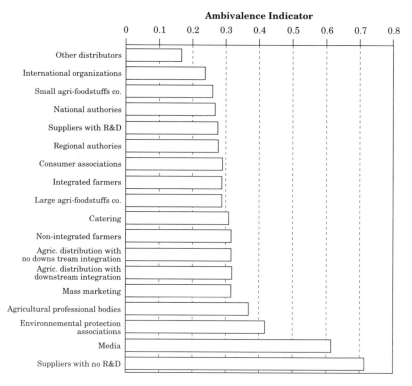

The more ambivalent an actor appears, the more caution should be exercised when considering alliances.

Legend: The ambivalence indicator - calculated here by integrating weightings by objective - may vary by convention from 0 (non ambivalent) to 1 (highly ambivalent).

Actors' Positions towards the Objectives

Outline of the Methodology

The data table ("actors/objectives" matrix) shows "valued" positions towards each objective. This reveals the extent of each actor's involvement in an objective, thus reflecting the importance they attach to each one.

The matrix of "non valued" positions (where positions towards objectives are shown only as positive, negative or neutral, regardless of degree) shows the number of actors concerned by each objective, whether they are for, against, or indifferent, and the number of objectives which concern each actor (for, against or indifferent).

In the matrix of "valued and weighted" positions, the power of influence of each actor is used to calculate a weighting for their involvement in the various objectives. This gives an idea of their degree of "commitment", or mobilization, and thus of their strength in relation to other actors.

Degrees of Commitment

Those concerned by all twenty-one objectives, and who are therefore to be reckoned with on all the battlegrounds, are the agricultural distributors (with or without food-processing) and the integrated farmers.

After these two groups come those highly concerned (by 18 to 20 objectives). They are the large and small agri-foodstuffs manufac-

Number of Objectives of Concern to Each Actor

21 objectives	– Agricultural distribution – Agricultural distribution with downstream integration – Integrated farmers
20 objectives	– Major agri-foodstuffs industries
19 objectives	– Small agri-foodstuffs industries – Mass marketing – Regional authorities
18 objectives	– Suppliers involved in R&D – Non integrated farmers
16 objectives	– Other types of distribution – Catering – Agricultural professional bodies – National authorities – Consumer associations
15 objectives	– Environmental protection associations
13 objectives	– International organizations
11 objectives	– Suppliers with no R&D
6 objectives	– Media

turers, mass marketing corporations, regional authorities, suppliers involved in R&D and farmers whose activities are integrated within a segment.

On the other hand, only six objectives concern the media. They are thus relatively independent in terms of the system. Obviously their stakes are elsewhere. The six objectives through which they interact with the system must be paid close attention, all the more so since they possess considerable powers of influence.

The least concerned are suppliers not involved in R&D (11 objectives) and international organisations (13 objectives). The remaining actors are still largely concerned by 15 to 16 objectives out of 21.

Objectives Involving the Largest Number of Actors

The objectives in which the largest number of actors feel involved are related to confidence, safety, controversies, and legal matters. These same objectives also have to do with informing the public: information, labelling and transparency.

Obviously, these are objectives of common interest, which are of concern not only to the technical segments, but also to the authorities at all levels, end users and associations.

Number of Actors Concerned by Each Objective

– Restore confidence in institutions	18
– Ensure health and safety – Ensure required transparency – Educate and inform the public at large – Develop quality labels, enhance local specialities – Inform public debate, foster controversies – Introduce new and rational regulations – Clarify legal and penal responsibilities	17
– Increase competitiveness through technical innovation – Avoid maximizing the use of the precautionary principle – Control environmental impacts	16
– Ensure nutritional quality and flavor	15
– Shopping basket assessments (safety, environmental impacts) – Develop incentives and eco-taxes	14
– Reflect downstream competitive pricing in upstream prices – Develop contract and partnerships	13
– Ensure added value upstream	12
– Shorten circuits – Develop integration from downstream	11
– Protect brand name image	7
– Promote distributor brand content	6

It would therefore be possible for the sector as a whole to establish cooperation strategies for these objectives, which are of concern to a high number of actors.

However, the objectives which concern the greater number are also those which will determine how the system evolves in the years to come, e.g. introducing rational regulations, mastering the precautionary principle or developing technical innovation.

Actors' Degrees of Commitment to the 21 Objectives

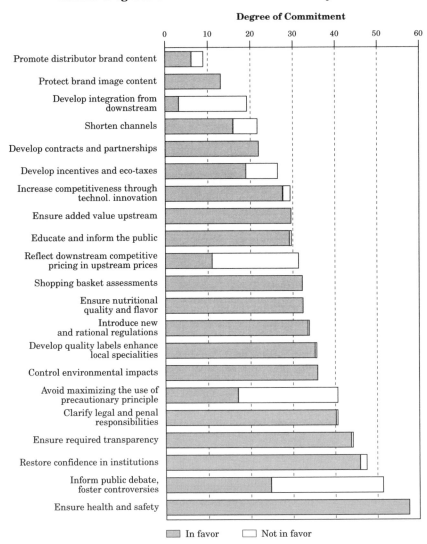

This table shows degrees of commitment (taking the balance of power into account), and which objectives create divisions (relative weight of positions for and against each objective).

On the other hand, the objectives which are of less widespread concern have more to do with internal issues of a technical, economic or managerial nature. These include distributor brands and brand-name products, integration from downstream segments and developing shorter channels.

When the balance of either power or influence are brought into play, we can go further and discern relative degrees of commitment for each objective for each actor.

The objectives which summon up the greatest degree of commitment, and around which the fiercest battles are likely to be fought when they are divisive – and which, *a contrario*, will rally the strongest support when they create a consensus - are those concerning safety, controversies, confidence and transparency, closely followed by legal matters and the precautionary principle.

Many Objectives Generate Agreement, Some Are Deeply Divisive

Depending on how positions for and against the objectives are distributed, they will generate either agreement or conflict in varying degrees. In addition, the actors involved in strategies specific to these objectives will have varying powers of influence. The scale of confrontation will also depend on the number of actors and their relative powers of influence over the system.

Divergence is obvious for the following two objectives, with about as many in favor of them as against:
– introduction of eco-taxes (7 pluses – those in favor – and 7 minuses – those against);
– ensuring added value downstream (5 pluses and 8 minuses).

Five of the objectives generate even greater conflicts of interest:
– fostering controversies (5 pluses and 12 minuses);
– shorter channels (8 pluses and 3 minuses);
– avoiding maximalist use of precautionary principle (10 pluses and 6 minuses);
– promoting the safety and environmental content of distributor brands (4 pluses and 2 minuses);
– developing integration from downstream (2 pluses and 9 minuses).

The table shows that several objectives bring a large number of protagonists into play and will therefore generate marked dissent. This is particularly true of the divisive objectives which are likely to weigh heavily on the way the system evolves in the medium- to long-term, and on the major mechanisms of arbitration:
– fostering controversies (17 actors concerned);
– avoiding maximalist use of the precautionary principle (16 actors concerned);
– introducing eco-taxes (14 actors concerned).

Other objectives are obvious causes of dissent within the system, but concern comparatively fewer actors:
- developing shorter circuits;
- protecting downstream added value;
- highlighting the safety and "environment" content of distributor brands;
- developing integration from downstream.

All the other objectives generate either a high degree of agreement (with only one against and all others in favor) or complete agreement (no opponents). This is particularly true of all the objectives of general interest to society as a whole – those concerning safety, confidence, transparency or environmental impacts, for example – and of those which are internal to the system, concerning partnerships, upstream added value and branded products (but not distributor brands). It should be noted that mass distribution needs branded products when consumers ask/clamor for them. However, this consensus does not apply to distributor's brands which independent farmers or small companies, but especially the other distribution channels oppose.

Varying Powers of Influence over Divisive Objectives

When powers of influence are taken into account; i.e., the capacities of those involved in various objectives to exert pressure and thus determine the outcome of battles over divisive objectives, this can reverse the powers of reciprocal influence between actors engaged in conflict or with opposing interests.

This does indeed occur for three of the most divisive objectives:
- avoiding maximalist use of the precautionary principle;
- introducing eco-taxes;
- fostering controversies over new technologies.

Moreover, these divisive objectives, together with the direction in which conflicts are resolved, will largely determine how the system evolves in the medium- and long-term.

Will the direction taken be rather favorable to the system; i.e., a tendency to rely on innovation, on possibilities for implementing new techniques and on the public confidence, or will the balance of power encourage trends in the opposite direction, with strict application of the precautionary principle, and constant uncertainty as to the risks or social usefulness of new technologies?

In the case of the three divisive objectives that are internal to the system, the powers of influence do not tip the balance either way between degrees of commitment hence:
- those in favor of shortening circuits are in the majority;
- those against reflecting competitive pricing downstream in purchase prices upstream seem to be more highly committed than those in favor;
- those in favor of integration from downstream are in the minority.

Towards Eco-Taxation

With the "eco-taxes" objective, the balance of power shifts towards those in favor of eco-taxation when degrees of commitment, where powers of influence come into play, are taken into account (+ 19 et – 8), but the situation is reversed when only involvement is considered (+ 12 and – 14).

"Developing incentives and eco-taxes in the agri-foodstuffs sector"

Involvement regardless of powers...		...commitment including powers of influence	
In favor	Not in favor	In favor	Not in favor
12	**14**	**19**	**8**

Actors for	Actors against	For	Against
		Suppliers, Large Agri-foodstuffs co.	Agricultural distribution Farmers
		National authorities	Small Agri-foodstuffs co.
		Regional authorities	Agric. professional bodies
		International organisations	
		Consumer associations	
		Environmental protection protection	

Those in favor (suppliers with R&D, large agri-foodstuffs manufacturers, public authorities in general and associations) outscore those against (upstream segments).

Towards Maximum Use of the Precautionary Principle

The pattern appears the same for the objective on "promoting the maximum use of the precautionary principle". This objective was originally entitled "avoiding maximum use of the precautionary principle", but was changed here to "promoting maximum use of the precautionary principle" for greater clarity. However those against were in the majority when classified by involvement (– 28, + 14), the situation is reversed when degrees of commitment (bringing powers of influence into play) are considered.

The index of commitment for those against this objective is – 17. For those in favor, who are often opposed to the introduction of new technologies, the index of commitment is + 24.

Those in favor of maximizing use of the precautionary principle are in the majority and hence defeat their opponents.

"Promoting maximum use of the precautionary principle"

Involvement regardless of powers...		...commitment including powers of influence	
Not in favor	In favor	Not in favor	In favor
28	**14**	**17**	**24**

Actors against	Actors for	Against	For
		Suppliers	Mass marketing
		Agricultural distribution	National authorities
		Farmers	Regional authorities
		Agri-foodstuffs co.	International organisations
		Agric. professional bodies	Consumer associations
			Environmental protection associations

Regional, national and international authorities and both types of associations outscore those against this objective (all of influence upstream segments).

Towards Permanent Controversy

In terms of "fostering controversies", the outcome (+ 15 and – 35) was more favorable to those against when involvement was considered (where bringing powers of influence are not taken into account). Bringing powers of influence into play merely results in a balanced situation, with commitment indices at + 25 and – 27.

These figures reveal a much weaker position than was previously thought among those opposing this objective.

The Three Divisive Objectives within the Sector

Three other objectives are divisive, but mainly concern issues that are internal to the system. Bringing powers of influence into play does not shift the initial balance between those in favor and those against these objectives.

Relative powers of influence as they emerge here from the interplay of strategies may be characterized as follows:

– favorable to those supporting shorter distribution circuits;

– favorable to those opposing any reflection of competitive pricing downstream in purchase prices upstream;

– unfavorable to those supporting the development of integrated activities from downstream.

"Supporting public debate, including by fostering controversies over new technologies"

Involvement regardless of powers...

...commitment including powers of influence

In favor	Not in favor		In favor	Not in favor
15	**35**		**25**	**27**

Actors for   Actors against

For
Mass marketing, Media
Agric. professional bodies
Consumer associations
Environmental protection
associations

Against
Suppliers, Farmers
Agricultural distribution
Agri-foodstuffs co.
National authorities
Regional authorities
International organisations

Upstream segments and public authorities on the one hand, and mass marketing, APBs, the media and the associations on the other (in favor of controversy).

"Shortening distribution channels (from farmers to consumers)"

Involvement regardless of powers...

...commitment including powers of influence

In favor	Not in favor		In favor	Not in favor
15	**8**		**16**	**6**

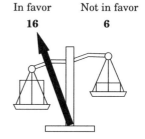

Actors for   Actors against

For
Farmers
Agric. professional bodies
Mass marketing & other
Regional authorities
Consumer associations
Environmental protection
associations

Against
Agricultural distribution
Large Agri-foodstuffs co.

Those in favor (local actors) outscore those against (agricultural distribution agencies and large agri-foodstuffs manufacturers).

"Reflecting competitive downstream pricing in upstream purchase prices"

Involvement regardless of powers...

In favor   Not in favor

14   29

Actors for   Actors against

...commitment including powers of influence

In favor   Not in favor

11   20

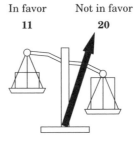

For	Against
Mass marketing & other	Suppliers with R&D
Catering	Agricultural distribution
National authorities	Farmers
Regional authorities	Agri-foodstuffs co.
	Agric. professional bodies

Those against (upstream) outscore downstream actors and the authorities.

"Developing integration from downstream"

Involvement regardless... of powers...

In favor   Not in favor

3   23

Actors for   Actors against

...commitment including powers of influence

In favor   Not in favor

3   16

For	Against
Mass marketing	Agricultural distribution
	Farmers
	Agri-foodstuffs co.
	Agric. professional bodies
	Regional authorities

Those against (upstream and regional actors) outscore mass marketing.

Main Results Regarding Food Safety and the Environment

Strong Actors, Weak Actors and Four Future Battlegrounds

Participants from the agricultural sector walked away with the following lessons, as summarized below:
- actors upstream are dominated;
- many objectives are consensual and only a few are very conflictual;
- mass distribution plays a lynch pin role,
- four battle lines will shape the future: distribution of added value, application of the principle of precaution, implementatin of eco-taxes, scientific and technical controversies.

Actors upstream are dominated

Actors dominating the system include public authorities (international and national), associations, the media and mass distributors. Contrary to popular belief, large companies in the agri-industry branded products play a role equal in importance to that of mass distribution. As a whole, with influence on the system is largely outside the actual agricultural channel of suppliers, agricultrual distributors and farmers.

Many consensual objectives and few conflictual objectives

Overall, the actors' role in food safety and the environment reveals a large number of subjects which generate consensus, e.g. "guarantee innocuity" "clarify legal and penal liablity", "master environmental impact" and "implement new rational regulations".

In fact, the number of conflictual objectives is small and includes "development of incentives and eco-taxes, redistribution of added value, controversy, precautionary principle".

In this context, those active in the agri-food sector must avoid two parallel pitfalls: first, hushing up diverging viewpoints and talking only about commonground; second, splitting up on a conflictual goal to the detriment of converging interests.

The pivotal role of major food distributors

Given the stance adopted by major food distributors on various issues and goals, they are in a position for double-dealing since opinions converge significantly between distributors and players upstream in the market as well as with the consumer, who seems very close to distribution. The role played by distribution in changing the system will therefore be a key one. Distributors will have to make some choices in order to ensure a coherent strategic front.

The four battles of the future: distribution of added value, precautionary principle, eco-taxes and controversy

If we take into account the balance of power among the actors the most involved in the goals that create dissent potentially serious conflict in four areas arises, namely:

– the main issue of the distribution of declining added value in the sector, given the consumer's decreasing willingness to pay plus the additional costs linked to food safety and environmental conservation;

– a very favorable balance of power for those who support developing eco-taxes on the use of chemical products, water usage, etc.

– similarly, a favorable position for those who support a maximialist application of the precautionary principle. This should generate greater restrictions in technical innovations;

– an equal balance of power in terms of controversy because the food safety debate is likely to become permanent.

Let us consider then constantly renewed controversies and a permanent state of doubt, as well as a rather maximalist application of the precautionary principle, lastly, the implementation of eco-taxes and increased integration of environment-related external costs by the sector. In a mature market, the struggle for added value will only intensify.

Three Topics for Strategic Thinking

This section describes the main points arising from the comments and discussions on these findings within the Futures Studies Group on food safety and the environment.

The Future Role of Integrated Farming

Discussion focused mainly on the likely role of integrated farming in crop production, over both the medium- and long-term. On the one hand, industrial users of agricultural products, who occupy an intermediate position in the sector, must ask whether integrated farming is likely to become the dominant norm in agriculture. This would obviously have an impact on agricultural practices and techniques, and in turn, on the nature of plant protection products and fertilizers and their sales volume. On the other hand, in the area of food marketing, would distributors decide to turn integrated farming to their competitive advantage, or would it become the norm for everyone, with only a few companies benefitting from their image as pioneers in the field?

Food Safety and Environmental Issues as a Key to Common Interests

There is also the question of the different actors' responsibilities with regard to food safety and the environment. Judging by the results and the number of topics generating consensus, it would seem that food safety and environmental protection are "pre-competitive" objectives. The fact that these objectives are supported by all the actors involved is a key to the economic future of agriculture and foodstuffs, and to long-lasting consumer confidence.

There is some doubt as to whether all the economic actors in the sector, especially in downstream activities, are fully aware of this fact. Some tend to take an immediate stance which parrots that of consumer associations – sometimes as a short-term reaction – and thus ensures favorable public opinion.

The Crucial Role of Communication

Communication and information, particularly for the general public, will therefore play a crucial role in shaping strategies on food safety and the environment. The public is often convinced that scientific knowledge on a given topic exists but remains concealed for economic or political reasons. This is the basic problem underlying the question of expert independence, or differences in expert opinion.

At present, inadequate information and communication is a fundamental problem. While food safety is improving objectively, perceptions of the food sector are increasingly negative.

The key question is therefore how to debate an issue which has not yet reached crisis proportions early enough to prevent it from ever developing into a crisis. What form should the debate take, and how should the public be encouraged to take an interest in it? There are three possible tacks to take in dealing with the public's lack of confidence: provide information, provide "science lessons" to increase public knowledge, or throw open a debate. The first two solutions have been tried, albeit unsuccessfully as measures were taken in haste, and with no attempt to anticipate results.

With regard to communication about what goes on in upstream segments, appropriate responses may include meeting controversies head-on or opening up farms and factories to public inspection. At present, communication on agriculture is often too fragmentary and many representatives of agricultural organisations are too defensive in their arguments, which tend to reflect an urge to justify past practice ("it's what we do already"). What the sector needs is to move forward and communicate differently as a coherent whole, rather than as isolated segments.

Four Avenues to Explore in Future Discussions

The Futures Studies Group felt that it would be useful to extend discussions in the four directions that were further explored by the four workshops organised during the Hendaye seminar:

– the future role of integrated agriculture and its consequences for the farming profession;

– guidelines for a charter setting out initiatives and responsibilities to be taken within the sector, regarding food safety and the environment;

– other practical initiatives for the short term, in areas that are common to all those involved in upstream activities (packaging, traceability, etc.);

– objectives and main lines of mutually agreed communication activities to be developed by the sector as a whole to target external audiences.

Summary of Discussions: Ten Key Points

Ten key points emerged from the discussions and workshops organised as part of the seminar in which the Futures Studies Group presented its findings to other members of the sector and external actors (public authorities and consumer associations). These ten points are summarized here, in no particular order of importance.

Dominant actors under pressure

Those who were not members of the Future Studies Group felt that the analysis of the influence exercised by the different actors on each other credited them with more influence than they possessed. One participant, Vincent Perrot, who heads a consumer protection group, felt that consumer associations had far less influence on the mass marketing sector than was suggested by the Group's findings. Consumers only appear to be able to act – and to put pressure on the industry – when major problems arise. Of course his impression would argue in favour of the need to anticipate problems that are likely to emerge.

Similarly, Nicole Zylbermann [1] thought that the amount of pressure brought to bear by public authorities, international organisations and consumer associations was overestimated. There is a possibility that this discrepancy in the perceptions of relative powers of influence stems from a lack of awareness of the way administrative bodies and government authorities really work. The authorities do not have absolute power, and they can be influenced, especially by the media and lobby groups. They are generally amenable to discussion and, in matters coming under their scope, they prefer to gain the best possible understanding of the interests of the different parties involved.

Exerting pressure on international organisations

The same is true for international organisations, which are not autonomous entities as the powers vested in them are those of their member governments. Anyone wanting to exert any influence on these organi-

---

1. Head of the health and safety department of the General Directorat for Competition, Consumer Goods, and Food Inspection, or DGCCRF).

sations has to take part in the major debates taking place within them. This means preparing material, identifying areas of common interest with other countries or governments, forging alliances, taking an active part in both formal and informal discussions, and following up the practical enforcement of all decisions in detail.

Active participation is particularly necessary in the technical and scientific discussions designed to establish a *Codex alimentarius* under the authority of the Food and Agriculure Organization (FAO). This *Codex* is being referred to more and more frequently by the World Trade Organisation (WTO) as a basis for its technical decisions, especially when disputes arise concerning the food industry.

Reversing traditional attitudes to agricultural production "from table back to stable"

Agriculture is experiencing profound changes as those involved become increasingly aware that they need to look at production from a completely different angle if they are to understand what is going on in the farming and agri-foodstuffs sectors. Farmers must realize that their job is to meet the needs of society, in other words that they have to match production to the markets associated with these needs. This means reversing traditional attitudes to agricultural production, taking downstream demand as a starting point and following through "from table back to stable" rather than the other way round.

Meeting the consumer's demand despite its contradictions and diversity

There is no single consumer profile, but rather a wide diversity of different and sometimes contradictory expectations which all must be met. The food system has to be in a position to meet many different types of demand, using organic as well as intensive methods, and by promoting integrated agriculture as well as local specialities.

Consumer perceptions of food safety and the environment are changing fast. For example, people are becoming more aware of some of the external costs or "externalities" involved in the food supply chain, particularly in the area of water use. Increasingly consumers feel that as their water bills steadily rise – as they have in France for the last few years – they are being made to pay for all the pollution for which the farmers are partly responsible.

In view of these changing attitudes among consumers, we need ways to gain a better understanding of how collective behavior patterns and consumer sensitivity are changing. What worries consumers today is "all those chemicals in the food we eat", but a clear distinction must be made between actual risks and risks as perceived by consumers.

Consumer attitudes can be contradictory indeed, as in the case of those who have high expectations with regard to organic or "natural" products, but completely different attitudes in other areas. A common example would be the amateur gardener who uses inorganic fertilisers and plant protection products to grow his own vegetables, [1] and whose attitudes could be summed up as "no chemicals please, except in my kitchen garden".

To address these fears and contradictions, reciprocal feedback between consumers and those involved in the agri-foodstuffs system is essential, together with regular debates organised through the various channels of opinion. The associations have a key role in this respect. Opportunities have to be created to listen to people's concerns, and provide, or seek, any relevant technical or scientific information that will answer their questions.

Food safety arguments should not be a competitive advantage

According to the foodstuffs industry – and this is corroborated by the other actors – while quality is obviously a valid argument for competing agri-foodstuffs companies, marketing approaches should exercise caution with regard to food safety and environmental protection objectives, both considered "pre-competitive".

Since any market is only as safe as its products, any suspicion regarding a given product – whatever the commercial brand – is a threat to the market as a whole. Marketing arguments based on product safety are therefore entirely inappropriate, since they are liable to have direct negative effects on other products marketed by the same company or by the sector in general. Similarly, from the consumer's point of view, environmental protection is no longer a negotiable option. In a sense, these two dimensions make up the foundations for sustainable development within the sector as a whole.

Seemingly, what the sector needs are more systematic efforts to develop integrated farming, so that this form of agriculture ultimately becomes the norm for the entire profession.

The pivotal role of the mass marketing sector

There have been many debates on the relationships between mass food marketing companies and the public. This sector will play a vital role in the future of the system, partly because of its economic and commercial strength, partly because of constant close contact with consumers, but also because of the acute competition among the different mass-marketing groups.

---

1. The same goes for heavy smokers or people who drink a lot of alcohol, or – in the United States – people who have no qualms about taking Viagra, despite the high risks which appear to be involved for those prone to cardiovascular diseases.

Contrary to conventional thinking in various quarters, the position of the distribution sector in the food supply chain, between the agri-foodstuffs industry and the consumer, is neither neutral nor intermediate. Survey results show that consumers see the mass marketing sector as a separate entity within the system, which is linked to the other segments of the food supply chain through the consumer's own concerns and demands.

Nevertheless, the discussions did bring out the various diverging interests involved, particularly with regard to the "appropriation" of added value, which determines how payment is made for services rendered among the different segments in the system, from farmers to mass marketing corporations.

The workshops organized during the seminar also contributed the following four points for further discussion:

Informing the public before problems emerge

The ultimate purpose of communication in this sector is to restore consumer confidence in the agricultural system. Priority actions and targets have both been identified: consumers should be given information on the means employed throughout the system to ensure food safety, and on the technical, scientific and managerial capacities used to do so. Communication activities should target the younger generations as a priority, together with teachers as opinion relays. Lastly, to prevent consumer rejection, timely information must be provided to the public on emerging technologies and their soundness (advantages and disadvantages), well before their marketing and general distribution is actually on the agenda.

Internal debate within the system — as a form of self-assessment — should take place both to evaluate past communication strategies and to analyse the reasons for their success or failure. These joint discussions should also help to improve reciprocal information networks and contents within the system, and strengthen its ability to construct consistent messages for external audiences.

The agricultural sector needs to take on more initiative and responsibility

The sector should not take action purely to meet legal requirements or expectations from downstream segments and consumers. A voluntary charter on initiatives and responsibilities should be established, which might include the following:

– the need to comply with current laws, regulations and codes of sound agricultural practice;

– encouragement to non-polluting techniques and efforts to reduce waste of all kinds;

– development of partnerships between different actors within the system, as a means of encouraging transparency, efficiency and proper observance of mutual undertakings;

– the need for communication strategies and as much transparency as possible throughout the system, in particular by implementing full traceability procedures, through to each finished product;

– commitments towards training and information for partners and other members of the sector to strengthen their involvement.

Upstream segments with enough leverage to implement practical actions in the short term

Other practical initiatives of common interest to upstream actors may be implemented in the short term, for example on traceability, certification or recycling. A short list is included:

– common reference documents could be drawn up on a partnership basis, to avoid tendencies towards over-specification from downstream segments;

– agricultural training and information on sound practices could be developed, particularly on product storage, shipping and handling, equipment adjustments and, more generally, on environmental protection techniques;

– approval criteria for agricultural distributors could be strengthened;

– more specifically, a number of immediate practical measures could be encouraged, such as rinsing out jerricans, recycling used packaging, organising visits for the general public to farm "headquarters" and head offices of upstream companies (e.g. farm visits or open house days organised jointly by farmers and members of the agri-foodstuffs industry).

Integrated agriculture will either become dominant or dormant

Clearly the big issue in the years to come will be establishing an agricultural system that guarantees food safety and environmental protection. The means to this end involve what has become known in France and other European countries as "integrated farming" *(agriculture raisonnée)*.

The working group on integrated agriculture concluded that if integrated agriculture is to succeed, the proportion of farmers adopting this method should ultimately reach 50 to 60%, but about 25% of all farmers should do so as soon as possible. This would counter any threat of marginalization or lack of recognition of the integrated approach in public opinion, and help to avoid unwanted effects, for example, on perceptions of product quality in relation to other types of agriculture.

If the integrated approach were to become widespread among farmers, the likely consequences would include the systematic use of specifications, compulsory traceability documentation, and possibly farm certification.

This shift would tend to enhance farmers' perceptions of their profession and strengthen their solidarity, as members of a group whose value is recognised by society at large. Training and information activities would be crucial to this change in perceptions. The use of specifications or certification procedures may in some cases cause prices to rise above the norm.

The countryside stewardship plans *(contrats territoriaux d'exploitation)* currently being discussed as France prepares to enact its new Agricultural Planning Law *(Loi d'Orientation Agricole)* may well encourage this type of agriculture. However, this does not mean that integrated farming should rely exclusively on such plans or programes to become established.

From Anticipation to Strategic Management Processes

Futures Research and the Sectorial Procedure

Futures-thinking exercises proved extremely valuable as a means to animate interprofessional debate or discussion in which highly competitive actors find themselves obliged to consider one another's opinions.

Indeed, at the initial meeting in Venise, we brought together fifty-odd distributors who often compete amongst themselves. However, the methods adopted not only generated a series of avenues to explore together, as a group, but also encouraged half of the participants to ask for further futures-thinking opportunities.

During later sessions, it became clear that the tools enabled us to wipe out conventional thinking or preconceived notions, poll the actors present, list future issues. Once again, we allowed each participant to tease out avenues or immediate measures to be taken according to his/her own company.

BASF particularly appreciated the fact that a large number of companies located in all four corners of France were open to having their managers participate in this futures-thinking exercise and enrich their own files. In fact, we polled participants on their participation while consulting them on the environment through the Delphi questionnaire method.

We also measured the importance of outside input from interviews with experts, specific speeches or discussions during meetings of the steering committee, *extramuros* skills or any research, in terms of enriching files.

Lastly, when a theme surpasses that set out at the beginning of the exercise, it is particularly important to expand the circle to actors other than those intially selected. In this case, experience taught us that by opening up a circle composed primarily of distributors to include other partners (farmers, industrialists, mass distributors), we gained in power through a broader base of confrontation.

Futures-Thinking Exercises: the Strategic Utility for BASF

The initiative BASF undertook to meet its distribution partners' expectations through a futures-thinking process makes perfect sense for any corporate leader who wants to anticipate an uncertain future within the context of the global agricultural economy, the expected upset caused by EU structures and the arrival of the euro.

Given France's privileged geographical position, the French agricultural context provides the fullest range of the various aspects of European agriculture. The French scene thus serves as a point of reference for the BASF Group whether in terms of increasing productivity, enhancing the quality of agricultural production or improving agronomic procedures while integrating various ecological, environmental and economic characteristics.

The lessons learnt from this futures-thinking exercise helped BASF clarify its perception of a number of hypotheses. The company were thus able to contribute handsomely to the collective thinking process. Examples cover several fields; for instance, in terms of developing basic research, the BASF Group had decided several years previously to commit to genetic engineering as a means of improving agrochemical processes.

Reflection confirmed our position and encouraged BASF to take specific orientations. The decision to invest heavily in R&D led BASF to sign agreements with several research centres in Switzerland and Germany, in 1989. The initial thrust of the research consisted of injecting plants with genes capable of resisting chemicals, e.g. herbicides, infections or insect attacks. However, this had not been BASF's original priority.

BASF's goal is to improve its knowledge of genomes, genetic mutation and the introduction of genes into vegetables as well as come up with concrete applications that will complete the action of fertilisers and phytosanitary products on plant growth and quality.

On the basis of future needs, BASF decided to orient its research toward a more complex field. More specifically, researchers are making plant behaviour change so as to meet chronic or sporadic stress situations caused by climatic or pedological phenomena or other external factors.

Another research area involves using plants as tools capable of synthesising and creating interesting substances that will improve food products or health, intensify protein production and develop other substances such as aminoacids.

BASF has also opted to continue developing management of environmental factors, notably through intensified research on nitrification inhibitors designed to manage nitrogen better. There is also the battle against insects using "sexual confusion", a technique which helps limit reproduction.

Futures thinking has helped us not only in R&D but also more locally in making decisions and reorienting our merchandising procedures in the French agricultural context.

BASF has thus integrated the notion of a production channel. The company is committed to taking into account each crop in its marketing and commercial structures in France. This "crop" process, implemented for flower, vegetable and tree growing enables BASF to offer distributors and growers a full range of products so that the entire channel can meet new needs. The same process has just begun in the French winegrowing market.

BASF has also redefined procedures in terms of grains and industrial crops by developing the "channel approach" which goes beyond the farmer and coop to include the processor, the regulator, and tomorrow, even the superstore or any other agri-foodstuff distributor.

While progressing through these various stages, BASF strengthened ties with its distributor-clients. The company is currently moving from a "buyer-seller" to a "actor-actor" relationship. In fact, the "channel" *(filière)* approach led us to integrate parameters from expertise garnered at different levels. The readymade solution is simply not satisfactory anymore.

Indeed, alongside its partners, BASF learnt to evaluate what will be at stake in the future. With each partner, we tried to study the best positions to take in order to meet farmers' expectations.

Of course, "conventional thinking" and "preconceived notions" die hard. As creatures of habit, we all change and break down barriers slowly.

Futures Thinking and Managing Corporate Collaboration

Beyond the initiatives mentioned, we found it necessary to take into account how BASF could appropriate the results of the procedure its collaborators had undertaken. Obviously a new strategic orientation may be acquired intellectually with little trouble; however, its implementation by the players involved requires an adapted, voluntary, managerial approach. On this point, BASF suggested that perhaps they were too optimistic and did not integrate enough corporate actors in the futures exercise.

This was the conclusion that we reached after two years of work. Although the team which made up the strategic orientation committee participated fully in the futures-thinking process at BASF France, and teased out the guidelines for a new approach at BASF, most corporate collaborators did not readily see the basic changes that this process would have on their own behavior.

Through daily contact with their usual cohorts, both internal and external, our collaborators often remained "under the influence of the event". It should be added that the increased power of ecological restrictions, the Mad Cow scare and the uncertainty in which famers live, contributed to this type of attitude.

The question that corporate managers and their mangement team must ask when starting a futures-thinking exercise is how and when should corporate collaborators participate. The thinking process does not stop at the highest echelon of the company instead it must be cultivated at each level of the organisation likely to set up its own managerial procedure.

The notion of a channel obliges technical teams, assigned the task of implementing a developmental program for new products, to take into account new factors which may require additional partners and lead to setting new goals. The same may be said about a team mandated to develop agri-business in the grain or any other crop sector with a clientele concerned about the future of products on the market.

Marketing teams must also integrate this new approach in drawing up their strategy. Of course many other examples may be found up and down the corporate ladder.

In fact, two years ago, the need to integrate the channel approach throughout the company led BASF to commit to a follow-up program as part of training for executives. BASF hopes to develop managerial aptitudes in each executive by accentuating management by leadership so that they will take on a project individually and ensure its implementation as an entrepreneur rather than as a mere group leader or the supervisor of old.

The futures process provides the means to develop this managerial aptitude and the individual capacity of each executive in his/her own position to anticipate future developments, identify as well as implement the appropriate responses and initiatives.

Futures thinking has become part of the BASF France way of doing business on a daily basis. Naturally the company is eager to take its research futher in order to anticipate decisions better. Consequently, in 1999, we will continue working on the theme of food safety within a Circle expanded to include mass distribution representatives. Their inclusion should help determine the impact of distribution in setting up a statement of requirements that links all actors along the agri-food channel. Hopefully, all of the Futures Studies Group's endeavors will serve to judge the performance of products or techniques better.

Furthermore, within the company, BASF has decided to improve its ability to appropriate the new marketing orientations of our collaborators. BASF will try to improve its ability to take into account the expectations and reactions of actors or stakeholders playing a role in the company and with whom it shares both the same stakes and battlefield.

9

THE HUMAN FACTOR MAKES THE DIFFERENCE

Thinking collectively about the present and future is an important step, but reflecting upon changes in the environment should not become an end in itself. Similarly, we do not want to shine a spotlight on the exterior while leaving the interior in the dark. Yet sometimes people do just that and fool themselves by believing that the future of a company depends on smart strategic choices alone without any change whatsoever in internal structures or behaviors. However, this necessary transformation of structures and behaviors is conditioned by the answers to the following basic questions:

– How far should the subsidiarity principle be applied? In other words, should we decentralize or "recentralize"?

– How should we weigh and balance out short-term profitability and long-term development objectives?

– Should financial profitability and employment be considered a restriction or the result of a strategy?

The last question often proves crucial for the future. Should a company subordinate its strategy to maintain current staff, structures and behaviors? If so, what form of development should be promoted and what results should be expected? What strategic deficits should be accepted? In the opposite case, what are the consequences on the personnel, qualifications and structures according to the needs expressed in the strategy? Simply asking the question points to the answer: Activity is what creates employment and employment should not hold development strategy in check.

Any change in structures and behaviors depends not only on external changes but also on a corporation's identity, culture and history. In general, environmental complexity of the environment seems to be more readily mastered by simple structures, organized in a network according to the subsidiarity principle. This change sparks a veritable "mental revolution". In this chapter, we consider the revolution that change implies and then seek the out keys needed to motivate people. Motivation is a permanent challenge yet motivation makes everything possible. The future is truly the fruit of human will and initiative, as the examples presented herein have shown. Each example bears the same message: The difference between successful and unsuccessful companies lies in the human factor. A seemingly obvious fact of life, the human factor was found to be at the root of excellence and growth in a study carried out by an international consulting firm in 1998. [1]

Out of what we call "1001 individual initiatives", one movement might rise up in which people march toward the future differently. This is the hopeful message our last chapter gives.

---

1. Bain & Company France *Lettre d'information*, n°7, 1998.

Our "Growth Champions"...
Their Performance and Related Myths
Results from a 1998 International Comparative Survey
of 9,000 Companies
(Carried out by Bain and Company in conjunction
with Business Week magazine)

Growth does not depend on the economic sector.
In fact, only 20 percent of our "champion companies" are active in the so-called high growth sectors.
Growth does not come from size; in fact the correlation is low.
Growth does not depend on technological breakthroughs; in fact only 6 percent of the "champs" are in the high-tech sector
Lack of opportunity is not an obstacle or barrier to growth.
Fewer than one-quarter of executives give this reason or excuse.
Therefore it is not economic sector, size, technological breakthroughs, nor is it the opportunities available to the company that determine growth.
It is managerial behavior that makes the difference.
What are the priorities that "growth champions" set?
1. Focus on core competences and a leadership position
2. Seek out ways of expanding into neighboring activities or areas
3. Maximize or fight turbulence in the sectorial environment
4. Eliminate "growth inhibitors" within the company in a systematic way.

Changing Worlds and Adapting Structures and Behaviors

Strategic flexibility is a firm's capacity to adapt to changes in its environment. (This statement assumes that the firm has made a permanent effort in technological, commercial and economic foresight.) However, we know that flexibility does not suffice. Remaining competitive requires performance in terms of the price and quality of products or services. Of course performance must be constantly renewed through innovation. It soon becomes obvious that there are a multitude of possible strategic consequences of changes within a company's environment.

Without even attempting to be exhaustive in this chart, we have listed nine main trends that characterize change in the general business environment. Also indicated are the consequences for the organization and its corporate strategy.

Main Environmental Trends and Strategic Consequences

Uncertainty in the environment not only requires flexibility but also reinforces the need for a vision and projects, even if only to figure out where a company stands in terms of its objectives.

Environment	Strategic Consequences
1. Uncertainty	Flexibility
2. Interdependence and complexity	Overall view and simple structures
3. International Imbalances	Regulation via information and financial networks of "world systems"
4. Globalization	Internationalization of activities Local implantation
5. Irregular unequal growth	Struggle for market shares, Productivity, quality, differentiation
6. Technological Change + 7. Deregulation	Progress in processing rather than in products New competitors
8. Economy based on diversity Mass production of variety + 9. Autonomy, differentiation	Multi-small is profitable Independent, responsible teams Entrepreneurs and intrapreneurs

END OF HABITS
START OF MENTAL REVOLUTION

In the face of uncertainty, the rise in interdependence of phenomena makes understanding them all the more complex. More and more any action that should be taken requires panoramic vision. Actually, in attacking environmental complexity, complicated structures are definitely not needed; simple, light forms are preferable.

Persistent international imbalances (whether geopolitical, ecological, demographic or economic) within an international regulatory vacuum are compensated in part by new forms of regulation and new "world-systems", to use Fernand Braudel's term. The international financial network operates around the clock as well as around the planet. The same goes for information. Various international disturbances and non-tariff trade barriers have not prevented globalization, e.g. processes, products, markets, from developing and spreading. Every single year since 1945 has seen manufactured or finished product export figures rise faster than production figures. Companies are obliged to operate on a world scale. The result is globalization of the executive suite. However it takes time for foreign executives to be trained and "imbibed" in the corporate culture.

Basically the following three trends combine to stimulate competition:

1) irregular growth;

2) technological changes in processes, and;

3) deregulation.

In fact the struggle for market share is fought on the basis of the best price/quality ratio. Yet a company must simultaneously stand out, strive for greater automation wherever possible in order to reinforce productivity (progress in terms of process) and, last but not least, confront new competitors.

The human (and organizational) factor remains determining in terms of competitiveness. Equally decisive is the use of new information technology and communication networks according to the philosophy of "small is beautiful AND profitable". We have already entered the age of economic diversity so that the future trend is one of mass production of diversity and profitable production on a small scale. This technical and economic development is in sync with independence and differentiation. What does this mean for companies? It means setting up small, autonomous teams of responsible intrapreneurs. In this sense, new forms of management will progressively emerge and be seen in attitudes and behaviors throughout the organization.

External and Internal Front: Same Challenge

For many struggling companies, the reasons for sinking into the red can be found in internal managerial inadequacies rather than in the storm raging outside. As on the playing field, there can be no winning team without a good captain. Similarly strategy requires more than just the right game plan. It also needs a trained, motivated team to do the job. Hence the internal and external challenges of a company are really one and the same opponent in a battle that must be won on both fronts simultaneously or not won at all. In other words, when faced with strategic environmental changes, the future of a corporation depends largely on its internal and external strengths and weaknesses.

Of course the distinction between "strategic gap" and "performance gap" must be made, without forgetting "management gap". Let us consider, as an example, the following question: Is it absolutely essential to grow in order to be profitable?

In the late 1970s, automakers believed that only two or three large manufacturers in the world would survive up to the year 1990! In the name of this myth of minimum critical size within the global marketplace, PSA (Peugeot group) embarked on its Chrysler adventure and Renault followed suit with AMC (American Motor Car). Fiat, on the other hand, restored its competitiveness by withdrawing from the American market and refocusing its efforts on Europe. It may well be that the scale effect is becoming less and less dependent upon size, given the existence of network organizations.

In reality, smaller companies with better business figures do still exist in the same sector. The correct question, revised version of the previous one, is how can a company be profitable given its current size? In other words, the strategic gap; i.e., the ratio between growth objectives and volume, is perhaps less important than the performance gap. What counts is being profitable at the level where you are. It is worth noting that adopting a more Eurocentric strategy (even if only due to the enlargement of Europe) should not blind managers to the fact that in certain mature sectors like automobiles or electronics, an international company owes it to itself to be dominant at least in one of the poles of the triad and present in the other two, as Ken'ichi Omae (1985, 1991) demonstrated.

One of the conditions required to close the performance gap is, of course, catching up with the "management gap". The latter poses the question of adapting structures and behaviors within the company. The main factor limiting corporate development is the human factor; i.e., the time required to train men or women and create efficient teams. Yet wherever there is weakness in management or strategy, there is an opportunity to close the gap and catch up.

Of course management also implies considering an individual's fulfillment in his/her personal and professional lives, which are distinct yet indissociable. In this sense, during the 1980s, firms were able to reclaim a certain element of citizenship over and above their economic objectives. People were able to find a privileged place of fulfillment and shared objectives in the workplace. In many cases, however, the dynamics wound down, due to restructuring in the 1990s or because the procedures did not survive the departure of the individuals who had introduced them. Moreover, the general corporate climate deteriorated greatly in companies during the 1990s versus the 1980s. It seemed that the dream had faded, leaving many disillusioned.

In these circumstances, how can we (re)motivate people? Before attempting an answer, let us go back to the history of a corporation, or its roots, because the future always depends partly on the past.

Roots of the Future: Identity and Corporate Culture

Contrary to the popular belief held until recently, it is impossible to "mix and match" human resources like stock parts or machinery in modern corporations. People want to know why they are working, what their efforts achieve, and what kind of future they can expect within the company. They have ideas about what they do and react to the behavior of their supervisor, team leader or colleague.

In order to understand why certain organizations succeed while others flounder, we need to pay attention to the culture, history and identity of each organization. As the popular expression goes: To know where you are going, you have to know where you came from. Marc Mousli (1984) summed up this powerful idea in the following analogy: identity is to the company as personality is to the individual. Identity is recognition by difference and is defined by opposition. In this sense, identity operates on the zone between what is self and what is "other". Identity provides a sense of belonging and even existence to the corporation and its members (employees and executives) hence it offers them self-recognition through their differences. This identification process may be expressed through a logo, e.g. Renault's lozenge or Coca-cola's rounded lettering, through a successful product or a technological process that is solidly linked to the organization.

The corporate culture is a set of shared values, know-how, collective living habits, as well as a fairly strong sense of identity within each member or employee. The culture is based on a corporate image, collective memory, and, in many instances, on stories, myths and even legends. The organizational culture may be summed up in a few impactful words, e.g. quality, daring, tradition, and innovation. The exact words may vary from one organization to another but are not actually decreed anywhere. Remember, it took years to imprint them on the "corporate genetic code"!

Yet the corporate culture should not become a cult. All too often a corporation becomes a new church and the founding president becomes a self-styled prophet dictating his commandments. The nuance between religion and sect is not easily made, hence we find individuals scrambling to fit a mold, e.g. the white shirt plus blue blazer and red tie uniform, and giving the impression that they exist only for the glory of the company, now a totalitarian state of sorts. One anecdote describes the reaction of a Japanese businessman who landed in Paris with the firm conviction that Japanese civilization was superior to the French or, more broadly, the Western. As he put it: "We think that in all our activities we have reached the "five zeros"; i.e., zero defects, zero breakdowns, zero delays, zero inventory and zero dust. However after living for a while in your country [France], I realized that our system also had its flaws: zero vacation, zero humor, zero sex, zero space and zero freedom."

The vital harmonious relationship between strategy and culture must necessarily flow through structure. In the trilogy – structure, power and environment –, power is attacked by changes in the environment and defends itself through structures. One characteristic of structures is that they become the property of those who actually constitute the structures. In fact they tend to grow rigid for precisely that reason.

Adaptive or anticipatory structures? The debate continues and the jury is still out. Nevertheless Igor Ansoff's suggested dual structure, in which new forms coexist with old ones, seems realistic. Once again we have to consider that structures are influenced not only by strategy statements and the corporate environment but also by the intricate weave of company history and culture.

There is a conception of the company, its policies, goals, priorities and power plays behind the structures. As a result, an efficient structure must be adapted to the culture of a company as well as to the type of behavior displayed by its actors. Any reference to structure must be linked to behavior and management, but obviously there is no ideal structure just floating around somewhere. Blue chip and Fortune 500 companies have simply managed to harmonize strategy, culture and structure. If future performance depends on this harmony then past performance influences strategy, unites structure and shapes culture.

Subsidiarity and Simple Structures to Manage Complexity

Changes in the environment demand quick reaction time and flexibility. These capacities stem primarily from corporate structures. Now structures must not only adapt to such changes but also anticipate them because the inherent inertia in structures slows down adaptation to change.

Any and every structure runs the risk of becoming sclerotic, even fossilized, if it does not undergo reorganization and redistribution of its advantages and powers. Wherever possible, companies must introduce "habit busters", or factors to break habits within structures. Between the rigidity-sclerosis described above and agitation-alibi, which stirs up preoccupations and inefficiency, there has to be a suitable pace of transformation that can respond to changes in the corporate environment without upsetting the established balance unnecessarily. Seeking harmony implies a voluntary process which takes time and inertia into account. However these inertia should be lesser if we are dealing with simple, light structures.

Let us apply to corporations what has become known as the "subsidiarity principle", a key component of the EU's approach to handling administrative redundancy. In other words, we will decentralize everything that can be decentralized and centralize everything that must be centralized. To reach the point of "strategic centralization-operational decentralization", we have to blend rigor and flexibility, adopt a firm line or orientation while maintaining maximum individual autonomy.

The above paragraph raises the well-known debate over decentralization. Here decentralization means more autonomy and responsibility at the grass roots level but supposes that for consistency and overall efficiency, a certain central form of coordination is necessary.

Decentralized structures are best adapted to complex, evolving or geographically distant situations. Conditions within this type of structure may require some centralization beforehand. The key to successful decentralization is twofold:
– maintain a firm, central guideline on a certain number of basic values, e.g. production and service quality, internal rules;

– base the autonomy and responsibility of individuals or units on clear, respected rules through such processes as objective statements and contracts, evaluation of results, penalties, etc.

For example, responsibility means that each member of the team rather than one special department is responsible for quality control. Autonomy means development of an internal competitive spirit. The future belongs to flexible, decentralized, project-based structures made on a human scale. Autonomy and responsibility go hand-in-hand, and can be confirmed by the market reaction, balance sheet or performance review by objectives.

The End of Habits and the Start of a Mental Revolution

The trend of appropriation by individuals or groups of intrapreneurs within a company means that its executives and managers should have different qualities. For many corporations, the problem stems from inadequacies in internal management more than any outside danger. How else can we explain that some firms actually flourish under the same conditions?

Among the catalogue of internal weaknesses, we find an absence of power created essentially by permanent power struggles. It may sound paradoxical or not, but the fact is power struggles paralyze action. In these situations, the notion of power is less important than its twisted use or abuse. In other words, the pleasure of dominating others is often sought-after to the detriment of the power of self-domination, or self-control, which enables one to focus on creating or planning. The leader who knows how to base his/her authority on competencies and on motivation can let his/her team or employees take initiatives. The goals would not even need to be negotiated; they would be naturally generated or present.

The subsidiarity principle trickles down and throughout the organization. This operational decentralization assumes goal-based contracts or contracted goals, evaluations and monitoring later. In this new way of sharing responsibilities according to competence (sometimes called the German model), the operational units or inviduals should be remunerated since the hierarchical levels are fewer. If we are to apply a model that is open to communication and change, the size of production units should not be neglected, e.g. do not go beyond 300 people in an industrial or administrateive unit.

Of course within this ideal organization, responsibility is no longer hierarchical but rather collegiate. Although the boss and authority remain, the top of the corporate totem pole rises because of his/her leadership capacity; in other words, the ability to mobilize people, solve problems, and deal with human conflicts as well as financial risks. Co-opted rather than named, this leader's authority is earned through competence. Management is thus open and plural. Rather than challenge traditions, beliefs and values, mangement uses them as means of adaptation in specific regions or countries.

The entire organizational structure feels the tremor of the "mental revolution", similar to the revolutionizing effect of F.W. Taylor's "Scientific Management". The company is thus a grand social experiment. The bureaucratic rules of the game fall away as executives seek to acquire the same responsibilities that they have in their associative life. The economic efficiency of a company is not incompatible with individual aspirations if they draw upon autonomy, initiative and responsibility.

Training certainly plays a key role in this revolution; however, the type of training offered must promote collective self-teaching whenever possible. There is truth in the old adage that you only really learn or know something when you have to teach it. Hence this type of training should go beyond the banal to put theoretical knowledge into practice quite quickly.

Any training not followed up by action is just another drop in the ocean. Furthermore internal trainers should be the best, as was the case of executives acting as trainers at IBM, while awaiting promotions in the 1980s. In fact, being a trainer should be one of several stages in a career.

How can you spot the companies where this mental revolution has already begun? One simple test is to ask how things are going, as the work week begins. If the answer is "like a Monday", then the company is not faring well. Although it may sound simplistic, we stress that if people are unhappy in their work environment then they are not happy in the general social environment.

Towards Sustainable Motivation

Throughout this book, we referred to the human factor as a key to excellence. A double-edged sword, the human factor can spell success or failure.

According to the contingency principle, a key depends on the context. In which case yesterday's success might actually become the cause of tomorrow's failure. In order to adapt to a changing world, we have to know how to change habits, structures and behaviors. Fortunately change is also vital in motivating people.

Out with Routine, In with Motivation

When faced with future challenges, people will only mobilize if motivated. In the same vein, people only do really well what they understand. In the words of Henri Fayol, "if governing is foreseeing then obeying is understanding". Similarly, the ideal manager of pioneer management writer Mary Parker Follet does not issue orders but rather encourages initiatives which go along the same lines as the orders that could have been given. The quality of the leader remains a determining factor in business as well as in sports.

During the past two decades of consulting with clients in corporations or ministries, we have met a few of these ideal leaders. They were frequently but not exclusively in small firms. They were also usually in sectors experiencing difficulties rather than healthy ones. One law of human nature seems to be that when things are going well, companies can afford the luxury of mediocre managers or uselessly domineering ones. Similarly, a fundamental law of strategy states that generals should never fight their own army.

Multi-Small Is Profitable

The age of behemoth industrial groups or departments is not yet history, as the major corporate restructuring plans and mergers implemented or signed each week prove. Company size within a sector often expands like an accordion. If specific research functions, production units and marketing groups require greater strategic centralization within the context of the global economy, others may need to remain decentralized and "human size" in order to be efficient.

Like motivation, innovation requires stimulation. Operation structures assigning responsibility per project or per market seem preferable to structures that assign responsibility by larger function, e.g. studies, methods, purchasing, sales, etc. The most difficult thing is trying to cross two of these into so-called matrix structures. There are, of course, some corporate examples in which matrix structures do achieve harmony.

Usually the collection, boutique or shop organization works better. In this structure the departments/functions operate like an array of "almost small-to-medium-sized businesses". In some instances, a company can imitate outside competition in order to stimulate innovation and better performance. Organizing a company in small operational units, or what we call a human scale, may be the secret of constant adaptation as well as the key to ongoing innovation.

Moreover, globalization highlights the need for differentiation in terms of culture and local identification. These two feed off each other, as seen in the organization of the ABB Group, product of a merger between the Swedish ASEA and the Swiss Brown Boveri. At least this was the view of the company's president, Percy Barnevik. Since his successor took over the helm, ABB has since returned to a highly traditional organizational structure.

People are more easily motivated when part of small, independent, responsible teams in which individuals know one another, at least by sight, than when in large anonymous groups. We should remember that the longevity and performance of companies are not related to their large size. Remember how IBM, the big blue machine, learned a lesson or two about size when threatened by Apple then Microsoft.

There are countless other interesting examples to prove that companies operating on a human scale are more apt to motivate people and develop team spirit among staff. There must be some logic to numbers in that a football team rarely exceeds 11 players and the army covers territory by dispatching squadrons of 12 soldiers. What a difference from the mammoth corporations paralyzed by their elephantine proportions! Inside most of these dinosaurs, internal energy is spent on turf wars and executive power struggles. Employees are considered like so much weaponry by leaders chosen for their particular allegiance rather than their competence. In companies with a human face or operating on a human scale, individual employees can meet other employees and recognize something of themselves in their managers, who, in turn, are capable, open, accessible or simply well-adjusted.

Of course flexibility requires a certain amount of rigor to be efficient and to distinguish between that which must remain centralized and that which may be decentralized. Also required is a shared values system within a vision and along side corporate projects which act like living cement to bond the small units inside the company.

One Future Vision and Several Short-Term Projects

Our conviction has long been that it is far better to start a corporate project without saying so than to talk about it without really doing anything. Similarly, it is better to initiate small concrete projects rather than an illusory megaproject because the appropriation process counts more than the project itself. In fact, by the end of the 1990s, little appropriation and lots of talk had cheapened the concept of the corporate project in Europe. This situation likely contributed to the replacement of the term "project" by "vision", a similar word that seemed "new and improved" when introduced as an American import.

Regardless of terminology, a corporate future vision must be ambitious yet sufficiently realistic to be translated into concrete projects at the company's many levels. This future vision, although shared, must not claim to translate one grand, unique project that will be imposed uniformly upon one and all. The vision should be translated to a host of projects within the multiple facets of the company or group.

We believe that a vision and projects are necessary both as privileged vectors, capable of mobilizing intelligence within the company and as decisive advantages in the quest for competitiveness and excellence.

The discourse of the top brass, the attention paid to inhouse communication and the talent of consultants can not justify a coporate vision and ensure the success of corresponding projects. Prior serious reflection and proper precautions are also required at all levels of the company. In the end, the corporate vision fashion is not "ready to wear" but rather "made to measure". Each company must define the moment, form and content of the most suitable vision and projects.

With respect to corporate vision and projects, we turn to the following three questions: Why? how? and what are the pitfalls to be avoided?

Why one future vision and several short-term projects? The answer is twofold. First, a project is needed to avoid going off into never-neverland. Flexibility alone leads nowhere. Faced with uncertainty and a turbulent environment, reactivity may be desirable in the short-term but if not oriented toward long-term corporate objectives, it leads nowhere, too. In fact flexibility is not really strategic unless it helps a corporation stay on course. If we indulge in one last ship metaphor: when buffeted by contradictory winds, you do not necessarily change course but you do adjust the sails.

Strategic flexibility can only be fruitful and profitable if it becomes part of a shared ambition or what Harrington Emerson (1916) called "a clearly defined ideal". In fact, Emerson made flexibility the first of his twelve principles of efficiency. He felt that if all the ideals driving the organization, from top to bottom, could be aligned to pull in the same direction, the resulting force would be extremely powerful, but if these ideals pull in different directions, the resulting force could only be slightly positive, insignificant or occasionally even negative.

Yet the connection between foresight and strategic will is not enough to put companies on track to competitiveness and excellence. The third dimension that a project can bring is missing; i.e., the collective mobilization of intelligence to target strategic objectives as well as to confront threats or opportunities in the environment.

The Four Dimensions of a Vision Explained Clearly

A corporate vision normally includes four dimensions: an ambition for the future, a collective desire, a shared values system, major medium-term strategic axes.

The first dimension, ambition, rides on the aims and overarching objective that a company must define through debate then state both openly and clearly. There are several courses of action open, but there are also the uncertainties in the environment to consider. For example, a major corporation could have leadership in specific markets for certain products/services/techniques as a long-term ambition. Often expressed openly and qualitatively, this ambition is part of the dream needed to build any reality.

The collective will to stay the course especially when the seas are rough implies that each partner or participant maintain the same open communication under all circumstances. This will, or desire, to reach the objectives that correspond to the company's aims must be everybody's business. It must be permanent and functional across the board.

A values system shared by the corporate partners or actors in terms of recognition of roles and differences is vital. Such a system ideally includes

- listening;
- dialogue;
- access to information;
- trust in others' behavior;
- pride in belonging to the same group, in creating quality products or services, in being competitive and in playing a key role in innovation despite social, economic and technological changes.

Here the idea is to prefer a few major projects, set as short- and medium- term priorities, e.g. self-financing, investment, market share, training, and working conditions, but also to have a few long-term projects in R&D, for example.

All in all, a corporate vision can not be summed up as a statement of goals or aims but rather an expression of a collective will to achieve them. It is thus the recognition of a shared values system and the mobilization of people moving towards objectives and their corresponding overall aims which have been debated and clearly stated.

Five Pitfalls to Avoid

A lengthy catalogue of pitfalls can discourage any reader, so we have drafted a short list that will, hopefully, help lessen the number of abandoned efforts at corporate visions and projects.

These pitfalls put the corporate project out of fashion, although the concept occasionally resurfaces with the name "future vision". The unfortunate demise of the corporate vision or project represents a lost opportunity for companies looking for other ways to initiate the necessary transformation in structures and behaviors in the face of change.

The Future: Fruit of Will and Initiative

Throughout this book, we have worked to keep futures thinking or scenario planning "fresh" while underscoring the rigor applied in our approach. The fact that tested methods exist is an essential asset. The accumulated heritage of *la prospective,* foresight, futures studies, scenario building, as well as strategic analysis reveals the converging forces and complementarities among these approaches along with the possibility of listing the thinking tools in a single container, a "mental" toolbox. We can thus define our problem and look for the right tool. Contrary to popular opinion, the disorder of creative thinking does require some organization.

Five Pitfalls

• The first pitfall is to confuse collective mental gymnastics with strategic mobilization. Group mobilization and any warm-ups involved do not ensure flexiblity and performance in all circumstances. With hindsight, the intellectual gymnastics should be considered as efforts that were necessary to avoid threats and take advantage of opportunities arising from changes in the environment. Strategic culture can not be reduced to jogging on the spot.

• The second pitfall is the absence of any real content. In this sense vision is used as an executive toy or gadget because communication is poor. Worse, any vision in this case does not engage the life force within the company through a futures-thinking exercise. There is also the risk of seriously demotivating those who initially expressed interest in working on a corporate vision. One way of avoiding this trap is to build a corporate vision without saying so and then start the collective process without revealing the result in advance.

• The third pitfall would then be to consider a corporate vision as the be all and end all rather than a mere means to an end. The main advantage of developing a corporate vision is the opportunity for structured thinking and debate that it provides the group. How else will the company really know its strengths and weaknesses when facing the present and future threats or opportunities in the environment? As already mentioned in this chapter, the process counts more than the result.

• The fourth pitfall would be to contract out the vision or buy off the rack from specialists who reduce complexity to a few simple, attractive, images. In their enthusiasm to shed light, they can easily dazzle clients. The idea of adopting a vision and projects according to a menu of corporate lifestyles may appeal to some. However, is it reasonable to play with the future of a company on the basis of a fleeting snapshot? Would it not be better to ask about changes in the environment that might affect peoples' aspirations and behaviors? This type of question, based on mechanisms that link and oppose the forces of change with the forces of inertia, is vital to both understanding the inevitable resistances to change and to identifying the levers, or drivers, which may start the necessary shift in structures and change in behaviors.

• The fifth and final pitfall appears as a shortcut to most. The idea is to launch a corporate project while hoping to not go through the change in structures and behaviors necessarily implied. This change metamorphosis is more accurate here – involves executives and managers first. A corporate project forces them to undergo a real mental revolution which will place authority on competence and leadership rather than function or title. The true power of a leader is measured not through domination but through the capacity to develop intitiative and responsibility among his/her subordinates.

Of course the tools mentioned are neither panaceas nor ends in themselves. They should be used as needed according to the problem presented, the time allotted and funding budgeted. Unlike some kind of deck of cards for solitaire, they should be used to provide some shared language and method for collective thinking exercises.

Note that these methods have proven effective time and time again in Europe. They do not guarantee the quality of ideas but they do structure thinking by stimulating the imagination. Futures thinking and scenario building are an art which requires many talents, e.g. non-conformism, intuition and common sense. To use an analogy, playing scales is not enough to create a great pianist, but a pianist must practice scales everyday to remain great.

Of course there are other possible approaches. In fact it is a good idea for researchers and practitioners to keep trying to innovate while using established approaches in scenario building or strategic analysis. Their innovation will represent real progress if it makes their questioning or that of the participants more relevant, if it reduces inconsistencies in logic, and if it enhances the realism and importance of the conjectures. However, these new methods must be sufficiently simple to be appropriated. Complication is not the best weapon in fighting complexity. As primary school teachers used to tell their pupils: Clear thinking is clear writing.

Nevertheless, we need progress in the pedagogy of implementation more than we need new methods of analysis and thought to understand the world around us. For most major problems, e.g. training, unemployment or health, the diagnosis and prescription are well known. What is not known is how to take action before it is too late.

This leads to another question: How to replace urgency and reactivity by foresight and preactivity? If futures thinking, or scenario planning, is to be translated into action, it can no longer be the art of enlightened captains of industry but must be the concern of the largest number. Everyone should be interested in the future because that is where he/she will spend the rest of his/her life!

If there is no appropriation, there is rejection. This logic applies to ideas in that the best ideas are not usually the ones we have but rather the ones that we generate or encourage. Throughout this book, we have referred to motivation and talent as the distinctive feature that actually makes the difference between successful companies or regions and their unsuccessful counterparts. As a corollary, problems are also often part of the human factor. Without a good leader or captain, there is no winning team. In this sense, people are not only social animals, to paraphrase Aristotle, but also animals with desires. Dreams and projects are needed to build reality and, more prosaically, to score goals. In other words, the passage from futures thinking to strategic action can not take place without debate and awareness (group and individual) of the responsibilities that we share *vis-à-vis* the generations to come. We owe them at least some hope for an open world in which liberty and initiative thrive.

People need challenges and projects to give some meaning to their lives. Forward-looking people, who are moving towards the future unconventionally, find along the way what they seek in life – social links and mutual recognition – two elements found in any shared adventure. As the German proverb goes, *der Weg ist das Ziel* or the path is the goal. Some might say that "the aim of life is living".

Organisations will increasingly need to shed light on their actions according to possible and desirable futures. They will be able to do so in an even more effective manner since people's concerns will be a priority and, of course, individuals are necessarily behind all problems, solutions and wealth. In short, *strategic prospective* has acquired a solid heritage and has rediscovered the importance of Socrates' lesson, "know thyself". We must use our skills and know our strengths and weaknesses before setting out to conquer the future. As the French philosopher Vauvenargues observed: "knowing our strengths increases them; knowing our weaknesses reduces them".

Still open, the future will always be the fruit of the labors of those who care to work unconventionally towards it in regions or organizations. In the end, each one of us must take a stand: resignation, passive resistance or collaboration for an unconventional future. Collaboration has long been our choice, even though we know the long road stretching ahead of us.

As mentioned earlier there are two major roadblocks. The first stems from an excess of rationalism which leads to a blind, mechanical reliance on the very tools that were forged to spark the imagination, encourage reflection and facilitate communication. The second, almost symmetrical, comes from excessive pride; in other words, just because the tools are insufficient does not mean the mind alone is sufficient. It is a question of multiplying the strength of analysis and synthesis within the human brain through the use of "manmade" tools.

In sum, futures thinking helps us recapture a childlike curiosity and awe while applying rigor to our thinking. It keeps the human factor at the heart of matters and serves to shed light on people's actions thus guiding them towards a desirable future. Indeed, while creating futures, people find the social links and meaning they seek in their lives.

BIBLIOGRAPHY

Ackoff, R. *A Concept of Corporate Planning*. New York: John Wiley & Sons, 1970.

Alba, P. « Prospective et stratégie d'entreprise », *Futuribles*, n° 18, feb. (1989).

Albert, K.J. *The Strategic Management Handbook*. New York: McGraw-Hill, 1983.

Ansoff, I. *Corporate Strategy, An Analytic Approach to Business Policy for Growth and Expansion*. New York: McGraw-Hill, 1965.

Ansoff, I. *From Strategic Planning to Strategic Management*. New York: John Wiley, 1976.

Ansoff, I. *Strategic Management*. New York: McMillan, 1979.

Ansoff, I. *Implementing Strategic Management*. Englewood, NJ: Prentice Hall International, 1984.

Apostol, P. "Marxism and the Structure of the Future", *Futures*, vol. 4, Sept. 1972.

Archier, G. H. Sérieyx. *L'entreprise du 3ᵉ type*. Paris : Seuil, 1984.

Barel, Y. *Prospective et analyse du système*. Paris : Collection TRP, La Documentation Française, 1971.

Beaufre, A. *Introduction à la stratégie*. Paris : Ifri-Economica, 1963.

Bechmann, R. *Des arbres et des hommes, la forêt au Moyen Âge*. Paris : Flammarion, 1984. [Available in English. *Trees and Man, the Forest in the Middle Ages*. New York: Paragon House, 1990.]

Bell, D. « Prévision contre prophétie » in *L'historien entre l'ethnologue et le futurologue*. La Hague : Mouton, 1972.

Bell, D. *The Coming of Post-Industrial Society, a Venture in Social Forecasting*. 1st. ed. New York: Basic Books, 1976.

Benassouli, P., R. Monti. « La planification par scénarios, le cas AXA France 2005 », *Futuribles*, n° 203, nov., 1995.

Berger, G. « Sciences humaines et prévision », *La revue des deux mondes*, n° 3, feb., 1957.

Berger, G. *Phénoménologie du temps et prospective*. Paris : Presses universitaires de France, 1964.

Berger, G. *Étapes de la prospective*. Paris : PUF, 1967.

Boyer, L., N. Equilbey. *Histoire du management*. Paris : Éditions d'Organisation, 1990.

Camus, A. *Le mythe de Sisyphe*. Paris : Gallimard, 1962. [Available in English. Trans. O'Brien, J., *The Myth of Sisyphus and Other Essays*. New York: Vintage Books, 1955.]

Cazes, B. *Histoire des futurs*. Paris : Seghers, 1986.

Chandler, A. *Strategy and Structure: Chapters in the History of the Industrial Enterprise*. Garden City, N.J.: Doubleday, 1966.

Chesnais, J.-C. *Le crépuscule de l'Occident*. Paris : Éditions Robert Laffont, 1995.

Coates, J.F. *American Business in the New Millenium: Trends Shaping American Business*. New York: Coates & Jarrat, Inc., 1994.

Coates, J.F. *2025: Scenarios of US and Global Society Reshaped by Science and Technology*. Akron, OH: Oakhill Press, 1997.

Coates, J.F. *Issues Management: How to Plan, Organize, and Manage for the Future*. Mt. Airy, MD: Lomond, 1986.

Crozier, M., E. Friedberg. *L'acteur et le système*. Paris : Seuil, 1977. [Available in English as *Actors and Systems: the Politics of Collective Action*. Chicago: University of Chicago Press, 1980.]

Drucker, P. F. *Concept of the Corporation*. New York: New American Library, 1985.

Dupuy, J.P. *Ordres et désordres*. Paris : Seuil, 1982.

Follett, M.P. *Creative Experience*. New York: Longman's Green and Co, 1976.

Giget, M. « Arbres technologiques et arbres de compétences. Deux concepts à finalité distincte », *Futuribles*, n° 137, nov. 1989.

Giget, M. *La dynamique stratégique des entreprises*. Paris : Dunod, 1998.

The Global 2000 Study: "Report to the President of the United States: Entering the Twenty-First Century". New York: Pergamon Press, 1980.

Godet, M. "Smic: A New Cross Impact Method". *Futures*, vol. 7, Aug., 1975.

Godet, M. "Smic 74: a reply from the authors". *Futures*, vol. 8, August 1976.

Godet, M. Scenarios and Strategic Management. London: Butterworths, 1987.

Godet, M. "Integration of Scenarios and Strategic Management". Futures, vol. 22, Sept., 1990.

Godet, M. From Anticipation to Action. Paris: Unesco, 1994.

Godet, M. P. Chapuy, G. Comyn. "Global Scenarios of the International Context on the Horizon 2000", Futures, vol. 26, April, 1994.

Godet, M., F. Roubelat. "Creating the Future: the Use and Misuse of Scenarios". Long-Range Planning, vol. 9, n°2, April, 1996.

Grimaldi, N. Le désir et le temps. Paris : PUF, 1971.

Guillerme, A. Les temps de l'eau : la cité, l'eau et les techniques (fin IIIe-début XIXe siècles). Paris : Champ Vallon, 1983. [Available in English. The Age of Water: the Urban Environment of the North of France, A.D. 300-1800. College Station, TX: A&M University Press, 1988.]

Hall, D. J., M. A. Saias. "Strategy Follows Structure", Strategic Management Journal, vol. I.2, April-June, 1980.

Hamel, G., C.K. Prahalad. Competing for the Future. Boston: Harvard Business School Press, 1994.

Heijden, K. (van der) Scenarios, the Art of Strategic Conversation. London: John Wiley & Sons, 1996.

Interfuturs. Face aux Futurs. Paris : OECD, 1979.

Jantsch, E. Technological Forecasting in Perspective. Paris: OECD, 1967.

Jouvenel, B. (de) L'art de la conjecture. Paris : Éditions du Rocher, 1964. [Available in English, Trans. Lary, N., The Art of Conjecture. New York: Basic Books, 1967.]

Kapferer, J.N. Rumeurs, le plus vieux métier du monde. Paris : Seuil, 1987. [Available in English. Trans. Fink, B. Rumors: Uses, Interpretations, and Images. New Brunswick, NJ: Transaction Publishers, 1990.]

Keynes, J.-M., The General Theory of Employment, Interest and Money, London: Macmillan, 1974.

Lacoste, J. « Abondance pétrolière, jusqu'à quand? » in : L'énergie. Commissariat Général du Plan, Collection Plan et prospectives. Paris : Armand Colin, n° 6, 1970.

Le Roy Ladurie, E. Histoire du climat depuis l'an mil, vol. 1, Paris : Flammarion, 1967. [Now revised and updated in English as Times of Feast, Times of Famine: a History of Climate since the Year 1000. Garden City, New York: Double day, 1971.]

Lesourne, J. Les mille sentiers de l'avenir. Paris : Seghers, 1981.

Lesourne, J. Éducation et société pour demain. Paris : La Découverte, 1988.

Lesourne, J. *L'économie de l'ordre et du désordre*. Paris : Economica, 1981.

Lesourne, J. « Plaidoyer pour une recherche en prospective », *Futuribles*, n° 137, nov., 1989.

Lesourne, J., M. Godet. *La fin des habitudes*. Paris : Collectif, Seghers, 1985.

Lesourne, J., D. Malkin, « L'exercice interfuturs, réflexion méthodologique », *Futuribles*, n° 26-27, sept.-oct., 1979.

Linstone, H.A., M. Turrof. *The Delphi Method, Techniques and Applications*. Reading, MA : Wesley Publishing Co. 1975.

Lussato, B. « La culture en danger » (An interview with Prof. Michel Godet), *Futuribles*, n° 122, 1988.

Lussato, B. *L'échelle humaine : contre le gigantisme technologique et bureaucratique*. Paris : Robert Laffont, 1996.

Martino, J. P. *Technological Forecasting for Decision-making*. New York: North Holland, 1983.

Masse, P. *Le plan ou l'anti-hasard*. Paris : Idées Gallimard, 1965.

Mayo, E. *The Human Problems of an Industrial Civilisation*. New York: Viking Press, Compass Books Series, 1960.

Mintzberg, H. *Structure et dynamique des organisations*. Paris : Editions d'Organisation, 1982.

Mintzberg, H. *The Rise and Fall of Strategic Planning: Reconceiving Roles for Planning, Plans, Planners*. New York: The Free Press, 1994.

Morgenstern, O. *Précisions et incertitudes des données économiques*. Paris : Dunod, 1972. [Available in English. *On the Accuracy of Economic Observations*. Princeton, NJ: Princeton University Press, 1965.]

Nanus, B. "QUEST – Quick Environmental Scanning Technique", *Long Range Planning*, vol. 15, n° 2, 1982.

Orgogozo, I. *Les paradoxes de la qualité*, Paris : Éditions d'organisation, 1987.

Pascale, R. T. *Le management, est-il un art japonais?* Paris : Éditions d'Organisation, 1984.

Poirier, L. *Stratégie théorique II*. Paris : Economica, 1987.

Porter, M. *Competitive Strategy: Techniques for Analyzing Industries and Competitors*. New York: The Free Press, 1980.

Postel-Vinay, O. *Le Taon dans la cité : actualité de Socrate*. Paris : Édition Descartes et Cie., 1994.

Prigogine, I. « Loi, histoire et désertion » in : *La querelle du déterminisme*. Paris : Collection Le Débat, Gallimard, 1990.

Prigogine, I, I. Stengers. *La nouvelle alliance*. 2nd édition Paris: Gallimard, 1987.

Revel, J.F. *La connaissance inutile*. Paris : Grasset, 1988.

Ringland, G. *Scenario Planning*. New York: Wiley and Sons. 1998.

Roubelat, F. *La prospective stratégique en perspective : genèse, études de cas, prospective*. Thèse de doctorat en Sciences de gestion, Cnam, Paris, 1996.

Saaty, T.L. *The Analytical Hierarchy Process*. New York: McGraw-Hill, 1980.

Schwartz, P. *The Art of the Long View*. New York: Doubleday, 1991.

Sérieyx, H. *Le zéro mépris*. Paris : InterÉditions, 1989.

Simon, H. *Models of Bounded Rationality*. vol. 2, Cambridge, MA: The MIT Press, 1982.

Todd, E. *La troisième planète : structures familiales et systèmes idéologiques*. Paris : Seuil, 1983.

Toffler, A. *Future Shock*. New York: Random House, 1970.

Ville, J. *Étude critique de la notion de collectif*. Paris : Gauthier-Villars, 1937.

Wack, P. "Scenarios: Uncharted Waters Ahead." *Harvard Business Review*, Sept.-Oct. 1985, vol. 63, n°5.

Wack, P. "Scenarios: Shooting the Rapids." *Harvard Business Review*, novembre-décembre 1985, vol. 63, n° 6.

Zwicky, F. "Morphology and Nomenclatura of Jet Engires", *Aeronautical Engineering Review*, June, 1947.

INDEX

Réalisé en P.A.O. par STDI - Z.A. Route de Couterne - 53110 LASSAY-LES-CHÂTEAUX
Imprimé en France. - JOUVE, 18, rue Saint-Denis, 75001 PARIS
N° 290648V. - Dépôt légal : Février 2001